Good Housekeeping

the Supermarket Diet Cookbook

Janis Jibrin, M.S., R.D.
Susan Westmoreland

HEARST BOOKS

A division of Sterling Publishing Co., Inc.

New York / London
www.sterlingpublishing.com

Good Housekeeping

Rosemary Ellis	Editor in Chief
Richard Eisenberg	Special Projects Director
Susan Westmoreland	Food Director

The Good Housekeeping Cookbook Seal guarantees that the recipes in this cookbook meet the strict standards of the Good Housekeeping Research Institute, a source of reliable information and a consumer advocate since 1900. Every recipe has been triple-tested for ease, reliability, and great taste.

Cover Design by Roberto de Vicq de Cumptich
Book Design by Richard Oriolo

Photo Credits: Antonis Achilleos: pages 260 and 298. Quentin Bacon: page 238. James Baigrie: pages 8, 92, 121, 143, 171, 182, 189, 194, and 274. Beatriz Da Costa: page 130. Brian Hagiwara: pages 1, 6, 104, 107, 110, 124, 129, 144, 147, 152, 163, 167, 172, 178, 187, 190, 197, 198, 204, 206, 216, 223, 237, 265, 268, 297, 305, and 306. Rita Maas: pages 160, 177, and 244. Steven Mark Needham: pages 2 and 210. Alan Richardson: pages 148, 155, and 168. Mark Thomas: pages 181 and 193.

The Library of Congress cataloged the hardcover edition of this title as follows:
Jibrin, Janis.
  The Good housekeeping supermarket diet cookbook / Janis Jibrin & Susan Westmoreland.
    p. cm.
  Includes index.
  ISBN 978-1-58816-590-9
  1. Reducing diets—Recipes. I. Title: Supermarket diet cookbook. II. Westmoreland, Susan. III. Title.
  RM222.2.J5243 2006
  641.5'635—dc22
                          2006006046

10 9 8 7 6 5 4 3 1
First Paperback Edition 2009

Published by Hearst Books
A division of Sterling Publishing Co., Inc.
387 Park Avenue South, New York, NY 10016

Good Housekeeping and Hearst Books are trademarks of Hearst Communications, Inc.

www.goodhousekeeping.com

For information about custom editions, special sales, premium and corporate purchases, please contact Sterling Special Sales Department at 800-805-5489 or specialsales@sterlingpublishing.com.

Distributed in Canada by Sterling Publishing
c/o Canadian Manda Group, 165 Dufferin Street
Toronto, Ontario, Canada M6K 3H6

Distributed in Australia by Capricorn Link (Australia) Pty. Ltd.
P.O. Box 704, Windsor, NSW 2756 Australia

Manufactured in China

Sterling ISBN 978-1-58816-774-3

The Good Housekeeping Triple-Test Promise

At *Good Housekeeping*, we want to make sure that every recipe we print works in any oven, with any brand of ingredient, no matter what. That's why, in our test kitchens at the **Good Housekeeping Research Institute,** we go all out: We test each recipe at least three times—and, often, several more times after that.

When a recipe is first developed, one member of our team prepares the dish and we judge it on these criteria: it must be **delicious, family-friendly, healthy,** and **easy to make.**

1. The recipe is then tested several more times to fine-tune the flavor and ease of preparation, always by the same team member, using the same equipment.

2. Next, another team member follows the recipe as written, **varying the brands of ingredients and kinds of equipment.** Even the types of stoves we use are changed.

3. A third team member repeats the whole process **using yet another set of equipment and alternative ingredients.**

By the time the recipes appear on these pages, they are guaranteed to work in any kitchen, including yours. WE PROMISE.

Contents

Foreword

Ready to start cooking healthy meals and shaving off the pounds? *The Good Housekeeping Supermarket Diet Cookbook* is the perfect way to do it. As you may know, *The Supermarket Diet* is an easy, affordable, real-world program that shows you how to buy the right foods and put together tasty, healthful meals that keep your weight under control. *The Good Housekeeping Supermarket Diet Cookbook* does the diet one better by featuring more than 175 delicious, triple-tested recipes from the *Good Housekeeping* kitchens and more than 140 Meal Plans tailor-made to the diet.

Most of the recipes are quick as well as healthy, usually taking no more than 30 minutes to prepare. And our Meal Plans offer complete breakfast, lunch, and dinner menus, making meal prep that much easier.

The Good Housekeeping Supermarket Diet Cookbook also offers the helpful advice that you expect from *Good Housekeeping*. You'll learn how to choose the right foods when shopping the supermarket aisles (including how to read nutrition labels) and how to freeze and thaw foods properly.

Because this is a cookbook to help you diet, we have included plenty of weight-loss advice. For instance, we show you how to avoid the most common diet pitfalls, and we provide tips on how many calories you burn doing different types of exercise.

We think you'll find *The Good Housekeeping Supermarket Diet Cookbook* is a great companion to *The Good Housekeeping Supermarket Diet*. If you would like even more dieting advice and healthy recipes, be sure to visit www.goodhousekeeping.com. Best of luck, and here's to a long, healthy life!

The Editors of *Good Housekeeping*

1

It's Simple! How to Lose Weight on *The Supermarket Diet*

Hello, veterans of *The Supermarket Diet*, and welcome, newcomers! Our first book, *The Supermarket Diet*, laid out the basics of losing weight: how to shop smart in the supermarket, how to stock your kitchen with slimming foods, plus an exercise routine and loads of menu plans and recipes.

Now, in *The Supermarket Diet Cookbook*, you get more than 175 brand new recipes and more than 140 brand new meal plans in a convenient cookbook format. With the two books, you could truly stay on this plan—and maintain your weight loss—for the rest of your life!

Remember: People who eat at home are thinner than those who eat out often. If you're truly serious about losing weight and keeping it off, you've got to get in the kitchen. Let *Good Housekeeping* hold your hand, guiding you as you prepare delicious pound-paring meals.

Not a big fan of the kitchen? Well, even if you're not much of a cook, you can deal with the convenient recipes here. Most take no more than 30 minutes to prepare, many no more than 20 minutes. That's less time than picking up take-out. For instance, Cool and Creamy Shrimp Salad (page 125) takes all of 10 minutes to make. You'll have the Asian Flounder Bake (page 232) on the table in just 20 minutes. And if you *are* a cook, you'll revel in whipping up sophisticated—but still speedy—dishes such as Glazed Pork with Pear Chutney (page 169) or Thai Noodles with Cilantro and Basil (page 261).

The Supermarket Diet meals are super-nutritious, not only helping you lose weight, but lowering the risk for heart disease, cancer, diabetes, and other diet-related chronic diseases. But even the most impressive fat, fiber, and vitamin stats aren't going to lure you to the table: Ultimately, the dishes have to taste good. Just flip through the book and you'll see how yummy these recipes are. And they work: They've all been triple-tested in the *Good Housekeeping* Test Kitchen.

Have a sweet tooth? Don't worry, there's even room on this plan for sweets and other occasional not-entirely-nutritious fare. For example, it's OK to have a glass of wine, a light beer, chocolate, ice cream, chips, and the like.

HOW THE DIET WORKS

Losing weight on the *The Supermarket Diet* is straightforward: Simply choose from a wide variety of meals, prepare them, and eat them! Each day, just choose any breakfast, lunch, dinner, and calcium-rich snack (Calcium Break) from our Meal Plans, add a treat, and you'll end up having consumed just 1,500 (for women) or 1,800 calories (for men).

If you're new to *The Supermarket Diet*, you may opt to start with the Boot Camp weight-loss plan, which you'll find at www.goodhousekeeping.com. (Enter "supermarket diet" into the search bar, scroll down to "The Good Housekeeping Supermarket Diet," select "menus," and click on the link for "1,200 calorie regiment.") At 1,200 calories a day for women and 1,500 calories a day for men, Boot Camp will get you off to a quick start as you can lose up to four pounds a week for two weeks. After the two weeks are up, the Keep On Losin' plan—featured in both *The Supermarket Diet* and this book—helps you to lose one half to two pounds each week. You can stay on the Keep On Losin' plan for as long as you like. You can also skip Boot Camp altogether and simply start with Keep On Losin'.

Women should follow the 1,500-calorie Keep On Losin' plan. Once you've reached your desired weight-loss goal, the 1,800-calorie Stay Slim plan will be your maintenance plan. However, if you find that you're too hungry on the Keep On Losin' plan or losing weight too quickly—more than two pounds a week—add 100 or 200 calories a day from the lists found in "Graduating to Your Maintenance Plan" on pages 81 to 83. Or if you're still feeling too hungry, simply jump to the 1,800-calorie Stay Slim plan. Once you've reached your weight-loss goal, whether on 1,500 calories a day or more, then simply add 200-300 calories daily to maintain that weight. You know you're doing it right when your weight stays put and you're not gaining or losing.

Men should follow the 1,800-calorie Stay Slim plan as a weight-loss plan. The Stay Slim plan is simply the Keep On Losin' plan plus an additional 300 calories daily. Once you've reached your desired weight, then you should have 2,100 calories a day for your maintenance plan. However, if you find that you're too hungry on the Stay Slim plan, or losing weight too quickly—more than two pounds a week—add 100 or 200 calories a day from the Graduating to Your Maintenance Plan lists on pages 81 to 83. Once you've reached your weight-loss goal, you should then have about 2,100-2,200 calories a day.

You get oodles of choices with *The Supermarket Diet*. For instance, one morning you might pick a frozen breakfast burrito (page 108). From a list of 34 lunches, you might make a Fresh Mozzarella and Tomato Sandwich (page 133). Dinner that night could be Provençal Salmon with Tomato-Olive Relish (page 226), one of 82 dinners. Also on that day, you might choose a skim latte (page 80) for your Calcium Break and a little chocolate for your 125-calorie treat. The next day, you can have a completely different menu. Since all the breakfasts are around 375 calories, with roughly the same nutrition content, you're in good shape no matter which you choose. Ditto for the 400-calorie lunches, the 500-calorie dinners, 100-calorie Calcium Breaks, and 125-calorie treats.

The Meal Plans for breakfasts, lunches, dinners, calcium breaks, and treats start on page 49; recipes for all the breakfasts, lunches, and dinners start on page 93. At times when you're too busy to figure out what to eat, or if you'd like a little help, just turn to Weekly Menu Plans on page 82; we've done the planning for you!

While you're eating right, you also need to get some exercise. Most weight-loss books focus only on what goes into your mouth. But, as you know, exercise is just as important as diet for losing weight, and *critical* for maintaining that weight loss. *The Supermarket Diet* provides a walking program and tips on how to strength train. That—or any other exercise program of your choice—is a necessary accompaniment to this diet plan. Chapter 5 of this book shows you how many calories you burn walking, playing golf, swimming, and doing other activities.

Both *The Supermarket Diet* and *The Supermarket Diet Cookbook* are about empowerment. Instead of spoon-feeding you a rigid menu plan, you get to choose which meals you want on any given day. And instead of just one level of calorie intake, we show you how to turn the diet into an 1,800-calorie plan (and we also help you figure out how to set it somewhere in between 1,500 and 1,800 calories). Chapter 4 even shows you how to design your own meals to fit into the plan. Plus, you get powerful tools to take into the grocery store so you can figure out which cereal, spaghetti sauce, salad dressing, and other foods are the most nutritious and slimming.

WHY THE DIET WORKS

On paper, losing weight is extremely simple: You drop pounds by lowering calories—either by eating less, burning more, or, ideally, a combo of the two. That's what *The Supermarket Diet* and *The Supermarket Diet Cookbook* offer: a reduced-calorie eating plan and exercise guidelines for burning calories.

But as anyone who's tried it knows, weight loss isn't so simple in reality. Busy schedules, emotional eating, genetics, post-pregnancy weight, a sedentary desk job, and all sorts of other issues life throws at you gum up the best-laid weight-loss plans.

So we've made *The Supermarket Diet* as do-able as possible. The calories are all worked out for you, the foods are easy to prepare, and even a couch potato can handle the exercise suggestions—mainly walking. So, this plan works, and it's not complicated or demanding. As for those other life issues… well, turn to Chapter 5, "Avoiding Diet Pitfalls," to help get a handle on them.

Meanwhile, enjoy your delicious meals.

2 The Healthy Kitchen

Your kitchen is going to make you slimmer. Stock it properly, cook the meals in this book, keep out the junk food, and your kitchen will become a healthy place instead of a den of overindulgence! This chapter offers lists of the very basic foods to stock; you'll find a more complete list—as well as foods to throw out—in *The Supermarket Diet*. Also, here you'll find out how long you can safely keep those leftovers in the fridge, as well as other important food safety information.

What's the ideal meal for weight loss? One that's based on:

- healthy carbs (including whole grains and vegetables)
- lean protein
- healthy fat

The healthy carbs contain fiber, which expands in your digestive system, making you feel fuller, longer. Fiber also slows the conversion of starch to blood sugar. This means sugar enters the blood slowly and evenly, instead of with the spikes and dips which can leave you feeling fatigued and hungry. Meanwhile, protein acts as an appetite suppressor and fat slows stomach emptying, contributing to that full, satisfied feeling.

Ever notice that you're hungry an hour after a bowl of fat-free cereal and skim milk? The missing element is fat. Likewise, an all-vegetable salad tossed with low-fat dressing for lunch won't get you through the afternoon. But add some chicken or tofu (protein), a full-fat dressing, and a small whole-wheat roll, and you'll make it through exercise class after work.

You'll find the healthy-carb/lean-protein/healthy-fat combination over and over again in *Supermarket Diet* recipes and meals. For instance, the hot cereal breakfast (page 51) has all the elements:

- multigrain hot cereal (whole-grain carbs)
- blueberries (more healthy carbs)
- skim milk (lean protein)
- walnuts (healthy fat)

Here's how the Dijon-Fennel Pork Tenderloin with Sweet Potato Fries dinner (page 62) breaks down:

- pork tenderloin (lean protein)
- sweet potato fries (healthy carbs)
- salad (more healthy carbs) tossed with olive oil–based dressing (healthy fat)

Stock Up!

Naturally, recipes in this book call for very different ingredients, but there are certain foods that appear in many recipes. Stock up on these, and you'll cut down on the time spent in the supermarket. You can focus your shopping trip on just the new or fresh ingredients particular to a recipe, secure in the knowledge that the other healthy standbys are already sitting in your kitchen. And when you can't make it to the grocery store, rely on these staples to create a healthy meal. Here are the healthy carbohydrates, lean protein, and healthy fats to keep on hand:

HEALTHY CARBS

High-fiber/low-sugar cereals

Your rule of thumb: at least 4 g dietary fiber and no more than 5 g sugar per 100 calories (that's at least 6 g dietary fiber and no more than 8 g sugar per

150 calories). Examples: Kellogg's Complete Wheat Bran Flakes, Kashi GoLean (regular, not GoLean Crunch), and Nature's Path Optimum Slim.

Bread

Make sure bread has no white flour (see Chapter 3 for tips on reading ingredient lists). So, 100 percent whole-wheat sliced bread, 100 percent whole-rye bread, multigrain breads where all the grains are whole, and 100 percent whole-wheat pitas all fit the bill. For example, Arnold's 100% Whole Wheat Bread or Pepperidge Farm 100% Whole Wheat Bread.

Grains

Whole grains used in this book: bulgur (whole wheat), brown rice, whole-wheat couscous (Fantastic Foods and Casbah make it), whole-wheat pasta, oatmeal, whole-wheat flour. Brown rice shows up a lot in the menu plans. If you don't have the 45 minutes to cook regular brown rice, Uncle Ben's Whole Grain Brown Ready Rice, which takes only 90 seconds, is a fine alternative. If you *do* have the time, try a brown basmati, brown jasmine, or brown Texmati rice. These varieties have a wonderful aromatic, slightly nutty quality.

Crackers

Check to make sure there's no white flour in the ingredient list. Instead, the products should be based on whole wheat (such as Ak Mak or Triscuits) or whole rye (such as most of the Wasa crackers and Ryvita).

Fruits and vegetables

While many of the fruits and vegetables in this book are fresh, here are the ones you can stock up on:
Frozen: unsweetened strawberries and blueberries, broccoli flowerets, frozen corn kernels
Canned: vacuum-packed, no-salt-added corn (such as Del Monte Fresh No Salt Added Whole Kernel Cut Corn) reduced-sodium or no-salt-added tomatoes (such as Hunt's Whole Tomatoes No Salt Added or Pomi Chopped Tomatoes)

LEAN PROTEIN

Eggs

If you can find them (and afford them) buy omega 3–enriched eggs. Be careful though: Some of these eggs contain ALA, the less potent omega-3 (also called linolenic acid or alpha-linolenic acid). ALA is still good for you, but it's hardly worth the extra price of the eggs. What you want to see on the label is DHA and maybe a little EPA, the potent omega-3s found in fish (chickens are fed fish meal to produce the DHA). For instance, Eggland's Best, a nationally distributed brand, contains approximately 50 mg DHA and 50 mg ALA per egg. That's a good standard from which to judge other omega 3–enriched eggs.

Canned beans

Kidney beans, garbanzo beans, black beans, white beans, lentils, and all other legumes are rich in both protein and carbohydrates. If you've got the time and inclination, make your own by boiling dry beans. Otherwise, look for canned beans with the lowest sodium levels. Health food stores and the health food section of many larger supermarkets are still the most reliable source of these beans. However, in a hopeful sign, Goya—a mainstream supermarket brand—came out with a great low-sodium line with no more than 120 mg sodium per $^1/_2$ cup. In your supermarket's health food section, or, if you make it to a health food store, look for Eden Organic no-salt-added beans or Westbrae's line of canned beans, or any other bean with no more than 140 mg sodium per $^1/_2$ cup (as opposed to the 350 mg in many other brands).

Canned fish

Canned tuna is getting a welcome makeover in pouches. Some brands have a little less sodium, such as Starkist Premium Albacore Tuna in Water, and the tuna is a little tastier and firmer. Also try the flavored varieties, but always compare labels for the lower-sodium products.

Frozen chicken and frozen shrimp

Skinless frozen chicken breasts or thighs are the basis of many dishes in this book. There are also a lot of shrimp recipes; use either frozen and thawed, or "fresh" shrimp from the seafood counter (which is simply frozen shrimp that they've defrosted for you).

HEALTHY FATS

Olive oil

This oil is rich in monounsaturated fat, which doesn't raise cholesterol and has been linked to heart health. Extra virgin oil is the least processed and has the richest flavor and antioxidant content.

Canola oil

When you want a neutral-tasting oil, this one is rich in monounsaturated fat, and also omega-3s, linked to heart and mental health.

Sesame oil

Keep this dark, flavorful oil refrigerated, as you probably won't use it as often as olive oil or canola oil, and the fats can oxidize, especially in a hot kitchen.

Light mayonnaise

Regular mayo's got 100 calories and 11 g fat per tablespoon, whereas the reduced-fat version slims down to about 50 calories and 5 g fat per tablespoon. And it's surprisingly good. Both Kraft Light and Hellmann's Light are fine. Kraft is a better choice because it has 90 mg of sodium per tablespoon compared with 120 mg in Hellmann's. Steer clear of the rubbery fat-free versions.

Nuts

They're all good for you, so buy your favorites. Walnuts are rich in omega-3s, and almonds, cashews, pecans, and peanuts are great sources of monounsaturated fat. Just make sure you buy unsalted, as called for in this plan. For the most flavor, buy roasted, unsalted nuts, which aren't always easy to find; Whole Foods and other health food stores usually carry them. Keep in mind that nuts are often less expensive in health food stores than in mainstream markets.

OTHER STOCK ITEMS

Honey

Get whichever brand you like.

Maple syrup

Get whichever brand you like.

Reduced-sodium broth (chicken)

Regular chicken broth, either in ready-to-use cans or cartons or from a bouillon cube, can have 900 mg sodium per cup. But reduced-sodium chicken broth brings sodium down to about 100 mg. So, look for reduced-sodium or low-sodium on the front of the label and carefully read the back to ensure you're getting a truly lower-sodium broth. You'll see brand name suggestions in the recipes, such as Campbell's Low Sodium Chicken Broth; Shelton's Fat

Free/Low Sodium Chicken Broth (regular or organic versions); and Health Valley Low Fat Chicken Broth No Salt Added.

Reduced-sodium broth (vegetable)

Again, the lower the sodium, the better. Aim for 350 mg per cup, such as Health Valley's Fat Free Vegetable Broth.

Soy sauce

Regular soy sauce has up to 1,350 mg sodium per tablespoon. That's a lot! Get the light versions, such as Kikkoman Lite or La Choy Lite with about 600 mg or less per tablespoon.

Vinegar

Get whichever brand you like.

The Safe Kitchen

Now that you're doing more cooking, you want to make sure you're turning out clean, safe food. Common sense cleanliness, a food thermometer, and knowing when to throw food out will prevent food poisoning. Foods get contaminated when harmful bacteria such as salmonella or E. coli are allowed to flourish. Make sure this doesn't happen by following the guidelines below.

KEEP IT COOL

When you get back from the grocery store, your first duty is to make sure cold—or frozen—foods stay that way. Here are tips from the U.S. Department of Agriculture on refrigerating foods:

1. **Use This Tool to Keep It Cool.** Use a refrigerator thermometer to be sure the temperature is consistently 40°F or below.

2. **The Chill Factor.** Refrigerate or freeze perishables, prepared foods, and leftovers within two hours of purchase or use. Always marinate foods in the refrigerator.

3. **The Thaw Law.** Never defrost food at room temperature. Thaw food in the refrigerator. For a quick thaw, submerge in cold water in an airtight package or thaw in the microwave if you will be cooking it immediately.

4. **Divide and Conquer.** Separate large amounts of leftovers into small, shallow containers for quicker cooling in the refrigerator.

5. **Avoid the Pack Attack.** Do not over-stuff the refrigerator. Cold air must circulate to keep food safe.

6. **Rotate Before It's Too Late.** Use or discard chilled foods as recommended in the USDA Cold Storage Chart (page 20).

7. **Don't Go Too Low.** As you approach 32°F, ice crystals can begin to form and lower the quality of some foods such as raw fruits, vegetables, and eggs. A refrigerator thermometer will help you determine whether you are too close to this zone.

BE A SAFE CHEF

Here are ways to make sure food stays clean and uncontaminated while you cook:

- Always wash hands before and after handling food.
- Wash fruits and vegetables before using.
- Don't cross-contaminate. Keep raw meat, poultry, fish, and their juices away from other food. After cutting raw meats, wash hands, cutting board, knife, and counter tops with hot, soapy water.
- Marinate meat and poultry in a covered dish in the refrigerator.
- Afterward, sanitize cutting boards by using a solution of 1 teaspoon chlorine bleach in 1 quart of water.

COOK THE LIFE OUT OF THEM!

Heating meat, poultry, and seafood to the proper temperature will kill the most common bugs that cause food poisoning. You really can't tell whether a food is cooked properly unless you use a meat thermometer. The guidelines:

- Cook ground meats to 160°F; ground poultry to 165°F.
- Beef, veal, and lamb steaks, roasts, and chops may be cooked to 145°F; all cuts of fresh pork, 160°F.
- Whole poultry should reach 180°F in the thigh; breasts, 170°F.
- Cook fish until it's opaque and flakes easily with a fork.
- Perishable food should not be left out more than two hours at room temperature (one hour when temperature is above 90°F).

KNOW WHEN TO TOSS

The handy chart below, courtesy of the USDA and the Food Marketing Institute, answers the "Is it still good?" question.

These short but safe time limits will help keep refrigerated foods from spoiling or becoming dangerous to eat. Because freezing keeps food safe indefinitely, recommended storage times are for quality only. Storage times are from date of purchase unless specified on chart. It is not important if a date expires after food is frozen.

Cold Storage Chart

PRODUCT	REFRIGERATOR (40°F)	FREEZER (0°F)
EGGS		
Fresh, in shell	3 to 5 weeks	Don't freeze
Raw yolks, whites	2 to 4 days	1 year
Hard cooked	1 week	Don't freeze well
Liquid pasteurized eggs, egg substitutes,		
opened	3 days	Don't freeze well
unopened	10 days	1 year
MAYONNAISE		
commercial refrigerate after opening	2 months	Doesn't freeze
DELI & VACUUM-PACKED PRODUCTS		
Store-prepared (or homemade) egg, chicken, ham, tuna, macaroni salads	3 to 5 days	Doesn't freeze well
HOT DOGS & LUNCHEON MEATS		
Hot dogs,		
opened package	1 week	1 to 2 months
unopened package	2 weeks	1 to 2 months
Luncheon meats, opened package	3 to 5 days	1 to 2 months
unopened package	2 weeks	1 to 2 months

PRODUCT	REFRIGERATOR (40°F)	FREEZER (0°F)
BACON & SAUSAGE		
Bacon	7 days	1 month
Sausage, raw from chicken, turkey, pork, beef	1 to 2 days	1 to 2 months
Smoked breakfast links, patties	7 days	1 to 2 months
Hard sausage—pepperoni, jerky sticks	2 to 3 weeks	1 to 2 months
Summer sausage—labeled "Keep Refrigerated"		
opened	3 weeks	1 to 2 months
unopened	1 to 2 months	3 months
HAM, CORNED BEEF		
Corned beef, in pouch with pickling juices	5 to 7 days	Drained, 1 month
Ham, canned—labeled "Keep Refrigerated"		
opened	3 to 5 days	1 to 2 months
unopened	6 to 9 months	Doesn't freeze
Ham, fully cooked vacuum sealed at plant, undated, unopened	2 weeks	1 to 2 months
Ham, fully cooked vacuum sealed at plant, dated, unopened	"use by" date on package	1 to 2 months
Ham, fully cooked, whole	7 days	1 to 2 months
Ham, fully cooked, half	3 to 5 days	1 to 2 months
Ham, fully cooked, slices	3 to 4 days	1 to 2 months
HAMBURGER, GROUND & STEW MEAT		
Hamburger & stew meat	1 to 2 days	3 to 4 months
Ground turkey, veal, pork, lamb & mixtures of them	1 to 2 days	3 to 4 months
FRESH BEEF, VEAL, LAMB, PORK		
Steaks	3 to 5 days	6 to 12 months
Chops	3 to 5 days	4 to 6 months
Roasts	3 to 5 days	4 to 12 months
Variety meats—tongue, liver, heart, kidneys, chitterlings	1 to 2 days	3 to 4 months
Pre-stuffed, uncooked pork chops, lamb chops, or chicken breast stuffed with dressing	1 day	Don't freeze well

PRODUCT	REFRIGERATOR (40°F)	FREEZER (0°F)
SOUP & STEWS		
Vegetable or meat added	3 to 4 days	2 to 3 months
MEAT LEFTOVERS		
Cooked meat and meat casseroles	3 to 4 days	2 to 3 months
Gravy and meat broth	1 to 2 days	2 to 3 months
FRESH POULTRY		
Chicken or turkey, whole	1 to 2 days	1 year
Chicken or turkey, pieces	1 to 2 days	9 months
Giblets	1 to 2 days	3 to 4 months
COOKED POULTRY		
Fried chicken	3 to 4 days	4 months
Cooked poultry casseroles	3 to 4 days	4 to 6 months
Pieces, plain	3 to 4 days	4 months
Pieces covered with broth, gravy	1 to 2 days	6 months
Chicken nuggets, patties	1 to 2 days	1 to 3 months
PIZZA		
Pizza	3 to 4 days	1 to 2 months
STUFFING		
Stuffing—cooked	3 to 4 days	1 month
BEVERAGES, FRUIT		
Juices in cartons, fruit drinks, punch	3 weeks unopened 7 to 10 days opened	8 to 12 months
DAIRY		
Butter	1 to 3 months	6 to 9 months
Buttermilk	7 to 14 days	3 months
Cheese, Hard (such as Cheddar, Swiss)	6 months, unopened 3 to 4 weeks, opened	6 months
Cheese Soft (such as Brie, Bel Paese)	1 week	6 months
Cottage Cheese, Ricotta	1 week	Doesn't freeze well
Cream Cheese	2 weeks	Doesn't freeze well
Cream—Whipped, ultrapasteurized	1 month	Doesn't freeze
Cream—Whipped, Sweetened	1 day	1 to 2 months

PRODUCT	REFRIGERATOR (40°F)	FREEZER (0°F)
DAIRY (CONTINUED)		
Cream—Aerosol can, real whipped cream	3 to 4 weeks	Doesn't freeze
Cream—Aerosol can, nondairy topping	3 months	Doesn't freeze
Cream, Half and Half	3 to 4 days	4 months
Eggnog, commercial	3 to 5 days	6 months
Margarine	4 to 5 months	12 months
Milk	7 days	3 months
Pudding	package date; 2 days after opening	Doesn't freeze
Sour cream	7 to 21 days	Doesn't freeze
Yogurt	7 to 14 days	1 to 2 months
DOUGH		
Tube cans of rolls, biscuits, pizza dough, etc.	Use-by-date	Don't freeze
Ready-to-bake pie crust	Use-by-date	2 months
Cookie dough	Use-by-date unopened or opened	2 months
FISH		
Lean fish (cod, flounder, haddock, sole, etc.)	1 to 2 days	6 months
Fatty fish (bluefish, mackerel, salmon, etc.)	1 to 2 days	2 to 3 months
Cooked fish	3 to 4 days	4 to 6 months
Smoked fish	14 days or date on vacuum package	2 months in vacuum package
SHELLFISH		
Shrimp, scallops, crayfish, squid, shucked clams, mussels and oysters	1 to 2 days	3 to 6 months
Live clams, mussels, crab, lobster and oysters	2 to 3 days	2 to 3 months
Cooked shellfish	3 to 4 days	3 months

3 Savvy Shopping

Ever found yourself stuck, staring, at the cereal aisle in complete bewilderment? Or wondering which mayonnaise is healthier, or whether that "light" olive oil will help you lose weight? You need to look no further than the back of the package for all the answers. Between the nutrition facts panel and the ingredient list, you can figure out which cereal gives you the most fiber, which tomato soup is lowest in sodium, and whether that brown bread is truly made with whole grains.

Labels and ingredient lists can be confusing, so take a little time to learn how to read them. You'll be richly rewarded with a kitchen full of superior, healthful ingredients. Here are the rock-bottom basics of label and ingredient reading (for more in-depth coverage, see Chapter 6 of *The Supermarket Diet*).

THE LABEL

The nutrition facts panel, or label, is on the back of most every food. On page 25 are portions of this label taken from two cereals—a bran-based cereal and a cornflake-style cereal. If you were in the store, here's how to compare those labels and walk out with the better product:

Bran-based cereal

Nutrition Facts

Serving Size 1 cup (52g/1.8 oz.)
Servings Per Container About 8

Amount Per Serving

Calories 140	**Calories from Fat 10**
	% Daily Value**
Total Fat 1g*	**2**%
Saturated Fat 0g	**0**%
Trans Fat 0g	
Cholesterol 0mg	**0**%
Sodium 85mg	**4**%
Potassium 480mg	**14**%
Total Carbohydrate 30g	**10**%
Dietary Fiber 10g	**40**%
Soluble Fiber 1g	
Insoluble Fiber 9g	
Sugars 6g	
Protein 13g	**20**%

Vitamin A 0%	•	Vitamin C 0%	
Calcium 6%	•	Iron 10%	
Phosphorus 20%	•		

Corn flakes-style cereal

Nutrition Facts

Serving Size 1 Cup (28g/1.0 oz.)
Servings Per Container About 12

Amount Per Serving	Cereal	Cereal with ½ Cup Vitamins A&D Fat Free Milk
Calories	100	
Calories from Fat	0	
	% Daily Value**	
Total Fat 0g*	**0**%	
Saturated Fat 0g	**0**%	
Trans Fat 0g		
Cholesterol 0mg	**0**%	
Sodium 200mg	**8**%	
Potassium 25mg	**1**%	
Total Carbohydrate 24g	**8**%	
Dietary Fiber 1g	**4**%	
Sugars 2g		
Other Carbohydrate 21g		
Protein 2g		

Vitamin A	10%
Vitamin C	10%
Calcium	0%

The first place to look is the **Serving Size**. Portion sizes on both of these labels are 1 cup; that makes it easy for you as you're comparing similar portion sizes. Next stop, **Calories**. Notice that the bran cereal has more calories than the other. That's fine, because on *The Supermarket Diet*, you are allowed 160 calories worth of cereal at breakfast.

Now let's close in on which cereal is more nutritious. Our criteria: **Dietary Fiber** and **Sugar**. As mentioned in Chapter 2, you should choose cereals with at least 4 g fiber per 100 calories (at least 6 g per 150 calories) and preferably no more than 5 g sugar per 100 calories (no more than 8 g per 150 calories). The higher-calorie bran-based cereal more than meets our criteria with an impressive 10 g fiber and just 6 g sugar per 150 calories. But the box of corn flakes isn't doing so well. Sure, it makes the grade for sugar, with just 3 g per 100 calories. But with a measly 1 g fiber, it should stay on the supermarket shelf. You'll also note that the high-fiber bran-based cereal is substantially lower in **Sodium**. Put it in your cart, it's a winner!

You can apply this little label-reading example to all sorts of foods. The most important rules of thumb:

- Start with the serving size to make sure you're fairly comparing equal amounts of two or more foods.

- Next, check out the calories. Higher calorie isn't always worse. For instance, in the case of cereal, it's OK if one cereal is higher in calories than another, as long as it meets our fiber and sugar criteria. You'll just use a little less of the cereal to meet the calorie suggestion on *The Supermarket Diet*. Or, if one tomato soup is a little higher in calories than another, but lower in sodium, it's better to choose the higher-calorie soup.

- Once you know you're comparing equal portions of foods, then look for the nutrients you're interested in. In our cereal comparison, we were most interested in finding the higher-fiber, lower-sugar product. With canned beans, tomatoes, soups, and other canned foods, go for the lower-sodium product. You might also look at fiber, saturated fat (the less the better), and vitamins and minerals.

Oh, and about the question about "light" olive oil? Next time you're in the store, look at the label. You'll notice that both light and regular olive oils have 120 calories and 14 g fat per tablespoon. The only "light" thing about one of them is the flavor and color!

THE INGREDIENT LIST

While the nutrition facts panel tells a lot about a food, you still need to glance at the ingredient list to complete the nutrition picture. By law, ingredients must be listed by weight, starting with the heaviest. So, the first two or three ingredients usually constitute the bulk of the food. How come some ingredient lists are so long? Sometimes, it's because the food is pumped up with sugar, starch, gums, and artificial colors and flavorings. For instance, compare these two chicken broth ingredient lists:

Broth A: Chicken Stock, Chicken Fat, Salt, Utilized Yeast, Monosodium Glutamate, Dextrose, Hydrolyzed Wheat Gluten, Corn Oil, Flavoring & Hydrolyzed Soy & Corn Protein.
Broth B: Filtered Water, Concentrated Chicken Broth, Chicken Fat, Onion Powder, Turmeric, Ground Celery Seeds, White Pepper.

The monosodium glutamate in Broth A is a flavor enhancer, but guess what? It's also a sodium-*contributor!* The MSG and the salt bring the sodium to a whopping 770 mg per cup. Other ingredients to note: *Dextrose* is another name for sugar, *gluten* is a plant protein.

For my money, I'd stick to Broth B, which is simply chicken broth with spices. No salt was added, so sodium stands at a nice and easy 130 mg per cup.

Checking the ingredient list is a *must* when trying to determine whether the food is made of whole grains. That box of crackers that looks so earthy-crunchy, or that brown "multigrain" bread? The packaging may have stalks of wheat on it, but odds are that the product is not whole grain. Unless the only grains in the ingredient list are barley, buckwheat, brown rice, oats, quinoa, whole wheat, whole rye, and/or wild rice, you haven't got a whole-grain product.

Check out the ingredient lists for these two breads (the names are real, but manufacturers' names have been omitted just in case they change formulation). Size 'em up and spot the 100 percent whole-grain bread:

Whole Grain Flax: Organic stone-ground whole wheat, water, wheat gluten, wheat bran, organic whole rye, flaxseed, sea salt, oat fiber, yeast, olive oil.

7-Grain: Unbleached Wheat Flour [Flour, Malted Barley Flour, Reduced Iron, Niacin, Thiamin Mononitrate (Vitamin B1), Riboflavin (Vitamin B2), Folic Acid], Water, Whole-wheat Flour, High Fructose Corn Syrup, Molasses, Cracked Wheat, Yeast, Raisin Juice Concentrate, Soybean Oil, Salt, Barley, Wheat Gluten, Rye, Whey, Triticale, Soy Flour, Millet, Oats, Mono- and Diglycerides, Ground Corn, Calcium propionate (Preservative), Soybeans, Brown Rice, Flaxseed, Skim milk, Soy Lecithin, Calcium Carbonate, Sesame Seeds, Hazelnut Meal, Walnuts.

If you named the Whole Grain Flax as the product with 100 percent whole grain, you were right. All the flour is whole grain: whole-wheat or whole-rye, with added wheat bran and oat fiber. Despite its wholesome name, the 7-Grain is a whole-grain dud. The first ingredient—unbleached wheat flour—is simply white flour. Sure, there's some whole wheat, but as the third ingredient, after water, you can't count on much of it. (For more on spotting a whole grain, check out Chapter 6 of *The Supermarket Diet.*)

SPEEDIER SHOPPING

As said earlier, people who eat at home are slimmer than those who frequently eat out. But one of the obstacles to home cooking is finding the time to get the ingredients. But it is possible to get away with grocery shopping twice a week, sometimes even just once. The more organized you are, the quicker you'll be in and out of the grocery store. Some tips:

1. **Keep a list of staples posted on the fridge.** Whenever you're low, make a mark next to the item. With a rich stock of staples (see Chapter 2 for suggestions), you'll always have enough to make *something*, so you don't have to run out to the store.

2. **Always bring a complete list to the store.** Sit down with this book and plan at least five breakfasts, five lunches, and five dinners for the week. Run through the recipes, jotting down anything you need.

3. **Do just one major shopping trip a week.** Often, this'll cover you for the week. And if it doesn't, the second trip should be a quick one. For instance, if you do your major shopping on Monday, but want to have fish on Friday, you can make a quick stop at the store for the fish (and maybe some fresh veggies) on Thursday or Friday.

4. **Avoid the junk aisles.** This will save you both time and calories. Although you can have almost any food on this plan—Twinkies, potato chips, cola, fries, you name it!—you've got to watch the portions. You can get away with about 125 calories of any less-than-nutritious food—that's two-thirds of a 12-ounce can of soda, or a little under an ounce of potato chips, or a medium-sized cookie. But with the size of your treat budget, the last thing you want is to cruise the snack food and cookie aisles, loading up on tempting high-calorie foods. As with the rest of your meals, plan your treat. This way, you can make a targeted hit: Picking up a box of Skinny Cow or Weight Watchers frozen treats, or a single cookie at the bakery. If possible, buy just one treat, not a box: After all, it's easier to resist it just one time at the supermarket rather than to keep resisting it all week once you get it home.

4

Be Your Own Nutritionist

Between this book and *The Supermarket Diet*, you have enough meals to keep you slender for the rest of your life. Even so, we may have missed some of your favorite dishes in the meal plans we offer. But that doesn't mean you have to miss out. This chapter shows you how to design meals that fit right into the 1,500- or 1,800-calorie plans. You'll find that it's not hard to be your own nutritionist and tailor meals to suit your tastes.

Skip this chapter entirely if you have no urge to stray from the many meals in this book and in *The Supermarket Diet*. But if you decide to give it a whirl, first follow the plan in this book for a few weeks. You'll be in the groove of balanced meals, making it easier to design your own.

THE FOOD EXCHANGE SYSTEM

Here's how it works: You're allotted a certain number of servings within five food groups. In nutritionist-speak, it's the *food exchange system*. As you can see from the lists beginning on page 30, the groups are protein, starches, vegetables, fruit, fat, and dairy. As usual, you should work in a daily treat, bringing calories up to either 1,500 or 1,800, depending on your target daily calorie consumption.

What's great about the exchange system is that you hardly ever have to count calories. And a grasp of the exchanges makes eating out less tricky because you can easily size up portions and serve yourself just enough. As soon as you learn what a serving looks like (for instance, a slice of bread is a starch serving, a medium-sized piece of fruit is a fruit serving), all you have to do is rack up the right number of servings in each group. It's worth spending a little time learning serving sizes for foods you regularly eat. But don't make yourself crazy learning all of them—you can always pick up the book to figure out how many dried apricot halves make a fruit serving.

The guidelines below give you serving sizes and number of servings necessary to meet a 1,500- or 1,800-calorie-per-day plan. While the calories per serving aren't exact, they're close enough to help you stay safely on a controlled-calorie diet plan. For instance, a starch serving is 80 calories, but one of the items on this list—a $1/2$ cup cooked pasta—is actually closer to 90 calories. But half an English muffin is closer to 60 calories. Don't worry, these little discrepancies won't foil your weight loss!

HOW TO SIZE UP YOUR MEALS

Protein (160 calories per serving)

1,500- and 1,800-calorie plans: Have 2 servings per day (1 at lunch and 1 at dinner).

Examples of 1 serving:

- 3 ounces cooked chicken, fish, or lean meat
- 1 cup cooked or canned beans or legumes (count also as 2 starches), such as black beans, garbanzo beans, lentils, etc.
- 1 cup tofu
- 2 eggs
- 2 ounces reduced-fat cheese
- $3/4$ cup 2% cottage cheese
- 1 cup 1% cottage cheese
- 3 tablespoons peanut butter (count also as 3 fats)

If you go with the lean protein choices, you are allowed all 5 of your fat servings. But if you choose a protein with a higher-fat content, such as a burger, ribs, or chicken with skin, that also includes 2 fat servings. In addition, 2 ounces regular cheese uses up 2 fat servings. So, if you have a grilled cheese sandwich using regular full-fat Cheddar, that uses 2 of your fat servings for that day. But 2 ounces reduced-fat cheese (70 calories per ounce) doesn't use up any fats. Count 3 tablespoons peanut butter as 1 protein and 3 fats.

Starches (80 calories per serving)

1,500-calorie plan: Have 6 servings per day (about 2 at every meal).

1,800-calorie plan: Have 7 servings per day (about 2 at every meal).

Examples of 1 serving:

- 1 slice bread (preferably whole-wheat)
- $^1/_4$ large bagel (preferably whole-wheat)
- $^1/_2$ English muffin (preferably whole-wheat)
- $^1/_2$ cup cooked rice, pasta, or other grain
- 80 calories of cereal (check label for amount of cereal)
- $^1/_2$ cup cooked oatmeal
- 1 (4-inch) pancake
- $^1/_2$ large baked potato or sweet potato
- heaping $^1/_2$ cup cooked potatoes (not fried!)
- $^1/_2$ cup cooked corn or peas
- $^1/_3$ cup beans (such as black beans)
- 1 (80-calorie) tortilla

Vegetables (25 calories per serving)

1,500- and 1,800-calorie plans: Have at least 4 servings per day (1 to 3 at both lunch and dinner).

Examples of 1 serving:

- 2 cups lettuce
- 1 cup chopped raw vegetable
- $^1/_2$ cup cooked vegetable

Fruit (60 calories per serving)

1,500-calorie plan: Have at least 1 serving per day (at breakfast). In addition, opt for fruit as often as possible as part of your 125-calorie treat.

1,800-calorie plan: Have at least 2 servings per day. In addition, opt for fruit as often as possible as part of your 170-calorie treat.

Examples of 1 serving:

- 1 piece fruit (e.g., apple, pear)
- 1 cup fruit
- 4 ounces juice

Fat (45 calories per serving)

1,500-calorie plan: Have 5 servings per day (1 or 2 at every meal).

1,800-calorie plan: Have 6 servings per day (1 or 2 at every meal).

Examples of 1 serving:

- 1 teaspoon oil, butter, margarine, or mayonnaise
- 1 tablespoon salad dressing, cream cheese, or light mayonnaise
- 1 slice bacon
- 2 tablespoons reduced-fat cream cheese or salad dressing
- 1 tablespoon nuts

Dairy (100 calories per serving)

1,500-calorie plan: Have 2 servings per day (1 at breakfast and 1 at another meal or as a snack).

1,800-calorie plan: Have $2^1/_2$ servings per day (1 or $1^1/_2$ at breakfast and the rest at another meal or snack).

Examples of 1 serving:

- 1 cup (8 ounces) skim milk, 1% milk, or soy milk
- $^3/_4$ cup (6 ounces) plain nonfat yogurt, plain low-fat yogurt, or artificially sweetened yogurt
- $1^1/_2$ ounces reduced fat cheese

Daily Treat

1,500-calorie plan: 125 calories per day

1,800-calorie plan: 170 calories per day

Examples of treats:

- Chocolate, potato chips, fruit, wine, or anything else you fancy!

FOOD EXCHANGE SYSTEM AT-A-GLANCE

Refer to this handy chart to quickly determine the number of servings of each food group you can have each day on the 1,500- and 1,800-calorie plans.

	1,500-CALORIE PLAN	1,800-CALORIE PLAN
Protein	2 servings	2 servings
Starch	6 servings	7 servings
Vegetables	4 servings	4 servings
Fruit	1 or more* servings	2 or more* servings
Fat	5 servings	6 servings
Dairy	2 servings	$2^1/_2$ servings
Daily Treat	125 calories	170 calories

* "or more" means you can have more fruit as part of your daily treat

HOW TO DESIGN YOUR OWN BREAKFAST

The breakfasts on the 1,500-calorie plan come to an average of 375 calories. You can stick with 375-calorie breakfasts on the 1,800-calorie plan, or, if you like a bigger breakfast, bolster it with either 1 fat serving plus $^1/_2$ starch serving, or 1 full starch serving. A great way to distribute these 375 calories (which allows for 10 calories of wiggle room) is:

- 2 starches (160 calories)
- 1 dairy (100 calories)
- 1 fruit (60 calories)
- 1 fat (45)

For instance, if you like bread and cheese for breakfast (a type of breakfast not on the list), here's how you could design it:

- 2 slices whole-grain bread (2 starches)
- $1^1/_2$ ounces reduced-fat cheese, which, according to the label, should come to 100 calories (1 dairy)
- 1 orange (1 fruit)
- 1 tablespoon almonds (1 fat)

Here's how a pancake breakfast breaks down:

- 2 buckwheat pancakes (2 starches): If you make them in a nonstick skillet with a little oil spray, no need to use up a fat. But if you use more oil or margarine to fry them, then you've used up 1 fat exchange per pancake.
- 2 teaspoons syrup (check label, these calories will have to come out of your daily 125-calorie snack)
- 1 cup berries (1 fruit)
- 1 cup skim milk (1 dairy)

HOW TO DESIGN YOUR OWN LUNCH

The lunches on the 1,500-calorie plan are about 400 calories; on the 1,800-calorie plan they are 500 calories. A balanced way to distribute the 400 calories:

- 2 starches (160 calories)
- 1 protein (160 calories)
- 2 vegetables (50 calories)
- 1 fat (45 calories)

OK, that comes to 415 calories, but remember, you've got 10 extra calories from breakfast, and these are just approximates!

For the 1,800-calorie plan, add 1 starch or $^1/_3$ protein (an extra ounce of chicken, for example), and 1 fat.

Say you're hankering for a roast beef sandwich. Here's how you'd figure the food groups to tally 400 calories:

- 2 slices whole-wheat bread (2 starches)
- 2 teaspoons light mayonnaise (1 fat)
- 3 ounces lean roast beef (1 protein)
- horseradish (so low-calorie it's free!)
- tomato slices
- On the side: the remaining tomato slices (1 vegetable) and $^1/_2$ cup baby carrots (1 vegetable)

Here's how to set portions for a 400-calorie meal consisting of soup, an open-faced sandwich, and a tomato-mozzarella salad. (Soups are trickier; here you have to use the nutrition label for help.) For instance:

- 1 cup chicken noodle or chicken and rice soup: Label tells you that it is 80 calories per cup; since there's usually not much chicken, count this as 1 starch.
- 1 ounce reduced-fat mozzarella ($^1/_2$ protein) melted on 1 slice whole-wheat bread (1 starch)
- 1 large tomato, sliced (2 vegetables) another ounce reduced-fat mozzarella ($^1/_2$ protein), drizzled with 1 teaspoon olive oil (1 fat)

HOW TO DESIGN YOUR OWN DINNER

Dinners on the 1,500-calorie plan are 500 calories; on the 1,800-calorie plan, dinners are 550-600 calories. Here is a nutritionally balanced approach to a 500-calorie dinner on the 1,500-calorie plan:

- 2 starches (160 calories)
- 1 protein (160 calories)
- 2 vegetables (50 calories)
- 2 fats (90 calories)

That leaves you with 40 calories to play with: perhaps a little bit more rice, a dab more salad dressing, or a little more meat.

If you're on the 1,800-calorie plan, add 1 starch, or 1 starch and 1 fat to raise the calories to 550-600.

For instance, here's how it works for a 500-calorie chicken-broccoli stir-fry:

- $3/4$ cup chicken (1 protein)
- 2 cups broccoli (2 vegetables)
- 2 teaspoons canola oil for stir-frying (2 fats)
- garlic, ginger, soy sauce (all so low-calorie they're free!)
- 1 cup brown rice (2 starches)

Here's how a 500-calorie fajita dinner breaks down:

- 2 small tortillas (check label, if the two come to about 80 calories, that's 1 starch serving)
- 3 ounces flank steak (it's a lean meat, so count as 1 protein, don't need to use up fats)
- 1 cup peppers and onions (2 vegetables) sautéed in 1 teaspoon olive oil (1 fat)
- 2 tablespoons reduced-fat sour cream (1 fat)
- 2 to 3 tablespoons salsa (take it, it's free!)

Remember, in addition to the breakfasts, lunches, and dinners, you need to tack on a Calcium Break and a daily treat to bring calories up to 1,500 or 1,800 per day.

5 Avoiding Diet Pitfalls

"Thirty pounds in 30 days!" "The pill that will melt off fat!" "Smell strawberries and lose weight!" (Yes, that really was a headline in a magazine!) You've seen the claims for quick and easy weight loss, you may have even tried them, but as any diet veteran knows, weight loss is not so quick and not so easy. And maintaining the weight loss is even more challenging, requiring permanent lifestyle changes.

However, research proves that many dieters *do* successfully maintain their weight loss. Often, it takes a few weight-loss/weight-gain cycles until it sticks, according to the National Weight Control Registry, a University of Colorado–based study tracking the habits of 4,500 successful maintainers. The average participant in that study lost approximately 60 pounds and has maintained that loss for roughly five years.

What works for you may not work for your husband, wife, or friend. There is no one-size-fits-all weight-loss strategy, beyond eating less and exercising more. *The Supermarket Diet* plan, with all its many meal choices and its 1,500- to 1,800-calorie range can accommodate nearly all individual tastes. That's the food part. But you need to plot out the rest of your weight loss strategy. Here are some common weight-loss/weight-maintenance pitfalls and how to avoid them. Spot the ones you need to address and get to work!

DENIAL

Somewhere in the back of your mind you know you've been overeating and not getting enough exercise, but you don't go there. Neither do you step on the scale or try on the pants that might be too tight now. Denial is the enemy of weight loss. Not only must you think and plan around eating and exercise, when you slide into the bad old habits, stare them right in the face and record them! Write down every bite you put in your mouth and all the exercise you're getting. *The Supermarket Diet* offers food diary tear-out sheets. You can also print them out by visiting www.goodhousekeeping.com, entering "Supermarket Diet food diary" into the search bar, and clicking "Downloading the Supermarket Diet." Writing down your eating habits helps catch the problem early; seeing it in black and white is often enough to help you correct it. So does stepping on the scale, at least once a week. If the scale makes you crazy, then get out the pants. In other words, keep close check on your weight. Remember: Even relatively small gains of two or three pounds are tough to reverse.

ALL-OR-NOTHING THINKING

Ever told yourself, "Well, now that I messed up by eating this big dessert, I might as well give up and eat whatever I want"? That's all-or-nothing thinking: You're either good or bad, fat or thin, exercising like a maniac or slouching around like a couch potato. Instead, think of working on a healthy weight as an ongoing, normal part of life. Some days you do it well, eating controlled portions and getting enough exercise, other days you don't. Just like some days you're frenzied, other days calm. One frenzied day doesn't make you a permanently frenzied person. Your mantra for diet success: "I won't give up because of one or two bad days. I'll just start again tomorrow."

OVER-SCHEDULING

There are so many justifiable excuses for skipping the supermarket or the gym. Work, family duties, housework—even guilt at the idea of taking time out just for yourself instead of spending that time with your family. "I mean, it's not like I'm wasting time leisurely strolling through the mall, I truly don't have time to cook and exercise," a client of mine said. Super-busy periods are when many people put on weight, as cooking and exercise often get bumped off the schedule because of other pressing issues. In addition, sometimes, people use food to cope with the stress of a busy life. There's no easy solution to this one, but one approach is to take a good look at your calendar and ruthlessly cut out anything you can. Your mantra: "Eating right and exercising are top priorities. I need to make time for them." And if you're one of the people who feels guilty about going to the gym, then tell yourself, "It's not selfish to make my health a top priority; being a healthier, slimmer person is not only good for me, it's good for everyone around me."

USING FOOD TO COPE

No doubt about it: Food is soothing and comforting. By turning to ice cream or chips to cope with a stressful day, a bad marriage, a boring job or other issues, you're on to something. You are trying to make yourself feel better, and that's healthy. The problem, of course, is that you're getting fat in the meantime, and that's only going to bring you more misery. So, take your good impulse—coping—and try on new styles. It might be taking a walk, watching a movie, writing an email, listening to music, painting, or other activities. And, of course, any time you can fix the root of the stress, all the better.

NOT EXERCISING

Think of it this way: The more you exercise, the more you can eat. Sure you can lose weight by dieting alone, but eventually you'll rebel against such a restrictive plan. Back comes the weight. When you exercise regularly, you don't have to severely restrict everything that goes into your mouth. Plus, you get all the other crucial benefits of being fit: reduced risk of Alzheimer's, arthritis, cancer, depression, diabetes, heart disease, and osteoporosis, to name a few.

Fortunately for all those people who don't care for the gym, there are other activities—walking, swimming, cycling—that work. But a short stroll or a five-minute spin on the bike isn't going to cut it unless you take *multiple* short strolls or many quick bike rides. Check out the chart on page 39 to get a rough estimate of the number of calories burned doing various exercises. And if you're not doing so already, start strength training. Invest in at least one session with a personal trainer who will show you how to safely lift weights or use weight machines and when to increase the weight as you get stronger.

EATING OUT

I recently renovated my kitchen and, for two months, the kitchen was completely unusable. Unless someone invited me over, I ate every meal out. Even with my nutrition background, I couldn't be sure of what I was eating. Sure, if I ordered a salad topped with seared tuna and dressing on the side, I knew what I was getting into. But the "low-fat" apple bran muffin at Jolt 'n

Burn, Baby, Burn

This chart offers *approximate* numbers for calories burned per a 10-minute bout of exercise. Just multiply according to the number of minutes you spent at a given activity. For instance, if you weigh 160 pounds and spent 20 minutes on an exercise bike at 10 miles per hour, you expended around 73 x 2, or 146 calories. The more you weigh, the more effort—and expended calories—it takes to perform an activity. And for any of you shaking your head, realizing that a 30-minute walk isn't going to undo that 450-calorie slice of pecan pie, think of it this way: You'd be in bigger trouble without the walk! Remember: Dropping just 50 calories daily either through exercise or diet translates to a five-pound weight loss over a year's time.

Try to burn at least 60 calories per day (if you're really out of shape or just starting an exercise routine) and work up to burning 250 calories per day.

ACTIVITY	CALORIES BURNED EVERY 10 MINUTES, IF YOU WEIGH			
	120 POUNDS	140 POUNDS	160 POUNDS	180 POUNDS
Basketball	75	88	100	113
Bowling	12	14	16	19
Cycling (10 mph)	55	64	73	82
Dancing (aerobic)	74	86	98	111
Dancing (social)	29	33	37	42
Gardening	50	59	67	75
Golf (pull/carry clubs)	46	54	62	70
Golf (power cart)	21	25	28	32
Hiking	45	52	60	67
Jogging	93	108	124	139
Running	114	132	151	170
Sitting quietly	12	13	15	17
Skating (ice and roller)	59	69	79	88
Skiing (cross-country)	75	88	100	113
Skiing (water and downhill)	57	66	76	85
Swimming (crawl, moderate pace)	78	90	103	116
Tennis	60	69	79	89
Walking	65	76	87	97
Weight training	66	76	87	98

(Data adapted, with permission, from the American Council on Exercise, San Diego, California.)

Bolt? The broccoli-tofu stir-fry at Hunan Garden? Even though I ordered healthful foods, it was anyone's guess as to the amount of sugar or fat—and calories—they contained. As a result, I gained a few pounds. *The Supermarket Diet* and *The Supermarket Diet Cookbook* ask you to commit to a little cooking. Not onerous, time-consuming, elaborate cooking. Most dinners take just 20 to 30 minutes total, lunches about 10 minutes. Those minutes mean everything to your health.

But you do have to eat out sometimes. Use the "Be Your Own Nutritionist" exchange system (Chapter 4) as a guide to ordering food. For instance, you know you can build a 400-calorie lunch with 2 starches (160 calories), 1 protein (165 calories), 1 fat (45 calories), and 1 vegetable (25 calories). So, in the deli, order turkey on whole-wheat and a side salad with 1 tablespoon dressing.

If you're eating at a chain restaurant, check and see if its website gives nutrition info. And check out "Good Choices at the Chains" (page 41) for meals that fit into *The Supermarket Diet*.

UNDER-EATING

And you thought weight loss was all *about* under-eating! Actually, it's about eating less (and expending calories with exercise). But you still need enough calories to keep you feeling satisfied. You should only be really hungry just before a meal, not for large swaths of the day. On too-few calories your body rebels; it's not going to put up with hunger. And that could mean going back to overeating. The 1,500-calorie plan in this book will keep many people satisfied while still losing weight. But if this amount is too low, don't suffer! Move up to 1,800 calories, using the suggestions provided, or fudge your way somewhere in between.

Ways that people under-eat: skipping meals, particularly breakfast. That comes back to bite you with roaring hunger that can trigger excessive snacking at night (the Ben & Jerry's in front of the TV syndrome). Another common problem: the salad meal. No, a simple green salad is *not* a meal! But a green salad which includes hard-boiled eggs, shrimp, or another protein and is accompanied by a slice of bread or other starch—*that* is a meal. So, you're not being good by having just a salad for lunch. That's actually *bad* for losing weight!

You probably figured out your diet pitfalls long ago, but hopefully, some of the suggestions here will be a wake-up call and help you deal with them.

But ultimately, you have to make some real decisions: Will I stop overeating or won't I? Will I start exercising or won't I? It's hard to give up the pleas-

Good Choices at the Chains

Here are examples from national chain restaurants of meals that fit right into *The Supermarket Diet* plan. Since companies change both dishes and formulations, check their websites to see whether calories have changed.

Applebee's. For a 500-calorie dinner, have the Tortilla Chicken Melt. Or order any of the following accompanied by a side salad (no cheese or croutons) with 1 tablespoon dressing: Tango Chicken Sandwich, Confetti Chicken, Teriyaki Steak and Shrimp Skewers, or Grilled Tilapia with Mango Salsa.

Baja Fresh. For a 400-calorie lunch, order the Savory Pork Carnitas Ensalada with Salsa Verde Dressing or the Charbroiled Chicken Ensalada with one-third of the Ranch Dressing. (Watch it! Don't get the bigger, more caloric salads that are similar but are served with a cheese-stuffed flauta.)

For a 500-calorie dinner, get the Savory Pork Carnitas Ensalada with $1/2$ serving of the Olive Oil or Ranch dressing or the Side-by-Side Charbroiled Chicken with Salsa Verde Dressing.

Chipotle. For a 400-calorie lunch, order a bowl containing 1 serving rice, 1 serving black beans, any salsa except corn, and lettuce.

For a 500-calorie dinner, order a bowl containing 1 serving black beans, 1 serving chicken, any salsa except corn, lettuce, and $1/2$ serving rice.

McDonald's. These meals are so much lower in fiber (and some higher in sugar) than *Supermarket Diet* meals: Please make going to McDonald's an infrequent event!

For a 375-calorie breakfast, get the Fruit 'n Yogurt Parfait with granola, plus an English muffin (it comes with margarine) and half a "small" (12-ounce) orange juice.

For a 400-calorie lunch, order a hamburger (smallest one), plus a Caesar Salad (no chicken) with a full packet of Newman's Own Low Fat Balsamic Vinaigrette. Or, the Caesar Salad with Grilled Chicken, $1/2$ packet of Newman's Own Creamy Caesar Dressing, and a serving of croutons.

For a 500-calorie dinner, get a cheeseburger (smallest one) plus Caesar Salad (no chicken) with a full packet of Newman's Own Low Fat Balsamic Vinaigrette and a package of Apple Dippers with $1/2$ the Low Fat Caramel Sauce. Or, get the California Cobb Salad with Grilled Chicken plus $1/2$ packet of Newman's Own Ranch Dressing, plus a Fruit 'n Yogurt Parfait without granola.

Subway. Any of the "6 grams of fat or less," 6-inch subs with 280 to 290 calories is fine.

For example, for a 400-calorie lunch, you can get the 6-inch Ham, 6-inch Roast Beef, 6-inch Turkey Breast, or 6-inch Turkey Breast & Ham sub; or the 6-inch Veggie Delite sub with an added serving of cheese. Pair the sub with a Veggie Delite salad and $1/4$ packet of regular dressing or a full packet of fat-free Italian (or 50 calories of any dressing).

Wendy's. For a 400-calorie lunch get the Mandarin Chicken Salad with all the add-ins except the crispy noodles and have $1/2$ the Oriental Sesame Dressing.

For a 500-calorie dinner, order a plain baked potato topped with a small chili.

ure of eating lots of sweets, or fries, or whatever. And, sometimes, it's hard to hustle over to the gym, or take time for a walk or an exercise CD. So, you have to decide that having a slimmer, fitter, more energetic body is worth it. And that changing habits to help prevent cancer, heart disease, diabetes, and other ills is also very much worth it.

Once you seriously decide to eat less and exercise more, be watchful for ways the devil sitting on the other shoulder tries to undermine your decision. "C'mon, you're on vacation, you can splurge!" Or, "You've had a bad day, reward yourself with food." Be mindful of that little devil and send him packing!

6

Your Menus and Meals

Time to dig in! If you've been on *The Supermarket Diet*, you know the drill. Newcomers, it's pretty easy: Choose any breakfast, any lunch, any dinner, any high-calcium snack (called a Calcium Break), and a treat. Women who want to follow the diet simply prepare the meals in this chapter and add a 125 calorie treat: This is your Keep On Losin' plan of 1,500 calories a day. Remember, if you're feeling too hungry on this plan, then slightly increase your daily calorie intake as described on pages 10-11. Men on the diet follow the Stay Slim plan of 1,800 calories, which is simply the Keep On Losin' plan plus 300 calories a day. Use the lists on page 81 for suggestions on ways to add 300 calories. (If you'd like to start with a more spelled-out 1,800 calorie plan, then please refer to the first book, *The Supermarket Diet.*)

All the meals are based on *Good Housekeeping*'s delicious, triple-tested recipes found in Chapter 7. The recipes are quick and easy and in some instances the recipe is your entire meal. For some other meals, we've simply added a slice of bread, a fruit, or a little salad to round out the meal. So, this chapter is your main guide to planning your meals, showing you just what to eat.

Each meal recommendation comes with important nutrition information to help you with particular health needs. For example, if you have high blood pressure, pay attention to the sodium levels so that you can keep your intake low. If you are diabetic, you can easily figure out which meals are best for you from the amounts of carbohydrates. If you need more fiber in your diet—and most of us do—you'll find the complete fiber count for every meal.

As explained at the beginning of the book, the weight-loss plan can also be turned into a weight-maintenance plan. Using the lists of foods on page 81, increase your daily calorie level by 300 calories when you're ready to graduate from the Keep on Losin' plan and start maintaining your weight loss on the Stay Slim Maintenance Plan.

Using the Meal Plans that follow, you can put together any combination of meals you'd like. In other words, you can have any breakfast, any lunch, any dinner, any Calcium Break, and any 125-calorie treat. So if you prefer to mix and match, everything you need is in the Meal Plans. However, if you'd like a little guidance, the Weekly Menu Plans starting on page 86 are for you!

In the Meal Plans, breakfasts average 375 calories; lunches, 400 calories; dinners, 500 calories; and calcium-rich snacks, 100 calories. Like real life, calorie counts of these meals may vary 10, 20, even 30 calories above or below the average. For instance, the on-the-go breakfast is 355 calories, while the hot cereal breakfast is 387 calories. For lunches, the Black Bean and Avocado Salad with Cilantro is 380 calories, while the Chicken Cakes with Roasted Tomato Salsa is 420 calories. Dinners also vary slightly. If you happen to be a stickler for knowing *exact* calorie counts: Relax! It all works out in the end because you'll be eating a variety of meals. One breakfast might be a little under, one lunch a little over, and dinner spot on—but your consumption will work out very close to 1,500 calories daily. And even if you *always* stick to the highest calorie meal the diet will still be under 1,600 daily calories—low enough to lose weight.

But you're *not* going to stick to the same meals, right? The more variety, the more nutrients you'll take in, and the healthier you'll be. And the slimmer you'll be, too: By avoiding a boring food rut, you're more apt to stick with the program.

Remember: If 1,500 calories a day is too low for you as you start your weight-loss program (see page 10), then add 100 calories to your daily intake. If that's still not enough, add another 50 or 100 or more until you hit the right balance of feeling satisfied while still losing weight. You'll find out how to increase calories on page 48. Also, don't sabotage your own efforts by thinking that the fewer calories you consume, the more you're going to lose. It doesn't work that way. If you take in too few calories a day, your body starts to conserve energy and you end up burning fewer calories as well as feeling hungrier: Your weight loss will slow down and you are very likely to fall off your diet very quickly.

Most of these meals are quick and easy to prepare, thanks to the use of convenience foods such as canned beans, prewashed salad greens, and rotisserie chicken. There are one-dish meals, like Macaroni and Cheese on the Light Side: In 25 minutes you've got a complete dinner. With many other meals, you simply round out the entree with a slice of whole-grain bread, some brown rice (90-second Uncle Ben's Whole Grain Brown Ready Rice is perfectly fine), or crackers. For instance, Warm Chicken Salad with Mustard-Thyme Vinaigrette, a lunch, takes just 20 minutes to make, and is served with Triscuits.

The downside to some convenience foods is sodium. Too much sodium raises blood pressure. If you're overweight and therefore at greater risk for high blood pressure, you need to be particularly watchful of your sodium intake; you should limit yourself to no more than 2,300 mg daily. In fact every adult—overweight or not—should try to limit sodium to 2,300 mg

The DASH Sodium Study and Your Risk of High Blood Pressure

Being overweight increases your risk for high blood pressure, which, in turn, puts you at greater risk for heart disease. (A blood pressure reading of 140/90 mmHg or higher is considered high. Normal blood pressure is less than 120/80 mmHg. In between these levels is a condition called "pre-hypertension"; people in this category are at increased risk for developing high blood pressure.) The DASH Sodium study—a large, government-funded study—compared diets of 3,000 mg sodium (typical American), 2,400 mg (the old recommended level, now dropped to 2,300 mg), and 1,500 mg daily. While blood pressure did drop at 2,400 mg, people got a more significant reduction on 1,500 mg, such a large reduction that many were able to lower or get rid of their blood pressure medication.

Based on the findings of the DASH Sodium Study, the Low-Sodium Weekly Menu Plan (see pages 90-91) caps sodium at 1,500 mg per day. In fact, these meals put you under 1,500 mg daily, so there's room for a little sodium in your 125-calorie treat. However, most people with high blood pressure need not cut sodium this low: 2,300 mg daily is probably fine. But if you give this menu plan a try for a month and find that your blood pressure drops significantly, then 1,500 mg daily may be your lucky number. Start with this week, then build your own menu plan from the sodium levels listed after each meal listed earlier in this chapter.

daily. Although the vast majority of meals in this book are low or moderate in sodium, some are high (800 mg or more). We point these out in the Meal Plans, and suggest you pick lower-sodium meals the rest of the day to balance your sodium intake. A lower-sodium breakfast has 300 mg of sodium or less; lower-sodium lunches and dinners have 600 mg sodium or less. Look for the **LS** icon in the Meal Plans that follow. In addition, those with high blood pressure can try the Low-Sodium Weekly Menu Plan on page 90.

Another nutrient to watch is fiber. Women need 25 g or more daily, men 35 g or more. (The average American gets just 11 g daily!) At the recommended levels, it's easier to lose weight and to maintain your weight loss, because fiber keeps you feeling fuller for a longer time on fewer calories. Fiber also binds up some of the fat in your meal, so your body gets rid of the fat along with the fiber before the fat has a chance to be absorbed by the body. Most *Supermarket Diet Cookbook* meals are fairly high to very high in fiber, but there's the occasional comfort-food fiber dud, like Cream Cheese-and-Chives Scrambled Eggs. Worth it, though, because it's so yummy, and you can simply choose a high-fiber lunch and dinner to make up for it. Don't worry. There are plenty of high-fiber meals to choose from.

Other ways to make this plan as healthful as possible: Have at least two fish meals a week and try to have a vegetarian meal a few times a week, or even daily. The evidence for the benefits of fish for the heart, brain, and developing fetus is very strong. And there's also research indicating that vegetable sources of protein—like beans and soy—help reduce the risk of chronic disease. One reason is that these sources of protein are low in saturated fat—the kind of fat that raises blood cholesterol and is linked to heart disease. Nearly all recipes in this book are low in saturated fat, so you don't have to worry about that. But still, check out the Vegetarian Weekly Menu Plan (page 88) for ideas on putting together a vegetarian day.

Get ready for some good news: The salads on this plan are very generous. One reader of *The Supermarket Diet* asked whether the 3- and 4-cup salads on the plan really serve one person. Yes, they do! The salads are so generous because the diet reverses the typical American meal that features large portions protein and starch (like rice, fries, pasta) and a small side salad. Instead, in *The Supermarket Diet*, greens often upstage protein and starches. A big salad helps fill you up on fewer calories (a great weight-loss strategy), plus it loads you up with vitamins and minerals. So remember all the salads in the following meals serve just you; and the recipes for salads in Chapter 7 clearly state how many they serve—usually four or six people.

About Beverages

Thirsty? Have some water, seltzer, unsweetened iced tea, hot tea, coffee, or one of the beverages from a Calcium Break. Skip the juice, soda, sweetened iced tea, and any other caloric beverages. The problem: unsatisfying calories. There's evidence that the body doesn't register the 150 calories from a soda, like it does the 150 calories in a snack of crackers and cheese. In other words, that 117-calorie cup of apple juice won't be nearly as satisfying 20 minutes later as an 80-calorie apple. So, if you really want the calorie-laden drinks, save them for your 125-calorie treat. And if you can't part with soda, have a diet drink. However, if the diet drinks backfire—they may make you start to crave sugary foods—then skip them. Diet drinks are saviors for some people, but may not help others.

TWEAKING THE PLAN: DOS AND DON'TS

Here's what you can—and can't—get away with on the Keep On Losin' plan. You're welcome to tweak meals as long as you don't fiddle much with the calorie counts. Some guidelines:

- **Shortening prep time.** The meals on this plan don't take much time or cooking skill. Most meals take 5 to 25 minutes to prepare. If you don't have the time or inclination to make these exact recipes, no problem: Take shortcuts. For instance, if you don't want to make your own skinless chicken breasts, use precooked chicken pieces.

- **Subbing ingredients.** It's perfectly OK to use romaine lettuce instead of mixed greens, chopped carrots instead of celery, flounder instead of halibut, margarine instead of oil, or similar swaps. But if you substitute an extra tablespoon of low-fat mayo for yogurt, you're adding 30 calories to the meal. Your rule of thumb: Substitute like foods for like foods. Swap lean protein (chicken) for lean protein (fish, scallops, lean meat, etc.), one fat for another fat (mayo for margarine), a starch for a starch (one slice of bread for $1/2$ cup rice), a fruit for a fruit, almonds for pecans, etc. The Food Exchange System on page 29 will help you figure out which foods are in the same group. While it's OK to make these substitutions occasionally, if you're tweaking this plan a lot, best buy a calorie-counter book or check a website to make sure you're making equivalent calorie swaps. The U.S. Department of Agriculture's nutrient database website offers nutritional analysis of foods at www.nal.usda.gov/fnic/foodcomp/search. Keep in mind that the bread in this plan should be 65 to 75 calories per slice, no more, so read labels carefully to determine equivalent portion sizes.

- **Switching lunch for dinner (and vice versa).** It's fine to do this, just don't have two of the same meal on the same day. If you have two dinners on the same day, you'll bust your calorie limit, and if you have two lunches, you won't get quite enough calories (and may go hungry). Also, dinners tend to have more vegetables, so with two lunches, you may be skimping on this important food group.

- **Increasing calories.** A daily intake of 1,500 calories might not be enough for you. Signs that you're not getting enough calories:

  You're hungry when you shouldn't be (one or two hours after eating).

  You're losing weight too quickly (more than two pounds a week for weeks on end).

  You don't have the energy to complete your workouts.

If any of these happens, try having your Calcium Break a half hour to an hour before working out or about an hour before your next meal. If this still doesn't ward off hunger until you eat again, you may need more calories. Try adding 100 (healthful!) calories at a time to the plan (see "Adding Calories to Breakfast" and "Adding Calories to Lunch and Dinner," page 81).

- **Lowering calories.** In most research studies—and with my clients—consuming 1,500 daily calories induces weight loss. In fact, female clients who came to see me eating 1,200 calories or less started losing *more* weight when I switched them to 1,500 calories. (At 1,200 calories, with regular exercise, their bodies were thinking "starvation" and slowing down their metabolisms. It took the extra 300 daily calories to reassure the bodies that it was OK to turn metabolisms back up.) So, if you take in 1,200 calories for a week or two (1,500 calories for men), after that you need to switch to 1,500 calories (1,800 calories for men) to avoid lowering your metabolism.

Meal Plans

The symbol (V) next to a meal indicates that it is vegetarian. The symbol (LS) next to a meal indicates that it is low in sodium.

BREAKFASTS (ABOUT 375 CALORIES)

Apple-Cinnamon French Toast (V) (page 96)

Have 2 slices of French toast with 1 cup skim milk.

Complete meal: About 363 calories, 19 g protein, 68 g carbohydrate, 4 g total fat (1 g saturated), 6 g fiber, 5 mg cholesterol, 494 mg sodium.

Apple, Oat, and Raisin Muffin (V) (page 100)

Cut the muffin and spread the muffin halves with a total of 2 teaspoons peanut butter (preferably no-salt-added). Serve with 1 cup skim milk and 1 cup cut-up cantaloupe (or strawberries or apples).

Complete meal: About 373 calories, 17 g protein, 59 g carbohydrate, 9 g total fat (2 saturated), 3 g fiber, 23 mg cholesterol, 333 mg sodium.

Asparagus, Red Potato, and Romano Frittata (V) (page 102)

Serve with 1 cup strawberries (fresh or frozen unsweetened) or $^1/_2$ cup blueberries. This meal is a little high in fat and saturated fat for a break-fast, so balance out your day with a lunch and dinner that total, together, no more than 33 g fat and 9 g saturated fat, such as the Corn and Black Bean Salad lunch (page 109) and the Spiced Grilled Turkey Breast with Peach Salsa dinner (page 207).

Complete meal: About 369 calories, 23 g protein, 34 g carbohydrate, 17 g total fat (6 g saturated), 7 g fiber, 435 mg cholesterol, 512 mg sodium.

Berry Blast Smoothie (V) (page 94)

Serve with half a slice of whole-wheat toast (about 45 calories) spread with 1 teaspoon zero g trans fat margarine.

Complete meal: About 368 calories, 18 g protein, 67 g carbohydrate, 5 g total fat (2 g saturated), 5 g fiber, 12 mg cholesterol, 317 mg sodium.

Breakfast Burrito with Salsa (V) (page 108)

Serve with 1 cup skim milk.

Complete meal: About 362 calories, 18 g protein, 52 g carbohydrate, 10 g total fat (1 g saturated), 6 g fiber, 5 mg cholesterol, 804 mg sodium.

Cream-Cheese-and-Chives Scrambled Eggs  (page 105)

Serve with a café au lait ($^1/_2$ cup heated skim milk with $^1/_2$ cup coffee) or $^1/_2$ cup skim milk. Since this breakfast is lower in fiber and higher in saturated fat than most, compensate by having a lunch and a dinner that, together, add up to at least 20 g fiber, and no more than 8 g saturated fat. For instance, have the Rich's Caesar Salad lunch (page 113) and the Black Bean and Sweet Potato Chili dinner (page 246).

Complete meal: About 384 calories, 24 g protein, 25 g carbohydrate, 21 g total fat (7 g saturated), 3 g fiber, 441 mg cholesterol, 515 mg sodium.

Eggs and Toast (V)

Have 2 eggs, poached or boiled, with 1 slice of 100 percent whole-wheat bread (whole-wheat should be the only flour listed and the bread should be about 80 calories and at least 2 g fiber per slice). Serve with 1 cup skim milk and 1 cup strawberries, raspberries, or blackberries.

Complete meal: About 370 calories, 25 g protein, 41 g carbohydrate, 13 g total fat (4 g saturated), 8 g fiber, 429 mg cholesterol, 392 mg sodium.

Fruit Salad Smoothie (V) (LS) (page 94)

Have just the smoothie for a complete breakfast.

Complete meal: About 379 calories, 9 g protein, 84 g carbohydrate, 4 g total fat (1 g saturated), 10 g fiber, 0 mg cholesterol, 66 mg sodium.

Gingery Strawberry-Orange Smoothie (V) (LS) (page 95)

Have the smoothie with 10 unsalted almonds.

Complete meal: About 383 calories, 17 g protein, 63 g carbohydrate, 9 g total fat (2 g saturated), 5 g fiber, 13 mg cholesterol, 198 mg sodium.

Ham-and-Egg Muffin (page 103)

Serve with an orange and $^1/_2$ cup skim milk. This breakfast is high in sodium, so balance out the day with lower-sodium lunch and dinner choices.

Complete meal: About 386 calories, 30 g protein, 47 g carbohydrate, 9 g total fat (3 g saturated), 6 g fiber, 235 mg cholesterol, 887 mg sodium.

High-Fiber Cereal (V) (LS)

Have 160 calories of cereal containing at least 4 g fiber and no more than 5 g sugar per 100 calories (such as Kashi Go Lean), topped with

Salt and Your Buds

By cooking with low-sodium beans, broth, canned tomatoes, and other reduced-sodium items, some of these recipes may taste a little less salty than normal. But remember that by consistently reducing the sodium content of your diet—a good idea for heart disease prevention and not getting bloated—your tastes will change, and you won't need as much sodium. However, if you want to add a little salt to these recipes, do so *after* you've served them by sprinkling a few grains of salt on the top of the food. The feeling of salt crystals on the tongue satisfies the salt urge much more than pouring lots of salt into food while it's cooking.

2 tablespoons almonds (or other nuts) and $^1/_2$ cup blueberries (or apple or pear slices, or 1 cup other berries), with 1 cup skim milk.

Complete meal: About 373 calories, 26 g protein, 58 g carbohydrate, 10 g total fat (1 g saturated), 14 g fiber, 5 mg cholesterol, 200 mg sodium.

Honey-Glazed Oat Muffin (V) (page 101)

Cut the muffin and spread the muffin halves with a total of 2 teaspoons almond or peanut butter (preferably unsalted). Serve with a 12-ounce skim latte (page 80) and an apple.

Complete meal: About 382 calories, 18 g protein, 57 g carbohydrate, 11 g total fat (1 g saturated), 6 g fiber, 23 mg cholesterol, 445 mg sodium.

Honey-Pecan Belgian Waffles (V) (page 97)

Serve 1 waffle topped with 1 teaspoon honey and $^1/_2$ cup raspberries (or other fruit) and have 1 cup skim milk.

Complete meal: About 367 calories, 17 g protein, 54 g carbohydrate, 11 g total fat (2 g saturated), 8 g fiber, 54 mg cholesterol, 528 mg sodium.

Hot Cereal (V) (LS)

Have 1 cup cooked plain oatmeal topped with $^1/_2$ cup blueberries (or 1 cup other berries or a small apple), plus 2 tablespoons walnuts (or other nuts) and 1 teaspoon brown sugar or honey. Serve with 1 cup skim milk.

Complete meal: About 387 calories, 17 g protein, 59 g carbohydrate, 11 g total fat (2 g saturated), 7 g fiber, 5 mg cholesterol, 107 mg sodium.

Multigrain Pancakes Ⓥ *(page 98)*

Have 2 pancakes topped with 2 teaspoons maple syrup and 1 cup sliced strawberries. Serve with 1 cup skim milk.

Complete meal: About 364 calories, 16 g protein, 58 g carbohydrate, 10 g total fat (2 g saturated), 6 g fiber, 41 mg cholesterol, 537 mg sodium.

On-the-Go Breakfast Ⓥ

1 Kellogg's All-Bran breakfast bar (or other 130-calorie bar with at least 5 g fiber), one 12-ounce skim latte (page 80), and a banana.

Complete meal: About 355 calories, 15 g protein, 71 g carbohydrate, 3 g total fat (1 g saturated), 8 g fiber, 5 mg cholesterol, 341 mg sodium.

Spinach and Jack Cheese Bread Pudding Ⓥ *(page 106)*

Serve with a navel orange or medium apple. This meal is a little high in fat (especially saturated fat) for a breakfast, so balance out your day with a lunch and dinner that total no more than 33 g fat and 9 g saturated fat, such as the Black Bean and Avocado Salad with Cilantro lunch (page 112) and the Cod with Peppers and Onions dinner (page 230).

Complete meal: About 364 calories, 21 g protein, 43 g carbohydrate, 14 g total fat (6 g saturated), 7 g fiber, 233 mg cholesterol, 564 mg sodium.

Wake-Up Smoothie Ⓥ *(page 95)*

Have 1 smoothie with a slice of whole-wheat toast spread with 2 teaspoons peanut butter (preferably no-salt-added) and a cup of sliced strawberries.

Complete meal: About 374 calories, 17 g protein, 60 g carbohydrate, 9 g total fat (3 g saturated), 6 g fiber, 12 mg cholesterol, 314 mg sodium.

Whole-Grain Carrot Muffin Ⓥ *(page 99)*

Have 1 muffin with 1 cup skim milk and a banana.

Complete meal: About 369 calories, 14 g protein, 71 g carbohydrate, 6 g total fat (1 g saturated), 8 g fiber, 23 mg cholesterol, 365 mg sodium.

Yogurt, Fruit, and Nuts Ⓥ

Combine 1 cup plain low-fat yogurt with a sliced banana and 1¹/₂ teaspoons honey. Top with 2 tablespoons pecans (or other nuts).

Complete meal: About 374 calories, 15 g protein, 54 g carbohydrate, 13 g total fat (3 g saturated), 4 g fiber, 15 mg cholesterol, 174 mg sodium.

SALAD LUNCHES (ABOUT 400 CALORIES)

Black Bean and Avocado Salad with Cilantro (V) (LS) *(page 112)*

The salad by itself is a complete lunch.

Complete meal (with no-salt-added beans): About 380 calories, 16 g protein, 49 g carbohydrate, 15 g total fat (2 g saturated), 17 g fiber, 13 mg cholesterol, 335 mg sodium.

Broccoli and Garbanzo Bean Salad (V) (LS) *(page 114)*

Serve with a 150-calorie whole-wheat pita.

Complete meal: About 416 calories, 17 g protein, 60 g carbohydrate, 14 g total fat (4 g saturated), 14 g fiber, 13 mg cholesterol, 444 mg sodium.

Chicken, Garbanzo Bean, and Grains Salad (LS) *(page 123)*

The salad by itself is a complete lunch.

Complete meal: About 394 calories, 26 g protein, 46 g carbohydrate, 13 g total fat (2 g saturated), 9 g fiber, 53 mg cholesterol, 577 mg sodium.

Chicken with Lentil Salad *(page 119)*

The salad by itself is a complete lunch.

Complete meal: About 411 calories, 48 g protein, 35 g carbohydrate, 9 g total fat (2 g saturated), 18 g fiber, 82 mg cholesterol, 703 mg sodium.

Cool and Creamy Shrimp Salad *(page 125)*

Serve with 2 slices crusty whole-wheat bread spread with a total of 2 teaspoons zero grams trans fat margarine.

Complete meal: About 406 calories, 38 g protein, 32 g carbohydrate, 14 g total fat (4 g saturated), 5 g fiber, 242 mg cholesterol, 785 mg sodium.

Corn and Black Bean Salad (V) (LS) *(page 109)*

The salad by itself is a complete lunch.

Complete meal (with no-salt-added beans): About 394 calories, 17 g protein, 62 g carbohydrate, 12 g total fat (2 g saturated), 17 g fiber, 0 mg cholesterol, 473 mg sodium.

Dilled Tuna-Stuffed Tomatoes (page 126)

Serve with 180 calories of whole-grain crackers (preferably with less than 100 mg sodium per 120 calories, such as 9 Low Sodium Triscuits).

Complete meal: About 390 calories, 26 g protein, 42 g carbohydrate, 14 g total fat (3 g saturated), 7 g fiber, 42 mg cholesterol, 733 mg sodium.

Edamame Salad with Chicken **LS** *(page 117)*

The salad by itself is a complete lunch.

Complete meal: About 402 calories, 37 g protein, 34 g carbohydrate, 15 g total fat (3 g saturated), 9 g fiber, 48 mg cholesterol, 302 mg sodium.

Edamame Salad with Tofu **V** **LS** *(page 116)*

Serve with 60 calories of whole-grain crackers (preferably with less than 100 mg sodium per 120 calories, such as 3 Low Sodium Triscuits).

Complete meal: About 386 calories, 30 g protein, 41 g carbohydrate, 14 g total fat (2 g saturated), 10 g fiber, 0 mg cholesterol, 509 mg sodium.

Greek Peasant Salad **V** *(page 111)*

Serve with crackers and sardines: Drain the oil from a 3.75-ounce can of sardines (compare labels and get the lowest-sodium brand—less than 350 mg of sodium per can is fine—and, if possible, get it canned in olive oil; Season Norway brand is a good choice). Lightly mash the sardines with lemon juice, to taste, and, if desired, $1/4$ teaspoon crushed garlic. Spread on 120 calories of whole-grain crackers (preferably with no more than 100 mg sodium per 120 calories, such as 6 Low Sodium Triscuits). This lunch is a little high in sodium—unavoidable because of the olives and feta. To counter it, have a lower-sodium dinner.

Complete meal: About 392 calories, 21 g protein, 31 g carbohydrate, 22 g total fat (8 g saturated), 6 g fiber, 123 mg cholesterol, 849 mg sodium.

No-Cook Barbecue Chicken Salad **LS** *(page 122)*

The salad by itself is a complete lunch.

Complete meal (with no-salt-added beans): About 409 calories, 30 g protein, 46 g carbohydrate, 13 g total fat (2 g saturated), 13 g fiber, 53 mg cholesterol, 318 mg sodium.

Panzanella with Chicken (page 118)

The salad by itself is a complete lunch.

Complete meal: About 396 calories, 22 g protein, 32 g carbohydrate, 20 g total fat (7 g saturated), 4 g fiber, 53 mg cholesterol, 632 mg sodium.

Rich's Caesar Salad **LS** (page 113)

Serve with a 150-calorie whole-wheat pita. If you like, fill the pita up with some salad, and enjoy the remaining salad as a side.

Complete meal: About 410 calories, 32 g protein, 38 g carbohydrate, 14 g total fat (3 g saturated), 6 g fiber, 72 mg cholesterol, 464 mg sodium.

Tofu Salad with Peanuts **V** **LS** (page 115)

Serve with 1/2 cup cooked brown rice.

Complete meal: About 430 calories, 17 g protein, 45 g carbohydrate, 21 g total fat (3 g saturated), 8 g fiber, 0 mg cholesterol, 474 mg sodium.

Warm Chicken Salad with Mustard-Thyme Vinaigrette (page 120)

Serve with 60 calories of whole-grain crackers (preferably with less than 100 mg sodium per 120 calories, such as 3 Low Sodium Triscuits).

Complete meal: About 412 calories, 36 g protein, 20 g carbohydrates, 21 g total fat (6 g saturated), 4 g fiber, 105 mg cholesterol, 708 mg sodium.

SANDWICH AND WRAP LUNCHES (ABOUT 400 CALORIES)

Bacon, Lettuce, and Tomato Sandwich with Basil Mayonnaise (page 135)

Serve with 12 baby carrots.

Complete meal: About 404 calories, 17 g protein, 43 g carbohydrate, 20 g total fat (5 g saturated), 8 g fiber, 33 mg cholesterol, 821 mg sodium.

Chicken Cakes with "Roasted" Tomato Salsa **LS** (page 136)

Have with a salad: 3 cups mixed greens tossed with 80 calories of salad dressing (or 2 teaspoons olive oil, a spritz of lemon juice, and salt, pepper, and herbs to taste).

Complete meal: About 415 calories, 25 g protein, 27 g carbohydrate, 24 g total fat (4 g saturated), 6 g fiber, 58 mg cholesterol, 541 mg sodium.

Corn and Black Bean Burrito (V) (page 127)

The burrito by itself is a complete lunch.

Complete meal: About 400 calories, 22 g protein, 60 g carbohydrate, 11 g total fat (4g saturated), 13 g fiber, 23 mg cholesterol, 647 mg sodium.

Corn and Jack Quesadilla (V) (page 128)

The quesadilla by itself is a complete lunch. This meal is a little high in sodium so balance out your day with lower-sodium breakfast and dinner choices.

Complete meal: About 400 calories, 18 g protein, 59 g carbohydrate, 14 g total fat (5 g saturated), 12 g fiber, 18 mg cholesterol, 804 mg sodium.

Falafel with Tzatziki Sauce (V) (page 132)

Serve with a green salad: 3 cups mixed greens tossed with $1^1/_2$ teaspoons olive oil, $^1/_2$ teaspoon vinegar, and salt and pepper to taste.

Complete meal: About 412 calories, 25 g protein, 67 g carbohydrate, 9 g total fat (1 g saturated), 15 g fiber, 3 mg cholesterol, 801 mg sodium.

Fresh Mozzarella and Tomato Sandwich (V) (page 133)

Serve with 2 stalks celery.

Complete meal: About 410 calories, 18 g protein, 39 g carbohydrate, 20 g total fat (9 g saturated), 5 g fiber, 40 mg cholesterol, 661 mg sodium.

Greek Salad Pita (V) (page 131)

The pita sandwich by itself is a complete lunch.

Complete meal: About 392 calories, 17 g protein, 54 g carbohydrate, 13 g total fat (4 g saturated), 10 g fiber, 18 mg cholesterol, 542 mg sodium.

Peanut Butter and Jelly Sandwich (V) (LS)

On 2 slices whole-wheat bread, spread a total of 4 teaspoons peanut butter and 2 teaspoons jam or jelly. Serve with 1 cup skim milk and $^1/_2$ cup carrots.

Complete meal: About 421 calories, 20 g protein, 59 g carbohydrate, 14 g total fat (3 g saturated), 7 g fiber, 5 mg cholesterol, 573 mg sodium.

Portobello Burger (V) (page 138)

Serve with 10 baby carrots.

Complete meal: About 399 calories, 16 g protein, 50 g carbohydrate, 17 g total fat (5 g saturated), 8 g fiber, 25 mg cholesterol, 781 mg sodium.

Steak Sandwich with Grilled Onions (LS) (page 139)

The sandwich by itself is a complete lunch.

Complete meal: About 416 calories, 42 g protein, 41 g carbohydrate, 8 g total fat (3 g saturated), 6 g fiber, 2 mg cholesterol, 477 mg sodium.

Tofu "Egg" Salad Sandwich (V) (page 134)

Serve with a salad: 3 cups mixed greens and $^1/_2$ a sliced tomato, tossed with 2 teaspoons olive oil, $^1/_2$ teaspoon lemon juice or vinegar, and salt, pepper, and herbs to taste.

Complete meal: About 402 calories, 20 g protein, 41 g carbohydrate, 18 g total fat (2 g saturated), 10 g fiber, 5 mg cholesterol, 631 mg sodium.

Turkey and Swiss Sandwich from the Deli (LS)

Have 2 slices whole-wheat bread with 2 ounces (2 thick slices) reduced-sodium turkey breast (such as from Healthy Choice or another brand that also has 80 mg sodium per ounce or less), 1 ounce (1 sandwich-size slice) Swiss cheese and a few tomato slices. Serve with a salad: 2 cups mixed greens, a few tomato slices, and 1 teaspoon olive oil with $^1/_2$ teaspoon vinegar or lemon juice and salt and pepper to taste. Although *The Supermarket Diet* plan generally recommends reduced-fat cheese, this sandwich is easy to order when you're eating out, so the recipe uses regular cheese to reflect a deli sandwich. Make sure to ask for 1 ounce of cheese, no more!

Complete meal: About 404 calories, 26 g protein, 41 g carbohydrate, 17 g total fat (7 g saturated), 7 g fiber, 53 mg cholesterol, 576 mg sodium (more, if it comes from a deli).

Turkey and Swiss Sandwich from Subway

Order a turkey sandwich and 1 serving Swiss cheese on a 6-inch sub. Also have a Veggie Delite salad with $^1/_3$ packet of Fat Free Italian dressing.

Complete meal: About 405 calories, 25 g protein, 61 g carbohydrate, 9 g total fat (4 g saturated), 8 g fiber, 33 mg cholesterol, 1,360 mg sodium.

SOUP LUNCHES (ABOUT 400 CALORIES)

Chicken Soup with Latin Flavors **LS** *(page 142)*

Serve with a kiwi for dessert.

Complete meal: About 412 calories, 25 g protein, 43 g carbohydrate, 18 g total fat (3 g saturated), 10 g fiber, 53 mg cholesterol, 248 mg sodium.

Cranberry Bean Soup **V** **LS** *(page 140)*

The soup by itself is a complete lunch.

Complete meal: About 408 calories, 17 g protein, 81 g carbohydrate, 7 g total fat (1 g saturated), 13 g fiber, 0 mg cholesterol, 555 mg sodium.

Pasta e Fagioli **V** **LS** *(page 141)*

Have a serving of the soup topped with 1 tablespoon grated Parmesan. Serve with a $^1/_2$ cup of carrot sticks or baby carrots.

Complete meal: About 399 calories, 20 g protein, 66 g carbohydrate, 8 g total fat (2 g saturated), 16 g fiber, 4 mg cholesterol, 549 mg sodium.

OTHER LUNCHES (ABOUT 400 CALORIES)

Greens and Ricotta Pie **V** *(page 150)*

Serve with 2 slices whole-wheat toast. This is a little high in saturated fat, so balance your day out with a breakfast and dinner that total no more than 8 g saturated fat. For instance, you could have the high-fiber cereal breakfast (page 50) and the Cashew Chicken Stir-Fry dinner (page 202).

Complete meal: About 399 calories, 24 g protein, 41 g carbohydrate, 17 g fat (7 g saturated), 6 g fiber, 172 mg cholesterol, 768 mg sodium.

Middle-Eastern Garbanzo Beans and Macaroni **V** **LS** *(page 149)*

The dish by itself is a complete lunch.

Complete meal (with low-sodium tomatoes and no-salt-added beans): About 420 calories, 16 g protein, 74 g carbohydrate, 8 g total fat (1 g saturated), 13 g fiber, 0 mg cholesterol, 417 mg sodium.

Onion, Spinach, and Pecorino Frittata Ⓥ *(page 146)*

Serve with 1 slice whole-wheat toast and a salad: 3 cups spinach tossed with $1^1/_2$ teaspoons olive oil and $^1/_2$ teaspoon balsamic vinegar, plus herbs, salt, and pepper to taste. This is high in fat, so balance your day out with a breakfast and dinner that total no more than 23 g fat. For instance, you could have the on-the-go breakfast (page 52) and the Shrimp and Scallop Kabobs dinner (page 219).

Complete meal: About 423 calories, 22 g protein, 26 g carbohydrate, 27 g total fat (6 g saturated), 6 g fiber, 427 mg cholesterol, 658 mg sodium.

Tomato and Cheese Pie Ⓥ *(page 145)*

Serve with a corn salad: $^3/_4$ cup fresh cooked corn (or canned no-salt-added corn such as Del Monte or Green Giant Niblets), tossed with $^1/_3$ cup diced red pepper and a dash of balsamic vinegar.

Complete meal: About 424 calories, 27 g protein, 47 g carbohydrate, 17 g total fat (8 g saturated), 6 g fiber, 251 mg cholesterol, 607 mg sodium.

BEEF DINNERS (ABOUT 500 CALORIES)

Beef and Barley with Mushrooms Ⓛⓢ *(page 156)*

Serve with a salad: 3 cups mixed greens tossed with 60 calories dressing of your choice, or 1 tablespoon Vinaigrette (page 281).

Complete meal: About 516 calories, 32 g protein, 73 g carbohydrate, 12 g total fat (2 g saturated), 16 g fiber, 49 mg cholesterol, 510 mg sodium.

Grilled Steak Caesar Salad *(page 159)*

Serve with a tangerine.

Complete meal: About 507 calories, 35 g protein, 32 g carbohydrate, 28 g total fat (3 g saturated), 5 g fiber, 79 mg cholesterol, 767 mg sodium.

Jamaican Beef with Sweet Potatoes and Greens *(page 158)*

The dish by itself is a complete dinner.

Complete meal: About 516 calories, 28 g protein, 74 g carbohydrate, 15 g total fat (4 g saturated), 9 g fiber, 57 mg cholesterol, 737 mg sodium.

No-Bake Tamale Pie (page 162)

Serve with 1½ cups steamed cauliflower (or broccoli or Brussels sprouts), tossed with 1 teaspoon olive oil, a spritz of lemon, and a little chopped cilantro. This dinner is a little high in sodium, so balance out the day with lower sodium breakfast and lunch choices.

Complete meal: About 511 calories, 31 g protein, 51 g carbohydrate, 22 g total fat (5 g saturated), 9 g fiber, 74 mg cholesterol, 994 mg sodium.

Pepper-Crusted Filet Mignon (page 151)

Serve with Fattoush (page 285) and end the meal with a kiwi or tangerine. This dish is a little high in sodium so balance out your day out with lower-sodium breakfast and lunch choices.

Complete meal: About 487 calories, 34 g protein, 47 g carbohydrate, 21 g total fat (5 g saturated), 12 g fiber, 76 mg cholesterol, 977 mg sodium.

Skirt Steak with Chimichurri Sauce (page 153)

Serve with Mixed Summer Squash with Parsley and Lemon (page 278) and a very thick slice (1½ ounces) of whole-grain crusty bread, brushed with 1 teaspoon olive oil and grilled along with the steak.

Complete meal: About 511 calories, 37 g protein, 32 g carbohydrate, 27 g total fat (7 g saturated), 1 g fiber, 67 mg cholesterol, 757 mg sodium.

Steak and Pepper Fajitas (page 164)

The fajita by itself is a complete dinner.

Complete meal: About 489 calories, 38 g protein, 44 g carbohydrate, 19 g total fat (6 g saturated), 8 g fiber, 67 mg cholesterol, 771 mg sodium.

Steak with Mushroom Sauce (page 154)

Start the dinner with a serving of Green Pea and Lettuce Soup (page 288), then serve the steak with a medium baked sweet potato (eat the skin, it's got lots of fiber!) topped with 2 to 3 tablespoons plain low-fat yogurt. This dinner is high in sodium, so balance out the day with lower-sodium breakfast and lunch choices.

Complete meal: About 487 calories, 37 g protein, 52 g carbohydrate, 13 g total fat (4 g saturated), 9 g fiber, 70 mg cholesterol, 1,088 mg sodium.

Tangerine Beef Stir-Fry LS (page 166)

Serve with $^2/_3$ cup cooked brown rice.

Complete meal: About 521 calories, 33 g protein, 60 g carbohydrate, 15 g total fat (4 g saturated), 6 g fiber, 48 mg cholesterol, 506 mg sodium.

Thai Beef Salad LS (page 165)

Serve with 1 cup cooked brown rice.

Complete meal: About 514 calories, 33 g protein, 61 g carbohydrate, 16 g total fat (2 g saturated), 9 g fiber, 58 mg cholesterol, 403 mg sodium.

Tuscan Steak and Beans (page 161)

Serve with a Roasted Rosemary Potato Packet (page 272) and $1^1/_2$ cups crudités (such as sliced radishes and red pepper).

Complete meal: About 489 calories, 41 g protein, 51 g carbohydrate, 12 g total fat (3 g saturated), 11 g fiber, 84 mg cholesterol, 679 mg sodium.

PORK DINNERS (ABOUT 500 CALORIES)

Brazilian Pork LS (page 180)

Serve with $^2/_3$ cup cooked bulgur wheat (or $^1/_2$ cup cooked brown rice) and a salad: 3 cups romaine (or other lettuce) tossed with 1 teaspoon lime juice, $1^1/_2$ teaspoons olive oil, 1 to 3 teaspoons chopped cilantro, and salt and pepper to taste.

Complete meal: About 485 calories, 42 g protein, 48 g carbohydrate, 15 g total fat (3 g saturated), 16 g fiber, 90 mg cholesterol, 507 mg sodium.

Chorizo and Bean Burritos (page 175)

Serve with $^1/_2$ cup baby carrots. This dinner is high in sodium so balance it out with a lower-sodium breakfast and lunch choices.

Complete meal: About 513 calories, 27 g protein, 56 g carbohydrate, 23 g total fat (8 g saturated), 15 g fiber, 43 mg cholesterol, 1,168 mg sodium.

Couscous with Ham and Tomatoes (page 183)

Serve with 1 cup steamed Brussels sprouts (or broccoli or cauliflower) drizzled with 1 teaspoon olive oil and a spritz of fresh lemon juice. This dinner is high in sodium so balance it out with lower-sodium breakfast and lunch choices.

Complete meal: About 506 calories, 27 g protein, 74 g carbohydrate, 13 g total fat (2 g saturated), 15 g fiber, 27 mg cholesterol, 1,010 mg sodium.

Dijon-Fennel Pork Tenderloin with Sweet Potato Fries *(page 174)*

Serve with a spinach and orange salad: 3 cups spinach, 1 sliced orange, 1 tablespoon chopped red onion, and 2 tablespoons Vinaigrette (page 281) or 120 calories of a dressing of your choice.

Complete meal: About 502 calories, 31 g protein, 56 g carbohydrates, 18 g total fat (3 g saturated), 11 g fiber, 74 mg cholesterol, 862 mg sodium.

Glazed Pork with Pear Chutney **LS** *(page 169)*

Serve with a salad: Chop the remainder of the red pepper (from the Pear Chutney) and toss with $^1/_2$ cup chopped cucumber, 1 teaspoon olive oil, and a dash of balsamic vinegar.

Complete meal: About 486 calories, 34 g protein, 68 g carbohydrates, 11 g total fat (3 g saturated), 8 g fiber, 98 mg cholesterol, 543 mg sodium.

Jerk Pork Tenderloins **LS** *(page 173)*

Serve with Grilled Eggplant, Peppers, Zucchini, and Summer Squash (page 277) and 1 cup cooked brown rice.

Complete meal: About 475 calories, 30 g protein, 66 g carbohydrate, 11 g total fat (1 g saturated), 9 g fiber, 70 mg cholesterol, 432 mg sodium.

Pork, Cabbage, and Apple Sauté *(page 179)*

Serve with a salad: 1 (5-ounce) bag baby spinach (about 5 cups) tossed with 2 tablespoons plain low-fat yogurt mixed with 2 teaspoons apple cider vinegar, 1 teaspoon olive oil, and 1 tablespoon fresh chopped dill or any other herb of your choice (if desired, add half a clove crushed garlic). Have with 1 medium slice (1 ounce) whole-grain crusty bread spread with 1 teaspoon unsalted trans fat–free margarine.

Complete meal: About 509 calories, 30 g protein, 63 g carbohydrate, 12 g total fat (2 g saturated), 4 g fiber, 59 mg cholesterol, 748 mg sodium.

Pork Chops with Tomatoes and Arugula *(page 176)*

Serve with 1 thick slice ($1^1/_4$ ounces) whole-wheat crusty bread dipped in $1^1/_2$ teaspoons olive oil or spread with 60 calories trans fat–free margarine (about 2 teaspoons).

Complete meal: About 364 calories, 31 g protein, 15 g carbohydrate, 20 g total fat (5 g saturated), 3 g fiber, 67 mg cholesterol, 676 mg sodium.

Tarragon Pork Tenderloins with Grilled Grapes (LS) *(page 170)*

Serve with Grilled Eggplant, Peppers, Zucchini and Summer Squash (page 277) and grill 1 medium slice whole-grain crusty bread drizzled with 1 teaspoon olive oil.

Complete meal: About 487 calories, 33 g protein, 46 g carbohydrate, 21 g total fat (4 g saturated), 10 g fiber, 73 mg cholesterol, 461 mg sodium.

POULTRY DINNERS (ABOUT 500 CALORIES)

Arroz con Pollo (LS) *(page 192)*

Serve with a salad: 2 cups mixed greens; $1/2$ cup cherry tomatoes; $1/4$ of a sliced avocado; and 1 tablespoon chopped cilantro tossed with 1 teaspoon lime juice, 2 teaspoons olive oil, and salt and pepper to taste.

Complete meal: About 512 calories, 24 g protein, 56 g carbohydrates, 23 g total fat (4 g saturated), 10 g fiber, 58 mg cholesterol, 544 mg sodium.

Cashew Chicken Stir-Fry (LS) *(page 202)*

The stir-fry by itself is a complete meal.

Complete meal: About 504 calories, 36 g protein, 55 g carbohydrate, 15 g total fat (2 g saturated), 6 g fiber, 66 mg cholesterol, 550 mg sodium.

Chicken and Prosciutto Roll-Ups *(page 186)*

Serve with 1 slice (1 ounce) crusty whole-grain bread spread with 1 teaspoon trans fat–free margarine and a salad: $1^1/2$ cups escarole, $1^1/2$ cups arugula (or 3 cups mixed greens) with 90 calories dressing (or $1^1/2$ tablespoons Vinaigrette Dressing, page 281). This dinner is high in sodium (because of the cheese and prosciutto) so balance out the day with lower-sodium breakfast and lunch choices.

Complete meal: About 506 calories, 48 g protein, 20 g carbohydrate, 26 g total fat (8 g saturated), 4 g fiber, 123 mg cholesterol, 1,012 mg sodium.

Chicken Breasts with Cumin, Coriander, and Lime *(page 201)*

Serve with steamed asparagus spears and $1/2$ cup couscous.

Complete meal: About 345 calories, 38 g protein, 26 g carbohydrate, 9 g total fat (1 g saturated), 3 g fiber, 82 mg cholesterol, 682 mg sodium.

Chicken Breasts with Cranberry-Balsamic Sauce and Brussels Sprouts (page 191)

Serve with Bulgur and Corn Salad (page 283).

Complete meal: About 481 calories, 48 g protein, 55 g carbohydrate, 12 g total fat (2 g saturated), 11 g fiber, 82 mg cholesterol, 738 mg sodium.

Chicken-Spinach Salad with Warm Mushroom-Onion Vinaigrette (page 184)

Serve with a Roasted Rosemary Potato Packet (page 272), but divide the potato recipe by four instead of eight—you get two portions instead of one! This dinner is a little high in sodium, so balance out the day with lower-sodium breakfasts and lunch choices.

Complete meal: About 520 calories, 30 g protein, 59 g carbohydrate, 20 g total fat (3 g saturated), 7 g fiber, 62 mg cholesterol, 873 mg sodium.

Curried Turkey with Apricot Raisin Sauce (page 211)

Serve with Fattoush (page 285) and a kiwi for dessert. If you like, have a larger pita (6-inch or 170 calories) in your serving of Fattoush. Since the dinner is high in sodium, balance the day with lower-sodium breakfast and lunch choices.

Complete meal: About 504 calories, 30 g protein, 62 g carbohydrate, 18 g total fat (3 g saturated), 11 g fiber, 5 mg cholesterol, 1,011 mg sodium.

Glazed Rotisserie Chicken Four Ways (LS) (page 188) (except Hoisin)

Have any of the glazed chicken versions with $2^{1}/_{2}$ cups steamed broccoli, seasoned with lemon juice, and 1 whole-wheat roll (100 calories, about $1^{1}/_{2}$ ounces, or $^{1}/_{2}$ Pepperidge Farm 100% Whole Wheat Kaiser Roll) spread with $1^{1}/_{2}$ teaspoons trans fat–free margarine. The only real difference, nutritionally, among the different recipes is sodium.

Complete meal: About 474 to 498 calories, 45 to 47 g protein, 43 to 50 g carbohydrate, 15 to 16 g total fat (4 g saturated), 8 to 9 g fiber, 105 mg cholesterol. Sodium: 429 mg with Apricot-Ginger Glaze, 940 mg with Hoisin and Five-Spice Glaze, 403 mg with Moroccan-Spiced Glaze, 581 mg with Honey-Mustard Glaze.

Greek Turkey Cutlets with Lentil Pilaf *(page 214)*

Serve with 10 medium or large spears steamed asparagus drizzled with 2 teaspoons olive oil and 1 teaspoon lemon juice. This dinner is high in sodium; balance out your day with lower-sodium breakfast and lunch choices.

Complete meal: About 476 calories, 36 g protein, 41 g carbohydrate, 21 g total fat (4 g saturated), 11 g fiber, 58 mg cholesterol, 893 mg sodium.

Grilled Summer Squash and Chicken *(page 199)*

Serve with 2 servings of Roasted Rosemary Potato Packets (page 272) and finish the meal with an orange.

Complete meal: About 505 calories, 37 g protein, 67 g carbohydrate, 11 g total fat (2 g saturated), 10 g fiber, 118 mg cholesterol, 689 mg sodium.

Jerk Rice and Beans **LS** *(page 200)*

Serve with 4 cups mixed greens tossed with 1$^{1}/_{2}$ tablespoons Vinaigrette Dressing (page 281).

Complete meal: About 497 calories, 35 g protein, 51 g carbohydrate, 18 g total fat (3 g saturated), 11 g fiber, 66 mg cholesterol, 519 mg sodium.

Lemon Turkey *(page 212)*

Serve with Fattoush (page 285) and 1 slice of crusty whole-wheat bread and a kiwi for dessert. Since the dinner is high in sodium, balance the day with lower-sodium breakfast and lunch choices.

Complete meal: About 498 calories, 32 g protein, 56 g carbohydrate, 19 g total fat (3 g saturated), 12 g fiber, 50 mg cholesterol, 1,120 mg sodium.

Quick Chicken Mole **LS** *(page 195)*

Serve with $^{2}/_{3}$ cup cooked brown rice and a salad: 3 cups romaine (or other) lettuce tossed with 1 to 2 teaspoons chopped cilantro, 2 teaspoons lime juice, 1 teaspoon olive oil, and salt and pepper to taste.

Complete meal: About 530 calories, 40 g protein, 50 g carbohydrate, 19 g total fat (4 g saturated), 7 g fiber, 97 mg cholesterol, 212 mg sodium.

Rotisserie Chicken with Acorn Squash with White Beans and Sage (page 279)

Serve 1 serving of the squash with a quarter of a rotisserie chicken, skin removed and have 1 orange for dessert. You can also substitute 3 ounces cooked salmon for the chicken.

Complete meal: About 480 calories, 31 g protein, 59 g carbohydrate, 15 g total fat (4 g saturated), 12 g fiber, 115 mg cholesterol, 700 mg sodium.

Smoky Almond Chicken (page 196)

Serve with 1 cup Bulgur and Corn Salad (page 283) and 1 cup broccoli or frozen broccoli/cauliflower/carrot combination, steamed and seasoned with lemon juice. The chicken recipe is a little high in sodium; balance out your day with lower-sodium breakfast and lunch choices.

Complete meal: About 495 calories, 37 g protein, 41 g carbohydrate, 20 g total fat (3 g saturated), 10 g fiber, 74 mg cholesterol, 721 mg sodium.

Spiced Grilled Turkey Breast with Peach Salsa (page 207)

Serve with Picnic Potato Salad (page 271). Prepare this meal when you've got a crowd to feed. Multiply the vegetable servings accordingly. Grill a vegetable along with the turkey: Rub 2 medium zucchinis (sliced lengthwise) or toss 2 cups cauliflower or broccoli with 1 tablespoon olive oil; grill until softened. This dinner is high in sodium, so balance out the day with lower-sodium breakfast and lunch choices.

Complete meal: About 492 calories, 44 g protein, 47 g carbohydrate, 16 g total fat (2 g saturated), 8 g fiber, 93 mg cholesterol, 877 mg sodium.

Thai Chicken Saté with Pickled Cucumbers (page 203)

Serve with $1/2$ cup cooked brown rice and $1/2$ cup steamed snow peas. This dinner is high in sodium so balance out the day with lower-sodium breakfast and lunch choices.

Complete meal: About 495 calories, 41 g protein, 53 g carbohydrate, 14 g total fat (6 g saturated), 4 g fiber, 82 mg cholesterol, 988 mg sodium.

Turkey Cutlets, Indian Style (page 213)

Serve with Wheat-Berry Salad with Spinach (page 284) and a side of cucumber raita: $1/4$ cup plain low-fat yogurt mixed with 2 tablespoons finely chopped cucumber and a pinch dried mint. This dinner is high in sodium; balance out your day with lower-sodium breakfast and lunch choices.

Complete meal: About 497 calories, 35 g protein, 67 g carbohydrate, 13 g total fat (3 g saturated), 9 g fiber, 50 mg cholesterol, 1,002 mg sodium.

Turkey with Warm Arugula Salad (page 209)

Serve with 1 scant cup dry whole-wheat penne, cooked according to package directions; when cooked, toss with 2 teaspoons olive oil and $1/4$ cup of the arugula salad from the turkey and topped with 1 tablespoon grated Parmesan cheese.

Complete meal: About 504 calories, 34 g protein, 43 g carbohydrate, 23 g total fat (4 g saturated), 7 g fiber, 56 mg cholesterol, 652 mg sodium.

Warm Chicken and Apple Salad (page 185)

Serve with a slice (1 ounce) whole-grain crusty bread.

Complete meal: About 511 calories, 34 g protein, 61 g carbohydrate, 17 g total fat (3 g saturated), 7 g fiber, 66 mg cholesterol, 727 mg sodium.

SEAFOOD DINNERS (ABOUT 500 CALORIES)

Asian Flounder Bake (page 232)

Serve with microwaved (or stovetop heated) vegetables: 1 cup frozen shelled edamame and $1/2$ cup corn kernels; season with a spritz of lemon juice and herbs of your choice.

Complete meal: About 511 calories, 58 g protein, 50 g carbohydrate, 12 g total fat (2 g saturated), 13 g fiber, 68 mg cholesterol, 625 mg sodium.

Asian Tuna Burger (page 233)

Serve with Baby Spinach and Beet Salad (page 281) and 1 cup cooked brown rice.

Complete meal: About 529 calories, 37 g protein, 70 g carbohydrate, 11 g total fat (2 g saturated), 9 g fiber, 45 mg cholesterol, 765 mg sodium.

Broccoli-Shrimp Curry **LS** (page 215)

The curry by itself is a complete meal.

Complete meal (using whole-wheat couscous): About 500 calories, 35 g protein, 63 g carbohydrate, 12 g total fat (5 g saturated), 6 g fiber, 172 mg cholesterol, 504 mg sodium.

Cod with Peppers and Onions (page 230)

Serve with Garlicky Spinach (page 282).

Complete meal: About 502 calories, 43 g protein, 54 g carbohydrate, 14 g total fat, (2 g saturated), 14 g fiber, 73 mg cholesterol, 660 mg sodium.

Grilled Sea Bass (page 229)

Serve with Grilled Corn on the Cob with Molasses Butter (page 280) and 3 chopped plum tomatoes tossed with 2 teaspoons olive oil and $1/2$ teaspoon balsamic vinegar.

Complete meal: About 484 calories, 46 g protein, 28 g carbohydrate, 22 g total fat (4 g saturated), 5 g fiber, 93 mg cholesterol, 747 mg sodium.

Grilled Shrimp with Black Bean Salad (page 220)

Serve with a salad: 3 cups mixed greens tossed with 60 calories salad dressing (or 1 tablespoon Vinaigrette Dressing (page 281), topped with 2 tablespoons toasted walnuts.

Complete meal: About 509 calories, 39 g protein, 45 g carbohydrate, 21 g total fat (3 g saturated), 16 g fiber, 155 mg cholesterol, 721 mg sodium.

Poached Salmon with Antipasto Salad (page 289)

Serve the salad with 4 ounces of salmon, steamed (simmer in a pan, with lid on, in salted water barely covering the fish with a lemon wedge and some peppercorns for 8 minutes) and $1/4$ cup dry whole-wheat couscous cooked according to package directions with $1/2$ teaspoon olive oil.

Complete meal: About 497 calories, 44 g protein, 50 g carbohydrate, 15 g total fat (3 g saturated), 9 g fiber, 89 mg cholesterol, 679 mg sodium.

Provençal Salmon with Tomato-Olive Relish (page 226)

Serve with Grilled Garlic and Herb Bread (page 291), and grill 1 cup of broccoli tossed in 1 teaspoon olive oil alongside the salmon. Make up for this higher-sodium dinner with lower-sodium breakfast and lunch choices.

Complete meal: About 499 calories, 38 g protein, 27 g carbohydrate, 27 g total fat (6 g saturated), 5 g fiber, 93 mg cholesterol, 971 mg sodium.

Salmon Fillets with Tomato Jam (page 225)

Serve with Garlicky Spinach (page 282) and a small slice of crusty whole-grain bread.

Complete meal: About 536 calories, 42 g protein, 29 g carbohydrate, 29 g total fat (5 g saturated), 5 g fiber, 100 mg cholesterol, 623 mg sodium.

Salmon Patty with Broccoli Slaw (page 224)

The patty and slaw make a complete meal. Since this meal is high in sodium, balance out the day with lower-sodium breakfast and lunch choices.

Complete meal: About 482 calories, 32 g protein, 50 g carbohydrate, 17 g total fat (5 g saturated), 7 g fiber, 58 mg cholesterol, 1,071 mg sodium.

Salmon Steak with Nectarine Salad (LS) (page 227)

Serve with Grilled Basil-Romano Bread (page 291). Top the grilled bread with 1 chopped plum tomato and a pinch of dried basil (or 1 teaspoon fresh chopped basil).

Complete meal: About 514 calories, 39 g protein, 38 g carbohydrate, 24 g total fat (5 g saturated), 5 g fiber, 92 mg cholesterol, 586 mg sodium.

Seafood with Zesty Tomatoes and Wine (page 222)

Serve with 2 ounces whole-wheat penne (about $3/4$ cup dry) or spaghetti ($1/8$ of a 16-ounce package), cooked according to package directions. Alternatively, serve over 1 cup cooked whole-wheat couscous (about $1/4$ cup dry, cooked according to package directions but with no added salt or fat).

Complete meal: About 517 calories, 45 g protein, 52 g carbohydrate, 12 g total fat (1 g saturated), 5 g fiber, 136 mg cholesterol, 744 mg sodium.

Sesame Shrimp and Asparagus (page 217)

The dish by itself is a complete meal.

Complete meal: About 467 calories, 34 g protein, 57 g carbohydrate, 12 g total fat (2 g saturated), 7 g fiber, 172 mg cholesterol, 708 mg sodium.

Shrimp and Grains Paella (page 221)

Serve with 1^1/$_2$ cups frozen, steamed, or microwaved broccoli or mixed vegetables (such as broccoli, cauliflower, carrots) tossed with 1^1/$_2$ teaspoons olive oil, fresh lemon juice to taste, and, if you have it, 1 tablespoon chopped fresh dill or other fresh herbs. Top with 1 tablespoon slivered almonds. This dinner is a little high in sodium, so make up for it with lower-sodium breakfast and lunch choices.

Complete meal: About 517 calories, 29 g protein, 57 g carbohydrate, 18 g total fat (2 g saturated), 12 g fiber, 129 mg cholesterol, 837 mg sodium.

Shrimp and Scallop Kabobs (page 219)

Serve with Grilled Plum Tomatoes (page 276; have one-fourth of the recipe instead of an eighth) and 2 servings of Grilled Garlic and Herb Bread (page 291). Since this meal is high in sodium, balance out the day with lower-sodium breakfast and lunch choices.

Complete meal: About 471 calories, 36 g protein, 58 g carbohydrate, 12 g total fat (4 g saturated), 8 g fiber, 138 mg cholesterol, 961 mg sodium.

Shrimp Saté with Cucumber Salad (page 218)

Serve with Soybean Salad (page 287) and ^{2}/$_3$ cup cooked brown rice.

Complete meal: About 502 calories, 39 g protein, 60 g carbohydrate, 14 g total fat (2 g saturated), 2 g fiber, 147 mg cholesterol, 613 mg sodium.

Spinach and Flounder Bake (page 231)

Serve with 2 cups steamed cauliflower, broccoli, or Brussels spouts, seasoned with 1^1/$_2$ teaspoons olive oil and fresh lemon juice to taste. Because of the au gratin mix, this dish is high in sodium, but convenient and nutrient-rich enough to have on occasion. Balance your day out with lower-sodium breakfast and lunch choices.

Complete meal: About 493 calories, 44 g protein, 48 g carbohydrate, 18 g total fat (4 g saturated), 8 g fiber, 82 mg cholesterol, 1,192 mg sodium.

Thai Snapper (page 234)

Serve with Multi-Colored Slaw (page 273) and 1 scant cup cooked brown rice.

Complete meal: About 495 calories, 41 g protein, 55 g carbohydrate, 12 g total fat (2 g saturated), 7 g fiber, 63 mg cholesterol, 706 mg sodium.

STEW AND CHILI DINNERS (ABOUT 500 CALORIES)

Barley-Vegetable Stew (V) *(page 241)*

Serve with a salad: 3 cups mixed greens tossed with 90 calories dressing or 1^1/$_2$ tablespoons Vinaigrette Dressing (page 281). Make up for this higher-sodium dinner with lower-sodium breakfast and lunch choices.

Complete meal: About 492 calories, 14 g protein, 77 g carbohydrate, 17 g total fat (2 g saturated), 16 g fiber, 1 mg cholesterol, 991 mg sodium.

Black Bean and Sweet Potato Chili (V) (LS) *(page 246)*

Serve with a tangerine or kiwi for dessert.

Complete meal: About 486 calories, 19 g protein, 88 g carbohydrate, 8 g total fat (3 g saturated), 21 g fiber, 16 mg cholesterol, 493 mg sodium.

Curried Vegetable Stew (V) *(page 249)*

Serve with ^{3}/$_4$ cup cooked brown rice.

Complete meal: About 489 calories, 19 g protein, 97 g carbohydrate, 6 g total fat (1 g saturated), 22 g fiber, 0 mg cholesterol, 750 mg sodium.

Jambalaya (page 240)

Serve with a salad: 3 cups mixed greens, 1 sliced tangerine, and 1 chopped green onion, tossed with 1^1/$_2$ tablespoons Vinaigrette Dressing (page 281) and topped with 1 tablespoon slivered almonds.

Complete meal: About 513 calories, 33 g protein, 52 g carbohydrate, 21 g total fat (3 g saturated), 13 g fiber, 71 mg cholesterol, 800 mg sodium.

Lentil-Sausage Stew *(page 235)*

Serve with 1 cup cooked brown rice tossed with 1 tablespoon toasted pine nuts (pignoli). Since this dinner is high in sodium, balance out the day with lower-sodium breakfast and lunch choices.

Complete meal: About 501 calories, 28 g protein, 65 g carbohydrate, 8 g total fat (3 g saturated), 9 g fiber, 59 mg cholesterol, 1,157 mg sodium (982 mg sodium if you use no-salt-added lentil soup).

Moroccan-Style Chicken Stew **LS** *(page 239)*

Serve with 1 cup cooked whole-wheat couscous (about $^1/_4$ cup dry, cooked according to package directions but with no added salt or fat).

Complete meal (using reduced-sodium beans and whole-wheat couscous): About 495 calories, 36 g protein, 73 g carbohydrate, 8 g total fat (2 g saturated), 13 g fiber, 94 mg cholesterol, 505 mg sodium.

Red Bean and Collard Gumbo **V** **LS** *(page 248)*

Serve with 1 cup cooked brown rice.

Complete meal (using reduced-sodium beans): About 515 calories, 20 g protein, 95 g carbohydrate, 7 g total fat (1 g saturated), 19 g fiber, 0 mg cholesterol, 530 mg sodium.

Southwest Chicken Stew *(page 236)*

Serve with a medium tomato, sliced.

Complete meal: About 505 calories, 39 g protein, 53 g carbohydrate, 15 g total fat (4 g saturated), 11 g fiber, 101 mg cholesterol, 737 mg sodium.

Sweet-Potato Chili con Carne *(page 243)*

Serve with heaping $^1/_2$ cup cooked brown rice.

Complete meal: About 515 calories, 26 g protein, 75 g carbohydrate, 13 g total fat (5 g saturated), 14 g fiber, 51 mg cholesterol, 657 mg sodium.

Tofu and Black Bean Chili **V** **LS** *(page 247)*

Serve with $^3/_4$ cup cooked brown rice.

Complete meal: About 491 calories, 23 g protein, 74 g carbohydrate, 11 g total fat (1 g saturated), 15 g fiber, 2 mg cholesterol, 475 mg sodium.

Vegetarian Chili **V** **LS** *(page 245)*

Serve with 1 scant cup cooked brown rice.

Complete meal: About 499 calories, 20 g protein, 86 g carbohydrate, 12 g total fat (2 g saturated), 0 mg cholesterol, 18 g fiber, 361 mg sodium.

Vegetarian Lentil Stew **V** **LS** *(page 242)*

Serve with Bulgur and Corn Salad (page 283) mixed with $^2/_3$ cup shelled frozen warmed edamame.

Complete meal: About 509 calories, 29 g protein, 77 g carbohydrate, 14 g total fat (2 g saturated), 20 g fiber, 0 mg cholesterol, 506 mg sodium.

PASTA DINNERS (ABOUT 500 CALORIES)

Broccoli Pesto and Chicken Spaghetti **LS** *(page 257)*

The pasta by itself is a complete dinner.

Complete meal: About 507 calories, 37 g protein, 57 g carbohydrate, 15 g total fat (3 g saturated), 9 g fiber, 73 mg cholesterol, 304 mg sodium.

Fusilli with Ricotta and Fresh Tomato Sauce **V** *(page 255)*

Serve with Garlicky Spinach (page 282).

Complete meal: About 530 calories, 24 g protein, 74 g carbohydrate, 16 g total fat (4 g saturated), 13 g fiber, 20 mg cholesterol, 710 mg sodium.

Macaroni and Cheese on the Light Side **V** **LS** *(page 256)*

The pasta by itself is a complete dinner.

Complete meal: About 520 calories, 28 g protein, 77 g carbohydrate, 17 g total fat (5 g saturated), 11 g fiber, 27 mg cholesterol, 358 mg sodium.

Pasta with Broccoli Rabe and Garbanzo Beans **V** *(page 251)*

The pasta by itself is a complete dinner.

Complete meal: About 528 calories, 21 g protein, 90 g carbohydrate, 10 g total fat (1 g saturated), 17 g fiber, 0 mg cholesterol, 735 mg sodium.

Pasta with Ham and Tricolor Peppers (page 253)

Serve with a salad: 3 cups mixed greens, 1^1/$_2$ teaspoons olive oil, ^{3}/$_4$ teaspoon lemon juice or vinegar, and a dash of salt. Add fresh herbs and a chopped green onion if desired.

Complete meal: About 504 calories, 20 g protein, 65 g carbohydrate, 20 g total fat (4 g saturated), 11 g fiber, 16 mg cholesterol, 684 mg sodium.

Pasta with No-Cook Tomato Sauce and Bocconcini *(page 250)*

The pasta by itself is a complete dinner. Since this dinner is high in saturated fat, balance out the day with meals low in saturated fat, such as the high-fiber cereal breakfast (page 50) and the Dilled Tuna-Stuffed Tomatoes (page 126) or Black Bean and Avocado Salad with Cilantro (page 112) lunches.

Complete meal: About 500 calories, 19 g protein, 51 g carbohydrate, 24 g total fat (9 g saturated), 7 g fiber, 40 mg cholesterol, 560 mg sodium.

Roasted Vegetables with Arugula and Fusilli **V** **LS** *(page 262)*

Serve with half of a rotisserie chicken breast, skin removed (^{1}/$_2$ cup cooked chicken pieces). Or, for a vegetarian meal, grill 4 ounces firm tofu (sliced into rectangles and rubbed with 1 teaspoon olive oil, ^{1}/$_2$ teaspoon cumin, and a dash of red pepper).

Complete meal with chicken: About 509 calories, 34 g protein, 72 g carbohydrate, 10 g total fat (1 g saturated), 11 g fiber, 60 mg cholesterol, 456 mg sodium.

Complete meal with tofu: About 514 calories, 22 g protein, 75 g carbohydrate, 14 g total fat (1 g saturated), 12 g fiber, 0 mg cholesterol, 405 mg sodium.

Shrimp Fra Diavolo **LS** *(page 254)*

Serve with a salad: 2 cups arugula (or other greens), ^{1}/$_2$ cup cherry tomatoes, and 1^1/$_2$ tablespoons Vinaigrette Dressing (page 281) or 90 calories dressing of your choice.

Complete meal: About 525 calories, 28 g protein, 67 g carbohydrate, 17 g total fat (2 g saturated), 11 g fiber, 115 mg cholesterol, 368 mg sodium.

Choosing a Whole-Grain Pasta

Now that "low-carb" is a distant bad memory, it's time to start enjoying pasta again, especially whole-wheat pasta, which is an excellent choice if you're trying to lose weight. And today's whole-wheat pastas taste better than earlier versions. They have more than twice the fiber as white pasta—important because research studies consistently show that people lose more weight on high-fiber diets.

Pasta recipes in this book call for whole-wheat pasta. Those made with 100-percent whole-wheat or 100-percent other whole grain are the best choices, since whole grains are so rich in antioxidants. But those that combine white flour with wheat bran or other high-fiber ingredients are also OK, as long as you're getting **at least 4 g fiber per 2 ounces of dried pasta**. Your supermarket should have at least one of the pastas in the chart below. Health food stores, such as Whole Foods, will have many more choices. The nutrient levels reported below are all for 2 ounces or about $^1/_2$ cup dried penne, ziti, or fusilli—but the numbers are nearly the same for any other shape of pasta.

Comparing Whole-Wheat and Added-Fiber Pasta

	Barilla Plus Penne*	Bionaturae Whole Durham Wheat Penne**	De Cecco Whole Wheat Fusilli	Dreamfields Penne Rigate***	Eden Organic Spelt Ziti Rigate, 100% Whole Grain
SERVING SIZE	2 ounces	2 ounces	2 ounces	2 ounces	2 ounces
CALORIES	200	190	180	190	210
FIBER	4 g	5 g	7 g	5 g	5 g
	Ingredients Semolina, grain and legume flour blend (lentils, chickpeas, oats, spelt, barley, egg whites, ground flaxseeds, wheat fiber), vitamins and minerals.	Ingredients Organic whoie durham wheat, water	Ingredients Whole wheat semolina, vitamins and minerals	Ingredients Enriched semolina, fiber blend (inulin, xanthan gum, pectin), sorbitol, wheat gluten, potassium chloride	Ingredients Organic Spelt

* This pasta is also rich in the plant form of omega-3 fats, called ALA, thanks to the added flax seed.
** Our personal favorite, available in Whole Foods and other natural food stores.
*** According to the company claims, fiber blend and the wheat gluten slow down the absorption of carbohydrates, making this a very low glycemic index food.

Spaghetti Primavera ⓥ (page 258)

The pasta by itself is a complete dinner.

Complete meal: About 516 calories, 22 g protein, 78 g carbohydrate, 15 g total fat (4 g saturated), 15 g fiber, 11 mg cholesterol, 693 mg sodium.

Spaghetti with Mussels and Fresh Tomatoes (page 259)

Serve with Mixed Summer Squash with Parsley and Lemon (page 278).

Complete meal: About 489 calories, 30 g protein, 68 g carbohydrate, 11 g total fat (1 g saturated), 10 g fiber, 42 mg cholesterol, 730 mg sodium.

Thai Noodles with Cilantro and Basil (page 261)

Serve with 1 cup sliced red peppers.

Complete meal: About 508 calories, 30 g protein, 61 g carbohydrate, 18 g total fat (4 g saturated), 6 g fiber, 56 mg cholesterol, 601 mg sodium.

Tortellini with Zucchini and Radicchio ⓥ (page 252)

The pasta by itself is a complete dinner.

Complete meal: About 486 calories, 19 g protein, 67 g carbohydrate, 16 g total fat (6 g saturated), 4 g fiber, 54 mg cholesterol, 753 mg sodium.

OTHER DINNERS (ABOUT 500 CALORIES)

Asian Rice Pilaf with Tofu ⓥ (page 263)

Serve with a salad: 2 cups watercress, 2 ounces diced firm tofu, and 2 teaspoons chopped cilantro tossed with 1 teaspoon vinegar, 2 teaspoons olive oil, $^1/_2$ teaspoon Asian sesame oil, 1 teaspoon chopped ginger, and a dash of salt. This dinner is a little high in sodium and low in fiber, so balance out your day with lower-sodium, high-fiber meals such as the high-fiber cereal breakfast (page 50) and the Broccoli and Garbanzo Bean Salad lunch (page 114).

Complete meal: About 472 calories, 17 g protein, 47 g carbohydrate, 25 g total fat (3 g saturated), 4 g fiber, 0 mg cholesterol, 969 mg sodium.

Couscous with Garbanzo Beans Ⓥ (page 264)

Serve with raita: $^1/_4$ cup plain low-fat yogurt mixed with 2 tablespoons chopped cucumber, dash dried mint, and, if desired, $^1/_8$ teaspoon crushed garlic. Make up for this slightly high-sodium dinner with lower-sodium breakfast and lunch choices.

Complete meal: About 504 calories, 22 g protein, 77 g carbohydrate, 14 g total fat (2 g saturated), 11 g fiber, 4 mg cholesterol, 813 mg sodium.

Falafel with Tahini Sauce Ⓥ (page 267)

Serve with $^3/_4$ cup carrot sticks or baby carrots. Since this meal is a little high in sodium, balance out the day with lower-sodium breakfast and lunch choices.

Complete meal: About 500 calories, 26 g protein, 86 g carbohydrate, 10 g total fat (1 g saturated), 19 g fiber, 0 mg cholesterol, 827 mg sodium.

Japanese Eggplant and Tofu Stir-Fry Ⓥ (page 266)

Serve with 1 cup cooked brown rice.

Complete meal: About 489 calories, 22 g protein, 71 g carbohydrate, 14 g total fat (1 g saturated), 11 g fiber, 0 mg cholesterol, 714 mg sodium.

Polenta with Spicy Eggplant Sauce Ⓥ (page 269)

Serve with a garbanzo salad: Mix $^1/_2$ cup canned reduced-sodium garbanzo beans (Eden Organic or Goya Low Sodium Chickpeas) with a chopped plum tomato and 1 tablespoon chopped parsley; toss with $^1/_2$ teaspoon olive oil and $^1/_2$ teaspoon balsamic vinegar.

Complete meal: About 526 calories, 20 g protein, 90 g carbohydrate, 10 g total fat (2 g saturated), 23 g fiber, 6 mg cholesterol, 819 mg sodium.

Tex-Mex Wrap Ⓥ (page 270)

Serve with a tangerine or kiwi.

Complete meal: About 500 calories, 23 g protein, 89 g carbohydrate, 9 g total fat (2 g saturated), 21 g fiber, 4 mg cholesterol, 667 mg sodium.

CALCIUM BREAKS

It's important to have one Calcium Break each day to ensure that you get enough calcium. In addition to its bone-strengthening properties, according to some preliminary research, calcium may be a weight-loss aid.

Women and men under age 51 need 1,000 mg calcium daily. Older than 51, you need 1,200 mg. You will get about 1,000 mg daily on this plan, thanks to: 300 mg calcium in the Calcium Break (except the cheese and crackers and the soup, which provide 250 mg calcium each); 300 mg calcium from the dairy serving at breakfast; and 300 to 400 mg from the rest of the Keep On Losin' plan (in cheese, milk, yogurt, and smaller amounts in beans and vegetables). Just for insurance, take a multivitamin, which provides 100 to 200 mg daily. If you're over 51, take a daily calcium supplement providing 200 to 500 mg calcium on top of your multi.

Cheese and Crackers

Have about 45 calories of any whole-grain cracker (such as 2 Ak Maks) and 1 slice reduced-fat cheddar or American cheese providing about 250 mg—or 25% DV—calcium per slice (such as Borden's 2% Singles or Cabot 50% Light Cheddar).

Each snack: About 113 calories, 8 g protein, 9 g carbohydrate, 6 g total fat (3 g saturated), 1 g fiber, 14 mg cholesterol, 373 mg sodium, 300 mg calcium.

Chilled Buttermilk and Corn Soup

This recipe is higher in calories than other Calcium Breaks, so have it no more than three times a week.

PREP 20 minutes plus chilling   **MAKES** about $2^1/_4$ cups or 3 servings

2 cups low-fat buttermilk

2 medium tomatoes ($^3/_4$ pound), seeded and chopped

$^1/_2$ small cucumber, peeled, seeded, and chopped

1 cup corn kernels cut from cobs (about 2 small ears)

$^1/_4$ teaspoon salt

$^1/_8$ teaspoon coarsely ground black pepper

6 large fresh basil leaves, thinly sliced

1. In large bowl, combine buttermilk, tomatoes, cucumber, corn, salt, and pepper. Cover and refrigerate until very cold, at least 2 hours.

2. To serve, spoon soup into 3 soup bowls and sprinkle with sliced basil.

EACH SERVING: About 135 calories, 8 g protein, 24 g carbohydrate, 2 g total fat (1 g saturated), 2 g fiber, 6 mg cholesterol, 365 mg sodium, 207 mg calcium.

Chocolate Milk

Mix $1^1/_2$ teaspoons chocolate syrup into 1 cup skim milk.*

Each snack: About 109 calories, 9 g protein, 18 g carbohydrate, 0 g total fat (0 g saturated), 0 g fiber, 5 mg cholesterol, 109 mg sodium, 306 mg calcium.

Flavored Steamer

Heat 1 cup skim milk* and add 1 tablespoon flavored syrup (such as from Torani) or 2 tablespoons sugar-free flavored syrup. Regular syrup puts this drink at 118 calories, a little more than the rest, so have this snack no more than three times a week. Sugar-free syrup is calorie-free, so no need to limit it.

Each snack (with regular syrup): About 118 calories, 8 g protein, 21 g carbohydrate, 0 g total fat, 0 g fiber, 5 mg cholesterol, 103 mg sodium, 306 mg calcium.

Flavored Yogurt

Keep in mind that the yogurts are a little higher in calories than the rest of the Calcium Breaks; however, the extra calories shouldn't impact your weight loss. If you want to stick very closely to 1,500 calories, shave 20 calories from your treat on the days you have these yogurts.

Maple yogurt: Stir 1 teaspoon maple syrup into $^2/_3$ cup plain low-fat yogurt.

Each snack: About 120 calories, 8 g protein, 16 g carbohydrate, 3 g fat (2 g saturated), 0 g fiber, 10 mg cholesterol, 114 sodium, 300 mg calcium.

Fruit yogurt: Mix $^2/_3$ cup plain low-fat yogurt with 1 teaspoon honey and 2 tablespoons chopped or crushed fresh fruit.

Each snack: About 132 calories, 9 g protein, 19 g carbohydrate, 3 g fat (2 g saturated), 0 g fiber, 10 mg cholesterol, 114 mg sodium, 300 mg calcium.

* Substituting soy milk (with 30% DV for calcium and no more than 100 calories per cup) adds 7 to 17 extra calories, which you can afford if you're following the rest of the plan faithfully!

Hot Chocolate

Heat 1 cup skim milk* (see footnote, page 79) and add $1^{1}/_{2}$ teaspoons chocolate syrup. Or prepare Swiss Miss No Sugar Added Hot chocolate.

Each snack: About 109 calories, 9 g protein, 18 g carbohydrate, 0 g total fat (0 g saturated), 0 g fiber, 5 mg cholesterol, 109 mg sodium, 306 mg calcium.

Skim Latte (12 ounces)

1 cup skim milk* (see footnote, page 79) with 2 shots (2 ounces each) espresso.

Each snack: About 84 calories, 8 g protein, 12 g carbohydrate, 0 g fat, 0 g fiber, 5 mg cholesterol, 104 mg sodium, 308 mg calcium.

Skim Milk*

1 cup.

Each snack: About 83 calories, 8 g protein, 12 g carbohydrate, 0 g fat, 0 g fiber, 5 mg cholesterol, 103 mg sodium, 306 mg calcium.

Soy Milk

1 cup (check labels for 30% DV for calcium and no more than 100 calories per cup, such as Silk Plain).

Each snack: About 100 calories, 7 g protein, 8 g carbohydrate, 4 g fat (1 g saturated), 1 g fiber, 0 mg cholesterol, 120 mg sodium, 300 mg calcium.

125- AND 170-CALORIE TREATS

I don't know about you, but for me, giving up chocolate or the occasional glass of wine or ice cream or other treats would be an unbearable sacrifice! I'd be off that diet plan after just one day. So the good news is that you get any treat you want on this plan, as long as you keep portions moderate. On both the Keep On Losin' 1,500-calorie plan, and on the Stay Slim 1,800-calorie plan, you'll get either 125 or 170 calories daily to play with.

The Supermarket Diet lists 125-calorie treats, such as 25 chocolate covered peanuts, or $^{1}/_{2}$ cup light ice cream with 1 teaspoon chocolate syrup, or 10 ounces beer, or 2 cups popcorn. To access an online list of 100-calorie treats go to www.goodhousekeeping.com, enter "100 calories or less," into the search bar, then click on the link for "Best Snacks—100 Calories or Less." You can have any of those or any other food (check labels carefully for calorie counts). Or try some of the new desserts offered in this cookbook; most have servings of 125 calories or less (if less, you can have something else to make up calories).

If you're one of those fortunate people who rarely hankers for sweets, chips, and other "nutritionally challenged" foods, then use your treat as an opportunity to have 2 servings of fruit or 2 or more servings of a mix of fruit and vegetables—fruit is 60 calories per serving and vegetables are 25 calories per serving. "How to Size Up Your Meals" (page 30) shows you what quantity of fruit or vegetables constitutes a serving.

GRADUATING TO YOUR MAINTENANCE PLAN

Whether you start your diet on the Keep On Losin' plan at 1,500 calories a day, or on the Stay Slim Maintenance plan at 1,800 calories, you will add 300 calories to your daily consumption when you are ready to start maintaining your new weight. Just add food from the lists below to your meals until you've accumulated an extra 300 calories daily. Need more ideas? See page 32 for ideas from the lists of food exchanges. Or see *The Supermarket Diet* for an 1,800-calorie plan. Hint: One very easy way to add 100 calories daily is simply to have two Calcium Breaks daily instead of one.

Adding Calories to Breakfast

(For fruits and vegetables, see page 31 for serving sizes and calories.)

- 1 teaspoon trans fat–free margarine (about 25 calories)
- 1 heaping tablespoon nuts (50 calories)
- more cereal (check labels and add 50 or 100 calories)
- 1 slice bread (check labels, should be about 75 calories)
- 1 egg (75 calories). If you have high cholesterol, check with your doctor about how many eggs you should eat each week. Although most studies don't show a connection between egg consumption and blood cholesterol, some people may be more sensitive.
- 1 large apple, pear, or banana (100 calories)

Adding Calories to Lunch and Dinner

(For fruits and vegetables, see page 31 for serving sizes and calories.)

Here are healthful ways to tack on extra calories to the 400-calorie Keep On Losin' lunches and 500-calorie Keep On Losin' dinners.

FATS

- 1 teaspoon canola or olive oil (40 calories)
- 1 tablespoon salad dressing (50 to 75 calories; check labels to make sure)
- 2 teaspoons peanut butter (65 calories); use 2 tablespoons instead of 4 teaspoons on the sandwich)
- $^1/_4$ of an avocado (75 calories)

PROTEIN

- 2 ounces tofu (50 calories, but check labels as products vary)
- 1 ounce cooked fish (60 calories for salmon; 40 calories for snapper, flounder, or other white fish or canned water-packed tuna or canned water-packed salmon)
- 1 ounce cooked beef (60 calories for lean beef—top round, sirloin, ground 90% lean beef)
- $^1/_3$ cup diced skinless chicken breast (75 calories)
- 1 ounce reduced-fat cheese (75 calories)
- Generous $^1/_2$ cup corn or 1 medium ear (80 calories)
- Generous $^1/_3$ cup beans (100 calories)

STARCHES

- Bigger bread (add about 50 calories per sandwich by using bread that's 90 calories per slice, instead of the 65- to 75-calorie bread recommended in the weight loss part of the program, but keep it whole grain!)
- 2 to 3 crackers (check labels and have about 50 calories)
- Generous $^1/_2$ cup cooked whole-wheat pasta (80 calories)
- $^1/_3$ cup rice (80 calories)

WEEKLY MENU PLANS

Need a little help putting together a day's or week's worth of meals? The Weekly Menu Plans starting on page 84 will help you create meal combinations that are right for you. So if you don't want to spend time selecting breakfasts, lunches, and dinners, these plans lay them all out for you. There are plans that take particular health needs into consideration, focusing on low-sodium or vegetarian concerns. You'll also find a plan specially adapted for a fast-paced lifestyle: Even hectic schedules can accommodate *The Supermarket Diet!*

Keep in mind that all of the menus:

- Limit sodium to 2,300 mg or less daily, which meets current guidelines.

- Offer at least 25 g fiber a day; the amount recommended for women. (Men need 35 grams, but since men on this diet will be eating more food, they should be getting 35 grams.)

- Limit saturated fat to less than 10 percent of total calories (that works out to 15 g or less a day) as recommended by the U.S. Department of Agriculture's Dietary Guidelines for Americans.

When reviewing the menu plans (over), note that the meals refer to the *entire* meal, not simply the recipe. The Meal Plans are found at the beginning of this chapter.

Basic Weekly Menu Plan

Use this plan for ideas on how to mix and match the meals. You'll notice that lower-fiber meals are balanced out by higher-fiber meals, ditto for sodium. Don't forget to add your 125- or 170-calorie treat each day.

	breakfast	lunch
MONDAY 1,730 mg sodium 29 g fiber 8 g saturated fat	Berry Blast Smoothie (page 49) 317 mg sodium 5 g fiber 2 g saturated fat	Chicken with Lentil Salad (page 53) 703 mg sodium 18 g fiber 2 g saturated fat
TUESDAY 1,951 mg sodium 30 g fiber 8 g saturated fat	High-Fiber Cereal (page 50) 200 mg sodium 14 g fiber 1 g saturated fat	Cool and Creamy Shrimp Salad (page 53) 785 mg sodium 5 g fiber 4 g saturated fat
WEDNESDAY 1,454 mg sodium 28 g fiber 8 g saturated fat	Apple, Oat, and Raisin Muffin (freeze any you don't use) (page 49) 333 mg sodium 3 g fiber 2 g saturated fat	Steak Sandwich with Grilled Onions (page 57) 477 mg sodium 6 g fiber 3 g saturated fat
THURSDAY 2,039 mg sodium 32 g fiber 11 g saturated fat	Eggs and Toast (page 50) 392 mg sodium 8 g fiber 4 g saturated fat	Corn and Black Bean Salad (page 53) 473 mg sodium 17 g fiber 2 g saturated fat
FRIDAY 1,193 mg sodium 40 g fiber 6 g saturated fat	Hot Cereal (page 51) 107 mg sodium 7 g fiber 2 g saturated fat	Corn and Black Bean Salad (leftover) (page 53) 473 mg sodium 17 g fiber 2 g saturated fat
SATURDAY 1,238 mg sodium 31 g fiber 14 g saturated fat	Cream Cheese-and-Chives Scrambled Eggs (page 50) 515 mg sodium 3 g fiber 7 g saturated fat	Chicken Soup with Latin Flavors (page 58) 248 mg sodium 10 g fiber 3 g saturated fat
SUNDAY 1,903 mg sodium 32 g fiber 5 g saturated fat	Apple, Oat, and Raisin Muffin (page 49) 333 mg sodium 3 g fiber 2 g saturated fat	Falafel with Tzatziki Sauce (page 56) 801 mg sodium 15 g fiber 1 g saturated fat

Thai Noodles with Cilantro and Basil (page 76)
601 mg sodium
6 g fiber
4 g saturated fat

Chocolate Milk (page 79)
109 mg sodium
0 g fiber
0 g saturated fat

Dijon-Fennel Pork Tenderloin with Sweet Potato Fries (page 62)
862 mg sodium
11 g fiber
3 g saturated fat

Skim Latte (page 80)
104 mg sodium
0 g fiber
0 g saturated fat

Red Bean and Collard Gumbo (page 72)
530 mg sodium
19 g fiber
1 g saturated fat

Maple Yogurt (page 79)
114 mg sodium
0 g fiber
2 g saturated fat

Salmon Patty with Broccoli Slaw (page 69)
1,071 mg sodium
7 g fiber
5 g saturated fat

Flavored Steamer (page 79)
103 mg sodium
0 g fiber
0 g saturated fat

Beef and Barley with Mushrooms (page 59)
510 mg sodium
16 g fiber
2 g saturated fat

Skim Milk (page 80)
103 mg sodium
0 g fiber
0 g saturated fat

Vegetarian Chili (page 73)
361 mg sodium
18 g fiber
2 g saturated fat

Maple Yogurt (page 79)
114 mg sodium
0 g fiber
2 g saturated fat

Cod with Peppers and Onions (page 68)
660 mg sodium
14 g fiber
2 g saturated fat

Hot Chocolate (page 80)
109 mg sodium
0 g fiber
0 g saturated fat

Speedy Weekly Menu Plan

Got a busy life? Or a particularly busy week coming up? This plan showcases some of the faster meals: Breakfasts are 5 minutes or less, lunches are 15 minutes or less, and dinners will be on the table in 35 minutes. Don't forget your 125- or 170-calorie treat each day.

	breakfast	**lunch**
MONDAY 1,590 mg sodium 25 g fiber 9 g saturated fat	On-the-Go Breakfast (page 52) 341 mg sodium 8 g fiber 1 g saturated fat	Bacon, Lettuce and Tomato Sandwich (page 55) 821 mg sodium 8 g fiber 5 g saturated fat
TUESDAY 1,616 mg sodium 27 g fiber 8 g saturated fat	High-Fiber Cereal (page 50) 200 mg sodium 14 g fiber 1 g saturated fat	Tofu "Egg" Salad Sandwich (page 57) 631 mg sodium 10 g fiber 2 g saturated fat
WEDNESDAY 1,431 mg sodium 30 g fiber 15 g saturated fat	Yogurt, Fruit, and Nuts (page 52) 174 mg sodium 4 g fiber 3 g saturated fat	Fresh Mozzarella and Tomato Sandwich (page 56) 661 mg sodium 5 g fiber 9 g saturated fat
THURSDAY 2,080 mg sodium 37 g fiber 13 g saturated fat	Whole-Grain Carrot Muffin (make the night before) (page 52) 365 mg sodium 8 g fiber 1 g saturated fat	Broccoli and Garbanzo Bean Salad (page 53) 444 mg sodium 14 g fiber 4 g saturated fat
FRIDAY 1,677 mg sodium 28 g fiber 8 g saturated fat	Whole-Grain Carrot Muffin (page 52) 365 mg sodium 8 g fiber 1 g saturated fat	Peanut Butter and Jelly Sandwich (page 56) 573 mg sodium 7 g fiber 3 g saturated fat
SATURDAY 2,192 mg sodium 21 g fiber 9 g saturated fat	Ham-and-Egg Muffin (page 50) 887 mg sodium 6 g fiber 3 g saturated fat	Tofu Salad with Peanuts (page 55) 474 mg sodium 8 g fiber 3 g saturated fat
SUNDAY 2,236 mg sodium 29 g fiber 8 g saturated fat	Hot Cereal (page 51) 107 mg sodium 7 g fiber 2 g saturated fat	Turkey and Swiss Sandwich (page 57) (from Subway) 1,360 mg sodium 8 g fiber 4 g saturated fat

dinner	calcium break
Broccoli Pesto and Chicken Spaghetti (page 73) 304 mg sodium 9 g fiber 3 g saturated fat	**Skim Latte** (page 80) 104 mg sodium 0 g fiber 0 g saturated fat
Pork Chops with Tomatoes and Arugula (page 62) 676 mg sodium 3 g fiber 5 g saturated fat	**Chocolate Milk** (page 79) 109 mg sodium 0 g fiber 0 g saturated fat
Black Bean and Sweet Potato Chili (page 71) 493 mg sodium 21 g fiber 3 g saturated fat	**Flavored Steamer** (page 79) 103 mg sodium 0 g fiber 0 g saturated fat
Chorizo and Bean Burrito (page 61) 1,168 mg sodium 15 g fiber 8 g saturated fat	**Skim Milk** (page 80) 103 mg sodium 0 g fiber 0 g saturated fat
Asian Flounder Bake (page 67) 625 mg sodium 13 g fiber 2 g saturated fat	**Maple Yogurt** (page 79) 114 mg sodium 0 g fiber 2 g saturated fat
Warm Chicken and Apple Salad (page 67) 727 mg sodium 7 g fiber 3 g saturated fat	**Skim Latte** (page 80) 104 mg sodium 0 g fiber 0 g saturated fat
Cod with Peppers and Onions (page 68) 660 mg sodium 14 g fiber 2 g saturated fat	**Chocolate Milk** (page 79) 109 mg sodium 0 g fiber 0 g saturated fat

Vegetarian Weekly Menu Plan

This plan is for ovo-lacto vegetarians, who eat dairy and eggs. There is no meat, poultry, or fish in the following meals. Even if you're not a vegetarian, it's a good idea to have a vegetarian meal a few times a week, or even daily. Why? Vegetarians are, on average, thinner and

	breakfast	lunch
MONDAY 1,150 mg sodium 25 g fiber 10 g saturated fat	Yogurt, Fruit, and Nuts (page 52) 174 mg sodium 4 g fiber 3 g saturated fat	Edamame Salad with Tofu (page 54) 509 mg sodium 10 g fiber 2 g saturated fat
TUESDAY 1,873 mg sodium 26 g fiber 9 g saturated fat	Berry Blast Smoothie (page 49) 317 mg sodium 5 g fiber 2 g saturated fat	Corn and Black Bean Salad (page 53) 473 mg sodium 17 g fiber 2 g saturated fat
WEDNESDAY 1,467 mg sodium 31 g fiber 12 g saturated fat	On-the-Go Breakfast (page 52) 341 mg sodium 8 g fiber 1 g saturated fat	Fresh Mozzarella and Tomato Sandwich (page 56) 661 mg sodium 5 g fiber 9 g saturated fat
THURSDAY 1,938 mg sodium 37 g fiber 8 g sat fat	Hot Cereal (page 51) 107 mg sodium 7 g fiber 2 g saturated fat	Tofu "Egg" Salad Sandwich (page 57) 631 mg sodium 10 g fiber 2 g saturated fat
FRIDAY 1,269 mg sodium 39 g fiber 3 g saturated fat	High-Fiber Cereal (page 50) 200 mg sodium 14 g fiber 1 g saturated fat	Cranberry Bean Soup (page 58) 555 mg sodium 13 g fiber 1 g saturated fat
SATURDAY 2,092 mg sodium 34 g fiber 12 g saturated fat	Multigrain Pancakes (page 52) 537 mg sodium 6 g fiber 2 g saturated fat	Greens and Ricotta Pie (page 58) 768 mg sodium 6 g fiber 7 g saturated fat
SUNDAY 1,817 mg sodium 35 g fiber 12 g saturated fat	Eggs and Toast (page 50) 392 mg sodium 8 g fiber 4 g saturated fat	Portobello Burger (page 57) 781 mg sodium 8 g fiber 5 g saturated fat

have lower blood pressure than the rest of the population. *The Supermarket Diet Cookbook* is chock full of truly tasty vegetarian meals; you won't miss the meat. Don't forget your 125- or 170-calorie treat each day.

dinner	calcium break
Macaroni and Cheese on the Light Side (page 73) 358 mg sodium 11 g fiber 5 g saturated fat	**Chocolate Milk** (page 79) 109 mg sodium 0 g fiber 0 g saturated fat
Asian Rice Pilaf with Tofu (page 76) 969 mg sodium 4 g fiber 3 g saturated fat	**Maple Yogurt** (page 79) 114 mg sodium 0 g fiber 2 g saturated fat
Vegetarian Chili (page 73) 361 mg sodium 18 g fiber 2 g saturated fat	**Skim Latte** (page 80) 104 mg sodium 0 g fiber 0 g saturated fat
Falafel with Tahini Sauce (page 77) 827 mg sodium 19 g fiber 1 g saturated fat	**Cheese and Crackers** (page 78) 373 mg sodium 1 g fiber 3 g saturated fat
Roasted Vegetables with Arugula and Whole-Wheat Fusilli (page 74) 405 mg sodium 12 g fiber 1 g saturated fat	**Chocolate Milk** (page 79) 109 mg sodium 0 g fiber 0 g saturated fat
Tex-Mex Wrap (page 77) 667 mg sodium 21 g fiber 2 g saturated fat	**Soy Milk** (page 80) 120 mg sodium 1 g fiber 1 g saturated fat
Red Bean and Collard Gumbo (page 72) 530 mg sodium 19 g fiber 1 g saturated fat	**Maple Yogurt** (page 79) 114 mg sodium 0 g fiber 2 g saturated fat

Low-Sodium Weekly Menu Plan

Remember: You'll only get the nice low sodium number with these meals if you use the reduced-sodium or no-salt-added foods recommended in the recipes, such as low-sodium chicken broth, low-sodium or no-salt added beans, and reduced-sodium or no-salt added canned tomatoes. Don't forget your 125- or 170-calorie treat each day.

	breakfast	lunch
MONDAY 978 mg sodium 25 g fiber 8 g saturated fat	Fruit Salad Smoothie (page 50) 66 mg sodium 10 g fiber 1 g saturated fat	Edamame Salad with Chicken (page 54) 302 mg sodium 9 g fiber 3 g saturated fat
TUESDAY 1,319 mg sodium 28 g fiber 8 g saturated fat	Hot Cereal (page 51) 107 mg sodium 7 g fiber 2 g saturated fat	Cranberry Bean Soup (page 58) 555 mg sodium 13 g fiber 1 g saturated fat
WEDNESDAY 1,217 mg sodium 29 g fiber 8 g saturated fat	Yogurt, Fruit, and Nuts (page 52) 174 mg sodium 4 g fiber 3 g saturated fat	Peanut Butter and Jelly Sandwich (page 56) 573 mg sodium 7 g fiber 3 g saturated fat
THURSDAY 1,142 mg sodium 35 g fiber 6 g saturated fat	Gingery Strawberry-Orange Smoothie (page 50) 198 mg sodium 5 g fiber 2 g saturated fat	Black Bean and Avocado Salad with Cilantro (page 53) 335 mg sodium 17 g fiber 2 g saturated fat
FRIDAY 1,213 mg sodium 35 g fiber 7 g sat fat	High-Fiber Cereal (page 50) 200 mg sodium 14 g fiber 1 g saturated fat	Greek Salad Pita (page 56) 542 mg sodium 10 g fiber 4 g saturated fat
SATURDAY 1,167 mg sodium 26 g fiber 12 g saturated fat	Asparagus, Red Potato, and Romano Frittata (page 49) 512 mg sodium 7 g fiber 6 g saturated fat	Chicken Soup with Latin Flavors (page 58) 248 mg sodium 10 g fiber 3 g saturated fat
SUNDAY 1,383 mg sodium 26 g fiber 10 g saturated fat	Whole-Grain Carrot Muffin (page 52) 365 mg sodium 8 g fiber 1 g saturated fat	No-Cook Barbecue Chicken Salad (page 54) 318 mg sodium 13 g fiber 2 g saturated fat

Tangerine Beef Stir-Fry (page 61)	**Skim Latte** (page 80)
506 mg sodium	104 mg sodium
6 g fiber	0 g fiber
4 g saturated fat	0 g saturated fat
Glazed Pork with Pear Chutney (page 62)	**Maple Yogurt** (page 79)
543 mg sodium	114 mg sodium
8 g fiber	0 g fiber
3 g saturated fat	2 g saturated fat
Vegetarian Chili (page 73)	**Chocolate Milk** (page 79)
361 mg sodium	109 mg sodium
18 g fiber	0 g fiber
2 g saturated fat	0 g saturated fat
Moroccan-Style Chicken Stew (page 72)	**Skim Latte** (page 80)
505 mg sodium	104 mg sodium
13 g fiber	0 g fiber
2 g saturated fat	0 g saturated fat
Shrimp Fra Diavolo (page 74)	**Skim Milk** (page 80)
368 mg sodium	103 mg sodium
11 g fiber	0 g fiber
2 g saturated fat	0 g saturated fat
Broccoli Pesto and Chicken Spaghetti (page 73)	**Flavored Steamer** (page 79)
304 mg sodium	103 mg sodium
9 g fiber	0 g fiber
3 g saturated fat	0 g saturated fat
Salmon Steaks with Nectarine Salad (page 69)	**Maple Yogurt** (page 79)
586 mg sodium	114 mg sodium
5 g fiber	0 g fiber
5 g saturated fat	2 g saturated fat

7

Slimming Recipes

lthough a few single-serving recipes are featured, most of the recipes in *The Supermarket Diet* make 4 or 6 servings. That way, you can feed your family (or friends), or, if you're doing this solo, freeze a few servings for a later date. However, feel free to cut these recipes back to just one or two servings by halving or quartering the ingredients, or even dividing by six. Likewise, go ahead and double or triple them for a crowd.

Remember to refer to Chapter 6 to see how the recipes can be supplemented—with fruit or bread, for example—to create an entire meal.

All the recipes that call for margarine or butter were analyzed with zero grams trans fat margarine. Current research shows that this kind of margarine appears to be better for your heart than butter or the traditional margarines that are filled with trans fat (see box on page 278.)

The symbol **v** next to a recipe indicates that the dish is vegetarian.

Berry Blast Smoothie ⓥ

PREP 5 minutes **MAKES** about 1³/₄ cups or 1 serving

1 container (6 ounces) mixed berry low-fat yogurt

1 cup frozen berry medley (strawberries, raspberries, blackberries, and blueberries; such as Dole Mixed Berries or Cascadian Farm Organic Harvest Berries)

¹/₃ cup nonfat (skim) milk

2 tablespoons instant nonfat dry milk powder

In blender, combine yogurt, berries, milk, and milk powder; blend until smooth and frothy. Pour into 1 tall glass.

EACH SMOOTHIE: About 299 calories, 16 g protein, 59 g carbohydrate, 2 g total fat (1 g saturated), 4 g fiber, 12 mg cholesterol, 219 mg sodium.

Fruit Salad Smoothie ⓥ

PREP 5 minutes **MAKES** 2 cups or 1 serving

¹/₂ cup calcium-fortified orange juice

¹/₂ cup plain soy milk (fewer than 100 calories per cup with at least 30 percent daily value of calcium, such as Silk or 8th Continent) or ¹/₂ cup nonfat (skim) milk

1 kiwi, peeled and cut into chunks

¹/₂ cup fresh pineapple chunks, or drained canned pineapple in juice

1 medium banana, cut into chunks

¹/₂ cup frozen strawberries

1 tablespoon toasted wheat germ

1¹/₂ teaspoons honey

In blender, combine orange juice, soy milk, kiwi, pineapple, banana, strawberries, wheat germ, and honey; blend until smooth and frothy. Pour into 1 tall glass.

EACH SMOOTHIE (WITH SOY MILK): About 379 calories, 9 g protein, 84 g carbohydrate, 4 g total fat (1 g saturated), 10 g fiber, 0 mg cholesterol, 66 mg sodium.

EACH SMOOTHIE (WITH NONFAT MILK): About 370 calories, 10 g protein, 86 g carbohydrate, 2 g total fat (0 g saturated), 9 g fiber, 58 mg sodium.

Gingery Strawberry-Orange Smoothie ⓥ

PREP 5 minutes   **MAKES** $1^3/_4$ cups or 1 serving

> **1 cup frozen strawberries**
>
> **1 container (6 ounces) vanilla low-fat yogurt**
>
> **$^1/_2$ cup calcium-fortified orange juice**
>
> **2 tablespoons instant nonfat dry milk powder**
>
> **$^1/_2$ teaspoon grated fresh ginger**

In blender, combine strawberries, yogurt, orange juice, milk powder, and ginger; blend until smooth and frothy. Pour into 1 tall glass.

EACH SMOOTHIE: About 312 calories, 14 g protein, 61 g carbohydrate, 3 g total fat (2 g saturated), 3 g fiber, 13 mg cholesterol, 198 mg sodium.

Wake-Up Smoothie ⓥ

PREP 5 minutes   **MAKES** about $1^3/_4$ cups or 1 serving

> **1 container (6 ounces) vanilla low-fat yogurt**
>
> **$^1/_3$ cup nonfat (skim) milk**
>
> **$^1/_3$ cup ice cubes**
>
> **1 teaspoon instant coffee powder**

In blender, combine yogurt, milk, ice, and coffee powder; blend until smooth and frothy. Pour into 1 tall glass.

EACH SMOOTHIE: About 180 calories, 10 g protein, 30 g carbohydrate, 3 g total fat (2 g saturated), 0 g fiber, 12 mg cholesterol, 149 mg sodium.

Apple-Cinnamon French Toast Ⓥ

PREP 10 minutes COOK 20 minutes MAKES 3 servings

2 apples, peeled, cored, and thinly sliced

3 tablespoons maple syrup

$1/2$ cup Egg Beaters egg product

$1/4$ cup nonfat (skim) milk

6 slices whole-wheat bread

confectioners' sugar (optional)

ground cinnamon (optional)

1. Spray 3-quart saucepan with cooking spray; heat over medium heat. Add apples and cook, stirring frequently, until tender-crisp, about 5 minutes. Stir in maple syrup; cook, stirring, 1 minute to heat through. Remove from heat; keep warm.

2. In pie plate, with fork, mix egg product and milk. Dip bread into mixture until evenly coated.

3. Spray 10-inch skillet with cooking spray; heat over medium heat. Add 3 bread slices and cook, turning once, until golden brown. Repeat with remaining bread and egg mixture. Serve with apple mixture. Sprinkle with confectioners' sugar and cinnamon, if you like.

EACH SERVING: About 280 calories, 10 g protein, 56 g carbohydrate, 3 g total fat (1 g saturated), 6 g fiber, 0 mg cholesterol, 391 mg sodium.

Honey-Pecan Belgian Waffles Ⓥ

PREP 20 minutes   **BAKE** 4 minutes per batch   **MAKES** 9 waffles or 9 servings

> 1¼ cups whole-wheat flour
>
> ½ cup all-purpose flour
>
> ¼ cup oat bran
>
> 1½ teaspoons baking powder
>
> 1 teaspoon baking soda
>
> ½ teaspoon salt
>
> 2 cups buttermilk
>
> ¼ cup margarine or butter, melted
>
> 2 large eggs, lightly beaten
>
> 2 tablespoons honey
>
> ½ cup toasted pecans, finely chopped
>
> canola oil, for brushing waffle baker

1. Preheat waffle baker as manufacturer directs. In large bowl, combine whole-wheat and all-purpose flours, oat bran, baking powder, baking soda, and salt. Add buttermilk, melted margarine, eggs, and honey; stir just until flour mixture is moistened (batter will be lumpy). Stir in pecans.

2. When waffle baker is ready, brush lightly with oil. Pour batter into center of griddle until it spreads within 1 inch of edges. Cover and bake as manufacturer directs; do not lift cover during baking.

3. When waffle is done, lift cover and loosen waffle with fork. Serve immediately or keep warm in oven (place waffle directly on oven rack to keep crisp). Reheat waffle baker before pouring in more batter.

EACH WAFFLE: About 230 calories, 8 g protein, 29 g carbohydrate, 11 g total fat (2 g saturated), 4 g fiber, 49 mg cholesterol, 425 mg sodium.

Multigrain Pancakes ⓥ

PREP 10 minutes   **COOK** 3 minutes per batch
MAKES 12 pancakes or 6 servings

$^2/_3$ **cup whole-wheat flour**

$^1/_3$ **cup all-purpose flour**

$^1/_3$ **cup oat bran**

2 tablespoons sugar

2$^1/_2$ teaspoons baking powder

$^1/_2$ **teaspoon salt**

1$^1/_4$ cups nonfat (skim) milk

3 tablespoons margarine or butter, melted

1 large egg, lightly beaten

canola oil, for brushing pan

1. In large bowl, combine whole-wheat and all-purpose flours, oat bran, sugar, baking powder, and salt. Add milk, melted margarine, and egg; stir just until flour mixture is moistened (batter will be lumpy).

2. Heat griddle or 12-inch skillet over medium heat until drop of water sizzles; brush lightly with oil. Pour batter by scant $^1/_4$ cups onto hot griddle, making a few pancakes at a time. Cook until tops are bubbly, some bubbles burst, and edges look dry. With wide spatula, turn and cook until underside is golden. Transfer to platter; keep warm.

3. Repeat with remaining batter, brushing griddle with more oil if necessary.

EACH SERVING (ABOUT 2 PANCAKES): About 197 calories, 6 g protein,
26 g carbohydrate, 9 g total fat (1 g saturated), 3 g fiber, 36 mg cholesterol,
431 mg sodium.

Whole-Grain Carrot Muffins ⓥ

PREP 20 minutes   **BAKE** 25 minutes   **MAKES** 12 muffins

1 cup nonfat (skim) milk

¹/₄ cup light (mild) molasses

¹/₄ cup canola oil

1 large egg, lightly beaten

1¹/₂ cups All-Bran cereal (do not use bran flakes, All-Bran Extra Fiber, or other similar cereal that include a sugar substitute)

1 cup shredded carrots

³/₄ cup whole-wheat flour

¹/₂ cup all-purpose flour

1 tablespoon baking powder

¹/₂ teaspoon salt

¹/₂ teaspoon ground cinnamon

1 cup dried pitted plums (prunes), coarsely chopped

2 tablespoons toasted wheat germ

1. Preheat oven to 400°F. Grease twelve 2¹/₂" by 1¹/₄" muffin-pan cups. In medium bowl, with fork, beat milk, molasses, oil, egg, cereal, and carrots until well blended; let stand 10 minutes.

2. Meanwhile, in large bowl, combine whole-wheat and all-purpose flours, baking powder, salt, and cinnamon. Add cereal mixture to flour mixture; stir just until flour mixture is moistened (batter will be lumpy). Stir in dried plums.

3. Spoon batter into prepared muffin-pan cups; sprinkle with wheat germ. Bake until muffins begin to brown and toothpick inserted in center of muffin comes out clean, about 25 minutes. Immediately remove muffins from pan. Serve warm or cool on wire rack to serve later.

EACH MUFFIN: About 181 calories, 5 g protein, 32 g carbohydrate, 6 g total fat (1 g saturated), 5 g fiber, 18 mg cholesterol, 261 mg sodium.

Apple, Oat, and Raisin Muffins ⓥ

PREP 10 minutes   **BAKE** 20 minutes   **MAKES** 12 muffins

$1^3/_4$ **cups old-fashioned or quick oats, uncooked**

$2/_3$ **cup whole-wheat flour**

$1/_3$ **cup all-purpose flour**

$1/_2$ **cup firmly packed brown sugar**

1 teaspoon baking powder

$1/_2$ **teaspoon baking soda**

$1/_2$ **teaspoon salt**

$1/_2$ **teaspoon ground cinnamon**

$1/_4$ **teaspoon ground nutmeg**

$3/_4$ **cup unsweetened applesauce**

$1/_3$ **cup nonfat (skim) milk**

2 tablespoons canola oil

1 large egg, lightly beaten

$1/_2$ **cup raisins**

1. Preheat oven to 400°F. Grease twelve $2^1/_2$" by $1^1/_4$" muffin-pan cups. In large bowl, combine $1^1/_2$ cups oats, whole-wheat and all-purpose flours, brown sugar, baking powder, baking soda, salt, cinnamon, and nutmeg.

2. In medium bowl, with fork, beat applesauce, milk, oil, and egg. Add applesauce mixture to flour mixture; stir just until flour mixture is moistened (batter will be lumpy). Stir in raisins.

3. Spoon batter into prepared muffin-pan cups; sprinkle with remaining $1/_4$ cup oats, patting gently. Bake until muffins begin to brown and toothpick inserted in center of muffin comes out clean, about 20 minutes. Immediately remove muffins from pan. Serve warm or cool on wire rack to serve later.

EACH MUFFIN: About 169 calories, 4 g protein, 31 g carbohydrate, 4 g total fat (1 g saturated), 3 g fiber, 18 mg cholesterol, 204 mg sodium.

Honey-Glazed Oat Muffins ⓥ

PREP 20 minutes   **BAKE** 20 minutes   **MAKES** 12 muffins

$^2/_3$ **cup buttermilk**

$^1/_2$ **cup plus 1 teaspoon orange juice**

$^1/_4$ **cup plus 2 tablespoons honey**

3 tablespoons canola oil

1 large egg, lightly beaten

1 teaspoon grated orange zest

1 cup old-fashioned or quick oats, uncooked

$^3/_4$ **cup whole-wheat flour**

$^1/_2$ **cup all-purpose flour**

$^1/_4$ **cup oat bran**

$2^1/_2$ **teaspoons baking powder**

$^1/_2$ **teaspoon baking soda**

$^1/_2$ **teaspoon salt**

1. Preheat oven to 400°F. Grease twelve $2^1/_2$" by $1^1/_4$" muffin-pan cups. In medium bowl, with fork, beat buttermilk, $^1/_2$ cup orange juice, $^1/_4$ cup honey, oil, egg, orange zest, and oats until well blended; let stand 10 minutes.

2. In large bowl, combine whole-wheat and all-purpose flours, oat bran, baking powder, baking soda, and salt. Add oat mixture to flour mixture; stir just until flour mixture is moistened (batter will be lumpy).

3. Spoon batter into prepared muffin-pan cups. Bake until muffins begin to brown and toothpick inserted in center of muffin comes out clean, about 20 minutes. Cool muffins in pan 5 minutes. Transfer to wire rack; cool 10 minutes.

4. Meanwhile, in small bowl, combine remaining 2 tablespoons honey and 1 teaspoon orange juice. Dip tops of muffins in honey mixture. Serve warm or cool to serve later.

EACH MUFFIN: About 122 calories, 4 g protein, 17 g carbohydrate, 5 g total fat (1 g saturated), 2 g fiber, 18 mg cholesterol, 272 mg sodium.

Asparagus, Red Potato, and Romano Frittata ⓥ

PREP 20 minutes   **MICROWAVE** 2 minutes   **COOK/BAKE** 20 minutes
MAKES 4 servings

2 medium red potatoes (6 ounces each), cut into 1-inch chunks

8 large eggs

¹/₂ cup freshly grated Romano cheese

¹/₂ cup whole milk

³/₄ teaspoon salt

¹/₈ teaspoon ground black pepper

1 tablespoon margarine or butter

1 bunch green onions, thinly sliced

12 ounces asparagus, cut crosswise into 1-inch pieces

1. Preheat oven to 375°F. Place potatoes in microwave-safe small bowl; add *2 tablespoons water.* Cover bowl with vented plastic wrap and cook on High, stirring once, until fork-tender, 2 to 3 minutes. Remove plastic wrap from bowl; discard water in bowl.

2. In medium bowl, with wire whisk, mix eggs, Romano, milk, ¹/₂ teaspoon salt, and pepper; set aside.

3. In nonstick oven-safe 12-inch skillet (if skillet is not oven-safe, wrap handle with double layer of foil), melt margarine over medium-high heat. Add green onions and cooked potatoes and cook, stirring occasionally, 2 minutes. Stir in asparagus and remaining ¹/₄ teaspoon salt, and cook, stirring frequently, until asparagus is tender, 5 to 6 minutes. Spread vegetables evenly in skillet.

4. Reduce heat to medium-low. Pour egg mixture over vegetables in skillet; cook, without stirring, until eggs begin to set around edge, 4 to 5 minutes. Place skillet in oven and bake, uncovered, until frittata is set and knife inserted in center comes out clean, 10 to 12 minutes. Cut into wedges to serve.

EACH SERVING: About 321 calories, 22 g protein, 22 g carbohydrate, 16 g total fat (6 g saturated), 4 g fiber, 435 mg cholesterol, 510 mg sodium.

Ham-and-Egg Muffin

PREP 5 minutes   **COOK** 4 minutes   **MAKES** 1 serving

1 large egg

1 large egg white

pinch salt

pinch ground black pepper

1 ounce lower-sodium deli ham with no more than 35 calories and 250 mg sodium per ounce (such as Healthy Choice Virginia Smoked Ham)

1 whole-wheat English muffin (such as Pepperidge Farm 100% Whole-Wheat or Thomas' Hearty Grains 100% Whole Wheat, both about 130 calories), split and toasted

2 tablespoons reduced-fat shredded Italian cheese blend (such as Sargento Reduced Fat 4 Cheese Italian)

1. In small bowl, whisk egg, egg white, salt, and pepper.

2. Spray small nonstick skillet with cooking spray and set over medium heat. Warm ham for about 30 seconds; transfer to plate.

3. Reduce heat to low. Add egg mixture to skillet; cook, stirring constantly with a heat-proof spatula or wooden spoon, until eggs are just set, 1 minute.

4. Place ham on bottom of muffin; top with eggs and sprinkle with cheese. Top with muffin top.

EACH MUFFIN: About 283 calories, 25 g protein, 25 g carbohydrate, 9 g total fat (3 g saturated), 3 g fiber, 233 mg cholesterol, 835 mg sodium.

Cream-Cheese-and-Chives Scrambled Eggs

Cream-Cheese-and-Chives Scrambled Eggs Ⓥ

PREP 5 minutes   **COOK** 5 minutes   **MAKES** 4 servings

1 bag (5 ounces) mixed baby salad greens

1 tablespoon olive oil

2 teaspoons red wine vinegar

pinch plus $1/2$ teaspoon salt

8 large eggs

2 tablespoons chopped fresh chives

$1/4$ teaspoon coarsely ground black pepper

$1/4$ cup water

2 teaspoons butter or margarine

4 ounces (half 8-ounce package) Neufchatel or light cream cheese, cut into $1/2$-inch pieces

4 slices multigrain bread, each toasted and cut diagonally in half

1. In medium bowl, toss greens with oil, vinegar, and pinch salt; set aside.

2. In large bowl, with wire whisk, beat eggs, chives, pepper, remaining $1/2$ teaspoon salt, and water until blended.

3. In nonstick 10-inch skillet, melt butter over medium-high heat; add egg mixture. With heat-safe rubber spatula, gently push egg mixture as it begins to set to form soft curds. When eggs are partially cooked, top with Neufchatel and continue cooking, stirring occasionally, until eggs have thickened and no visible liquid egg remains.

4. To serve, divide greens among 4 plates. Place 2 toast halves on each plate; spoon eggs over toast.

EACH SERVING: About 341 calories, 19 g protein, 19 g carbohydrate, 21 g total fat (7 g saturated), 3 g fiber, 439 mg cholesterol, 461 mg sodium.

Spinach and Jack Cheese Bread Pudding ⓥ

PREP 5 minutes   **BAKE** 25 minutes   **MAKES** 6 servings

6 large eggs

2 cups low-fat milk (1%)

¹/₄ teaspoon dried thyme

¹/₄ teaspoon salt

¹/₄ teaspoon coarsely ground black pepper

pinch ground nutmeg

1 package (10 ounces) frozen chopped spinach, thawed and squeezed dry

1 cup shredded Monterey Jack cheese (4 ounces)

8 slices firm whole-wheat bread, cut into ³/₄-inch pieces

1. Preheat oven to 375°F. Lightly grease a 13" by 9" ceramic or glass baking dish. In large bowl, with wire whisk, beat eggs, milk, thyme, salt, pepper, and nutmeg until blended. With rubber spatula, stir in spinach, Monterey Jack, and bread.

2. Pour mixture into prepared baking dish. Bake bread pudding until browned and puffed, and knife inserted in center comes out clean, 20 to 25 minutes.

3. Remove bread pudding from oven; let stand 5 minutes before serving.

EACH SERVING: About 296 calories, 20 g protein, 26 g carbohydrate, 14 g total fat (6 g saturated), 4 g fiber, 233 mg cholesterol, 563 mg sodium.

Spinach and Jack Cheese Bread Pudding

Breakfast Burrito with Salsa ⓥ

PREP 5 minutes   **COOK** 3 minutes   **MAKES** 1 serving

- $^1/_2$ **cup cherry tomatoes, quartered**
- **1 small green onion, thinly sliced**
- **1 tablespoon chopped fresh cilantro**
- **1 teaspoon fresh lime juice**
- $^1/_2$ **teaspoon olive oil**
- **pinch ground cumin**
- **pinch salt**
- **1 frozen Amy's Breakfast Burrito (6 ounces) or other burrito with about 250 calories, at least 5 g fiber, no more than 1 g saturated fat, and about 540 mg sodium or less**

1. To make salsa, in medium bowl, combine tomatoes, green onion, cilantro, lime juice, oil, cumin, and salt.

2. Meanwhile, microwave burrito according to package directions. Serve with salsa.

EACH BURRITO WITH SALSA: About 270 calories, 9 g protein, 40 g carbohydrate, 9 g total fat (1 g saturated), 6 g fiber, 0 mg cholesterol, 701 mg sodium.

Salads

Corn and Black Bean Salad Ⓥ

PREP 25 minutes   **COOK** 15 minutes   **MAKES** 4 servings

6 medium ears corn, husks and silk removed

$1/2$ cup loosely packed fresh cilantro leaves, chopped

$1/4$ cup cider vinegar

3 tablespoons olive oil

$3/4$ teaspoon salt

pinch ground black pepper

2 cans (15 ounces each) black beans (preferably fewer than 140 mg sodium per $1/2$ cup, such as Eden Organic or Goya Low Sodium), rinsed and drained

1 jalapeño chile (or 2 if you like the heat!), seeded and minced

2 tablespoons chopped red onion

2 cups chopped tomatoes

1. In 12-quart saucepot, heat *6 quarts water* to boiling over high heat. Add corn and cook, covered, 5 minutes; drain. When corn is cool enough to handle, cut kernels from cobs with sharp knife.

2. Meanwhile, in large bowl, whisk cilantro, vinegar, oil, salt, and pepper until mixed. Add corn, beans, jalapeño, onion, and tomatoes; toss until well coated. Serve salad at room temperature or cover and refrigerate up to 1 day ahead.

EACH SERVING: About 394 calories, 17 g protein, 62 g carbohydrate, 12 g total fat (2 g saturated), 17 g fiber, 0 mg cholesterol, 473 mg sodium.

Greek Peasant Salad

Greek Peasant Salad ⓥ

PREP 25 minutes **MAKES** about 6½ cups or 6 servings

4 kirby cucumbers (1 pound)

2 tablespoons fresh lemon juice

1 tablespoon olive oil

¹⁄₈ teaspoon ground black pepper

2 pounds ripe red and/or yellow tomatoes (6 medium), cut into 1-inch chunks

¹⁄₂ cup loosely packed fresh mint leaves, chopped

¹⁄₃ cup kalamata olives, pitted and coarsely chopped

¹⁄₄ cup loosely packed fresh dill, chopped

2 ounces feta cheese, crumbled (¹⁄₂ cup)

1. With vegetable peeler, remove 3 or 4 evenly spaced lengthwise strips of peel from each cucumber. Cut each cucumber lengthwise into quarters, then crosswise into ¹⁄₂-inch pieces.

2. In large bowl, with wire whisk or fork, mix lemon juice, oil, and pepper. Add cucumbers, tomatoes, mint, olives, and dill; toss until evenly mixed and coated with dressing. Top with feta.

EACH SERVING: About 125 calories, 4 g protein, 11 g carbohydrate, 8 g total fat (3 g saturated), 3 g fiber, 13 mg cholesterol, 579 mg sodium.

Black Bean and Avocado Salad with Cilantro (V)

PREP 30 minutes   **MAKES** about 16 cups or 4 servings

Cilantro Dressing

2 limes

6 tablespoons light mayonnaise (such as from Kraft or Hellman's)

$^1/_2$ cup plus 3 tablespoons packed fresh cilantro leaves

3 tablespoons reduced-fat sour cream

$^3/_4$ teaspoon ground cumin

$^1/_4$ teaspoon sugar

$^1/_8$ teaspoon salt

$^1/_8$ teaspoon coarsely ground black pepper

Salad

1 small head romaine lettuce (1 pound), cut into $^3/_4$-inch pieces (8 cups)

2 medium tomatoes, cut into $^1/_2$-inch pieces

2 kirby cucumbers (4 ounces each), unpeeled, each cut lengthwise into quarters, then crosswise into $^1/_4$-inch-thick pieces

1 ripe avocado, pitted, peeled, and cut into $^1/_2$-inch pieces

2 cans (15 ounces each) black beans (preferably fewer than 140 mg sodium per $^1/_2$ cup, such as Eden Organic or Goya Low Sodium), rinsed and drained

1. Prepare dressing: From limes, grate 1 teaspoon peel and squeeze $^1/_4$ cup juice. In blender, combine lime peel and juice, mayonnaise, cilantro, sour cream, cumin, sugar, salt, and pepper; puree, occasionally scraping down sides of blender, until smooth. Cover and refrigerate if not using right away. Makes about $^2/_3$ cup.

2. Prepare salad: In large serving bowl, combine romaine, tomatoes, cucumbers, avocado, and beans. Add dressing and toss until evenly coated.

EACH SERVING (WITH NO-SALT-ADDED BEANS): About 380 calories, 16 g protein, 49 g carbohydrate, 15 g total fat (2 g saturated), 17 g fiber, 13 mg cholesterol, 335 mg sodium.

Rich's Caesar Salad

PREP 15 minutes   **MAKES** 4 servings

2 anchovy fillets

1 garlic clove, minced

¹/₄ cup light mayonnaise (such as from Kraft or Hellman's)

¹/₄ cup grated Romano cheese

2 tablespoons fresh lemon juice

1 tablespoon olive oil

1 tablespoon Dijon mustard

1 teaspoon Worcestershire sauce

1 bag (12 ounces) romaine hearts, torn

2 cups shredded or diced skinless rotisserie chicken-breast meat, (10 ounces)

freshly ground black pepper

1. In large bowl, with fork, mash anchovies with garlic until almost smooth. Whisk in mayonnaise, Romano, lemon juice, oil, mustard, and Worcestershire until blended.

2. Add romaine and chicken to bowl with dressing; toss to coat. Sprinkle with pepper to taste.

EACH SERVING: About 262 calories, 26 g protein, 7 g carbohydrate, 14 g total fat (3 g saturated), 2 g fiber, 72 mg cholesterol, 449 mg sodium.

Broccoli and Garbanzo Bean Salad ⓥ

PREP 15 minutes **COOK** 1 minute **MAKES** 2 servings

1½ cups broccoli florets, cut into bite-sized pieces

1 cup canned garbanzo beans (preferably fewer than 140 mg sodium per ½ cup, such as Eden Organic or Goya Low Sodium Chickpeas), rinsed and drained

1 medium tomato, diced

2 tablespoons chopped red onion

4 Kalamata olives, pitted and chopped

4 teaspoons extravirgin olive oil

1½ tablespoons fresh lemon juice

1 ounce feta cheese, grated

1. Bring a medium saucepan of *water* to the boil. Add broccoli and cook until crisp-tender, 1 minute. Drain broccoli and rinse with cold water. Pat dry with paper towels.

2. In a medium bowl, combine broccoli, garbanzo beans, tomato, red onion, and olives. Drizzle with oil and lemon juice. Toss to combine. Sprinkle with feta cheese.

EACH SERVING: About 268 calories, 11 g protein, 29 g carbohydrate, 14 g total fat (4 g saturated), 10 g fiber, 13 mg cholesterol, 429 mg sodium.

Tofu Salad with Peanuts Ⓥ

PREP 15 minutes **MAKES** 2 servings

> **1¹/₂ tablespoons olive oil**
>
> **1¹/₂ tablespoons unseasoned rice vinegar**
>
> **1¹/₂ teaspoons reduced-sodium soy sauce (such as Kikkoman or La Choy Lite)**
>
> **1¹/₂ teaspoons grated fresh ginger**
>
> **pinch hot pepper flakes**
>
> **6 ounces baked tofu, cut into ¹/₂-inch cubes**
>
> **3 cups shredded iceberg lettuce**
>
> **³/₄ cup shredded carrot**
>
> **³/₄ cup cubed fresh pineapple**
>
> **3 tablespoons chopped cilantro**
>
> **1¹/₂ green onions, chopped**
>
> **3 tablespoons unsalted peanuts, chopped**

1. In a large bowl, whisk oil, vinegar, soy sauce, ginger, and hot pepper flakes.

2. Add tofu, lettuce, carrots, pineapple, cilantro, scallion, and peanuts to bowl with dressing. Toss to combine.

EACH SERVING: About 322 calories, 15 g protein, 22 g carbohydrate, 21 g total fat (2 g saturated), 6 g fiber, 0 mg cholesterol, 469 mg sodium.

Edamame Salad with Tofu ⓥ

PREP 15 minutes   **COOK** 10 minutes   **MAKES** 2 servings

8 ounces frozen shelled edamame

2 tablespoons seasoned rice vinegar

1½ teaspoons reduced-sodium soy sauce (such as Kikkoman or La Choy Lite)

1 teaspoon grated fresh ginger

1 teaspoon sesame oil

6 ounces firm tofu, drained and cut into ½-inch cubes

1 cup shredded carrots

2 green onions, thinly sliced

1.   Cook edamame according to package directions without salt. Drain and rinse with cold water; pat dry.

2.   In a medium bowl, stir vinegar, soy sauce, ginger, and sesame oil to combine.

3.   Add tofu, carrots, green onions, and edamame; toss to combine.

EACH SERVING: About 326 calories, 28 g protein, 30 g carbohydrate, 12 g total fat (1 g saturated), 9 g fiber, 0 mg cholesterol, 427 mg sodium.

Edamame Salad with Chicken

PREP 25 minutes   **COOK** 10 minutes   **MAKES** 2 servings

- **8 ounces frozen shelled edamame**
- **1 large navel orange**
- **2 tablespoons seasoned rice vinegar**
- **2 tablespoons snipped fresh chives**
- **1 teaspoon olive oil**
- **6 radishes, coarsely chopped**
- **1/2 medium cucumber, peeled, seeded, and thinly sliced**
- **1 cup shredded cooked chicken breast or flaked cooked salmon**

1. Cook edamame according to package directions without salt. Drain and rinse with cold water; pat dry.

2. Grate 1/2 teaspoon orange zest and place in a large bowl. Peel orange and cut away white pith. Slice orange and cut slices into quarters; set aside.

3. To bowl with orange zest, add vinegar, chives, and oil; stir to combine.

4. Add edamame, radishes, cucumber, chicken, and orange pieces to bowl with dressing; toss to combine.

EACH SERVING: About 402 calories, 37 g protein, 34 g carbohydrate, 15 g total fat (3 g saturated), 9 g fiber, 48 mg cholesterol, 302 mg sodium.

Panzanella with Chicken

PREP 40 minutes   **BAKE** 15 minutes   **MAKES** 6 servings

10 ounces country-style whole-wheat, whole-rye, or other whole-grain bread, cut into ³/₄-inch cubes (8 cups)

4 tablespoons olive oil

2 packages (4.1 ounces each) refrigerated bone-in roasted chicken-breast halves

3 large tomatoes (1¹/₂ pounds), cut into ³/₄-inch chunks

¹/₂ pound smoked mozzarella cheese, cut into long, thin strips (if unavailable, use fresh mozzarella or part-skim regular mozzarella)

2 kirby cucumbers (4 ounces each), unpeeled, sliced

¹/₂ medium red onion, thinly sliced

12 large fresh basil leaves, thinly sliced

3 tablespoons red wine vinegar

¹/₂ teaspoon salt

¹/₈ teaspoon coarsely ground black pepper

1. Preheat oven to 350°F. In 15¹/₂" by 10¹/₂" jelly-roll pan, toss bread cubes with 1 tablespoon oil. Toast bread in oven, stirring occasionally, until golden brown, 15 to 20 minutes. Cool bread in pan on wire rack.

2. Meanwhile, remove skin and bones from chicken and discard. Pull meat into shreds.

3. In large serving bowl, toss bread with chicken, tomatoes, mozzarella, cucumbers, onion, basil, vinegar, salt, pepper, and remaining 3 tablespoons oil until well combined.

EACH SERVING: About 396 calories, 22 g protein, 32 g carbohydrate, 20 g total fat (7 g saturated), 4 g fiber, 53 mg cholesterol, 632 mg sodium.

Chicken with Lentil Salad

PREP 35 minutes **GRILL** 10 minutes **MAKES** 4 servings

- **2 lemons, plus lemon wedges for serving**
- **3 cups water**
- **1 cup green French lentils or brown lentils, picked over and rinsed**
- **4 medium skinless, boneless chicken-breast halves (1$^1/_4$ pounds)**
- **1$^1/_4$ teaspoons salt**
- **$^1/_2$ teaspoon coarsely ground black pepper**
- **2 medium tomatoes, seeded and chopped**
- **1 kirby cucumber, unpeeled, diced (1 cup)**
- **1 cup loosely packed fresh parsley leaves, chopped**
- **$^1/_2$ cup loosely packed fresh mint leaves, chopped**
- **2 tablespoons olive oil**
- **1 bag (5 ounces) mixed baby greens (8 cups loosely packed)**

1. From the 2 lemons, with vegetable peeler, remove 2 strips peel, about 2" by $^3/_4$" each. Grate 2 teaspoons peel and squeeze 3 tablespoons juice; set aside.

2. In 2-quart saucepan, combine lemon-peel strips, water, and lentils and bring to a boil over high heat. Reduce heat to low; cover and simmer until lentils are just tender, 20 to 25 minutes.

3. Meanwhile, prepare charcoal fire or preheat gas grill for covered direct grilling over medium heat.

4. Rub chicken with grated lemon peel, $^1/_2$ teaspoon salt, and $^1/_4$ teaspoon pepper; place on hot grill rack. Cover grill and cook chicken, turning once, until juices run clear when thickest part of breast is pierced with tip of knife, 10 to 12 minutes.

5. Drain lentils in colander. Rinse under cold running water and drain again. Discard lemon peel. In medium bowl, with spoon, stir lentils, tomatoes, cucumber, parsley, mint, oil, lemon juice, and remaining $^3/_4$ teaspoon salt and $^1/_4$ teaspoon pepper.

6. Arrange greens on platter; top with lentil mixture, then with chicken. Serve with lemon wedges.

EACH SERVING: About 411 calories, 48 g protein, 35 g carbohydrate, 9 g total fat (2 g saturated), 18 g fiber, 82 mg cholesterol, 703 mg sodium.

Warm Chicken Salad with Mustard-Thyme Vinaigrette

PREP 15 minutes **COOK** 5 minutes **MAKES** 4 servings

- **3 slices bacon, cut into $1/2$-inch pieces**
- **3 green onions, thinly sliced**
- **$1/3$ cup cider vinegar or red wine vinegar**
- **1 tablespoon olive oil**
- **1 tablespoon Dijon mustard with seeds**
- **2 teaspoons fresh thyme leaves (or $1/2$ teaspoon dried)**
- **$1/2$ teaspoon salt**
- **3 cups coarsely shredded skinless rotisserie chicken, light or dark meat (15 ounces)**
- **1 Red Delicious, Gala, or Fuji apple, unpeeled, cored, and thinly sliced**
- **1 bag (10 ounces) baby spinach**

1. In nonstick 10-inch skillet, cook bacon over medium heat, stirring occasionally, until browned, 5 to 6 minutes. Add green onions and cook, stirring, 1 minute. Remove skillet from heat. Stir in vinegar, oil, mustard, thyme, and salt.

2. Meanwhile, in large serving bowl, toss chicken with apple and spinach until combined.

3. Pour hot dressing over chicken mixture. Toss until salad is evenly coated. Serve immediately.

EACH SERVING: About 352 calories, 35 g protein, 8 g carbohydrates, 19 g total fat (5 g saturated), 2 g fiber, 105 mg cholesterol, 671 mg sodium.

Warm Chicken Salad with Mustard-Thyme Vinaigrette

No-Cook Barbecue Chicken Salad

PREP 25 minutes   **MAKES** 4 servings

1/4 cup barbecue sauce (preferably fewer than 260 mg sodium per
2 tablespoons, such as Sweet Baby Ray's)

2 tablespoons cider vinegar

1 tablespoon water

2 tablespoons olive oil

1/2 head romaine lettuce (8 ounces), cut crosswise into 1-inch slices

2 cups (1/2-inch pieces) skinless rotisserie chicken, light or dark meat
(10 ounces)

1 1/2 cups corn kernels cut from cobs (about 3 ears) or 1 1/2 cups
no-salt-added canned corn (such as Del Monte or Green Giant Niblets)

2 medium tomatoes, cut into 1/2-inch chunks

2 1/2 cups (1 1/2 [15-ounce] cans) black beans (preferably fewer than
140 mg sodium per 1/2 cup, such as Eden Organic or Goya Low
Sodium), rinsed and drained

1 can (4 to 4 1/2 ounces) chopped mild green chiles, drained

1. In small bowl, with wire whisk, mix barbecue sauce, cider vinegar, and water. In slow, steady stream, whisk in oil.

2. On large deep platter, toss romaine with 1/4 cup dressing. Arrange chicken, corn, tomatoes, and beans in strips on top of romaine. Sprinkle with chiles and drizzle with remaining dressing. Toss just before serving.

EACH SERVING (WITH NO-SALT-ADDED BEANS): About 389 calories, 29 g protein, 42 g carbohydrate, 13 g total fat (2 g saturated), 12 g fiber, 53 mg cholesterol, 318 mg sodium.

Chicken, Garbanzo Bean, and Grains Salad

PREP 10 minutes   **COOK** 25 minutes   **MAKES** 4 servings

- **1 box (5.1 ounces) Near East Whole Grain Blends Roasted Garlic Pilaf Mix**
- **2 tablespoons olive oil**
- **1 lemon**
- **2 tablespoons finely chopped red onion**
- **$1/8$ teaspoon ground red pepper**
- **4 cups spinach leaves, coarsely chopped**
- **2 cups ($1/2$-inch pieces) skinless rotisserie chicken, light or dark meat (10 ounces)**
- **1 cup canned garbanzo beans (preferably fewer than 140 mg sodium per $1/2$ cup, such as Eden Organic or Goya Low Sodium Chickpeas), rinsed and drained**
- **1 cup cherry tomatoes, halved**
- **$1/2$ cup shredded carrots**

1. Prepare pilaf mix according to package directions, using 1 tablespoon of the olive oil.

2. Meanwhile, from lemon, grate $1/2$ teaspoon zest and squeeze 3 tablespoons juice. In small bowl, whisk remaining 1 tablespoon oil, lemon zest and juice, red onion, and red pepper.

3. Transfer pilaf mix to large bowl; stir in spinach, chicken, garbanzo beans, tomatoes, and carrots. Drizzle salad with dressing and toss to blend.

EACH SERVING: About 394 calories, 26 g protein, 46 g carbohydrate, 13 g total fat (2 g saturated), 9 g fiber, 53 mg cholesterol, 577 mg sodium.

Cool and Creamy Shrimp Salad

Cool and Creamy Shrimp Salad

PREP 10 minutes **MAKES** 4 servings

- **1 large head Belgian endive, leaves separated and thinly sliced crosswise**
- **1 bag (4 ounces) watercress**
- **$\frac{1}{2}$ cup reduced-fat sour cream**
- **2 tablespoons fresh lime juice**
- **$\frac{1}{2}$ teaspoon salt**
- **$\frac{1}{4}$ teaspoon ground black pepper**
- **1 pound cooked, peeled, deveined shrimp**
- **1 English (seedless) cucumber (12 ounces), cut lengthwise in half, then thinly sliced crosswise**
- **1 green onion, thinly sliced**

In large serving bowl, toss endive with watercress. In medium bowl, stir sour cream, lime juice, salt, and pepper until mixed. Add shrimp, cucumber, and green onion; toss to coat well. Spoon shrimp mixture on top of greens. Toss before serving.

EACH SERVING: About 227 calories, 33 g protein, 8 g carbohydrate, 6 g total fat (3 g saturated), 1 g fiber, 242 mg cholesterol, 511 mg sodium.

Dilled Tuna-Stuffed Tomatoes

PREP 25 minutes   **MAKES** 4 servings

>   2 cans (6 ounces each) solid white tuna in water, drained and flaked
>
>   5 tablespoons light mayonnaise (such as from Kraft or Hellman's)
>
>   2 kirby cucumbers, unpeeled, cut into $1/4$-inch pieces
>
> $1/4$ cup loosely packed fresh dill, finely chopped
>
>   2 tablespoons capers, drained and finely chopped
>
>   2 tablespoons fresh lemon juice
>
>   1 tablespoon Dijon mustard
>
> $1/4$ teaspoon ground black pepper
>
>   4 large ripe tomatoes (12 ounces each)

1. In medium bowl, combine tuna, mayonnaise, cucumber, dill, capers, lemon juice, mustard, and pepper.

2. Cut each tomato, from blossom end, into 6 attached wedges, being careful not to cut all the way through. Spoon one-fourth of tuna mixture into center of each tomato.

EACH SERVING: About 209 calories, 22 g protein, 12 g carbohydrate, 8 g total fat (1 g saturated), 2 g fiber, 42 mg cholesterol, 622 mg sodium.

Corn and Black Bean Burritos ⓥ

PREP 15 minutes   **COOK** 12 minutes   **MAKES** 4 servings

- **1 teaspoon canola oil**
- **1 small onion, chopped**
- **1¹/₂ cups chopped red or green peppers**
- **1 garlic clove, minced**
- **1¹/₂ teaspoons chili powder**
- **¹/₄ teaspoon ground cumin**
- **1 can (15 ounces) black beans (preferably fewer than 140 mg sodium per ¹/₂ cup, such as Eden Organic or Goya Low Sodium), rinsed and drained**
- **1 cup canned whole-kernel corn, no-salt-added, drained**
- **4 burrito-size flour tortillas, preferably whole-wheat (120 to 140 calories each), warmed**
- **¹/₂ cup shredded reduced-fat Cheddar cheese (such as Cabot 50% Light)**
- **2 green onions, thinly sliced**
- **¹/₄ cup reduced-fat sour cream**
- **¹/₄ cup salsa (with fewer than 140 mg sodium per 2 tablespoons)**

1. In nonstick 12-inch skillet, heat oil over medium heat until hot. Add onion, chopped pepper, garlic, chili powder, and cumin; cook until vegetables are tender, 10 minutes. Add beans and corn and cook, stirring, until mixture is heated through, 2 to 3 minutes. Remove from heat.

2. Spread equal amount of bean/rice mixture in middle of each tortilla. Top each with 2 tablespoons shredded Cheddar, about 1 tablespoon green onion, and 1 tablespoon sour cream. Roll each tortilla around filling, burrito-style. Serve with salsa.

EACH SERVING: About 400 calories, 22 g protein, 60 g carbohydrate, 11 g total fat (4 g saturated), 13 g fiber, 23 mg cholesterol, 647 mg sodium.

Corn and Jack Quesadillas ⓥ

PREP 10 minutes plus cooling **GRILL** 11 minutes **MAKES** 4 servings

3 large ears corn, husks and silks removed

4 burrito-size flour tortillas, preferably whole-wheat (120 to 140 calories each; see Note)

4 ounces reduced-fat Monterey Jack cheese, shredded (1 cup)

1/2 cup mild or medium-hot salsa (with fewer than 140 mg sodium per 2 tablespoons)

2 green onions, thinly sliced

1 head romaine lettuce, thinly sliced

1 tablespoon olive oil

1 tablespoon cider vinegar

1/2 teaspoon coarsely ground pepper

1/4 teaspoon salt

1. Prepare charcoal fire or preheat gas grill for covered direct grilling over medium-high heat.

2. Place corn on hot grill rack. Cover grill and cook corn, turning frequently, until brown in spots, 10 to 15 minutes. Transfer corn to plate and let cool until easy to handle. With sharp knife, cut kernels from cobs.

3. Place tortillas on work surface. Evenly divide Monterey Jack, salsa, green onions, and corn on half of each tortilla. Fold tortillas over filling to make 4 quesadillas.

4. Place quesadillas on hot grill rack. Cook quesadillas, turning over once, until browned on both sides, 1 to 2 minutes. Transfer quesadillas to cutting board; cut each into 3 pieces.

5. In large bowl, toss romaine with oil, vinegar, pepper, and salt. Serve quesadillas with romaine salad.

EACH SERVING: About 400 calories, 18 g protein, 59 g carbohydrate, 14 g total fat (5 g saturated), 12 g fiber, 18 mg cholesterol, 804 mg sodium.

NOTE: Also a good choice are whole-wheat/soy-flour tortillas, such as La Tortilla Factory's Whole-Wheat Low Carb Low Fat Tortilla, which are only 80 calories each, so you can use 4 ears of corn in the recipe.

Corn and Jack Quesadillas

Greek Salad Pitas

Greek Salad Pitas (v)

PREP 20 minutes   **MAKES** 4 servings

- 1 can (15 ounces) garbanzo beans (preferably fewer than 140 mg sodium per $1/2$ cup, such as Eden Organic or Goya Low Sodium Chickpeas), rinsed and drained
- $1/4$ cup plain low-fat yogurt
- 2 tablespoons olive oil
- 2 tablespoons fresh lemon juice
- $1/2$ teaspoon salt
- $1/4$ teaspoon coarsely ground black pepper
- $1/4$ teaspoon ground cumin
- 1 garlic clove, peeled
- 4 (6- to 7-inch) whole-wheat pita breads (about 150 calories each)
- 3 cups sliced romaine lettuce
- 2 medium tomatoes, cut into $1/4$-inch pieces
- 1 medium cucumber, peeled and thinly sliced
- 2 ounces feta cheese, crumbled ($1/2$ cup)
- 2 tablespoons chopped fresh mint leaves

1. In food processor with knife blade attached, or in blender, combine beans, yogurt, oil, lemon juice, salt, pepper, cumin, and garlic; puree until smooth.

2. Cut off top third of each pita to form pocket. Use half of bean mixture to divide evenly inside pockets.

3. Combine lettuce, tomatoes, cucumber, feta, and mint; use to fill pockets. Top with remaining bean mixture.

EACH SERVING: About 392 calories, 17 g protein, 54 g carbohydrate, 13 g total fat (4 g saturated), 10 g fiber, 18 mg cholesterol, 542 mg sodium.

Falafel with Tzatziki Sauce Ⓥ

PREP 25 minutes **BAKE** 25 minutes **MAKES** 4 servings

>**1 box (6 ounces) Near East Falafel Mix**
>
>**1 container (6 ounces) plain low-fat yogurt**
>
>**$1/2$ large cucumber, peeled, seeded, and grated**
>
>**1 small garlic clove, minced**
>
>**$1/8$ teaspoon dried dill**
>
>**4 (6- to 7-inch) whole-wheat pitas (about 150 calories each)**
>
>**$1^1/2$ cups cherry or grape tomatoes, halved**
>
>**3 cups shredded romaine lettuce**

1. Prepare falafel mix according to package directions, making 8 patties. Bake (don't fry) according to package directions.

2. In a small bowl, combine yogurt, cucumber, garlic, and dill.

3. Cut pitas in half. Fill each half with 1 falafel, tomatoes, and lettuce; spoon sauce over.

EACH SERVING: About 324 calories, 22 g protein, 62 g carbohydrate, 2 g total fat (0 g saturated), 12 g fiber, 3 mg cholesterol, 759 mg sodium.

Fresh Mozzarella and Tomato Sandwiches ⓥ

PREP 15 minutes   **MAKES** 4 servings

¹/₂ cup Salsa Verde (below)

8 slices (¹/₂ inch thick) whole-wheat Italian bread or other whole-grain crusty bread (may be difficult to find, but you might find a bread made with a mix of white and whole-wheat flour)

2 ripe medium tomatoes, each cut into 4 slices

8 ounces fresh mozzarella cheese, cut into 8 slices

Spread about 1 tablespoon Salsa Verde on 1 side of each bread slice. Place 2 tomato slices and 2 mozzarella slice on each of 4 slices. Top with remaining bread slices, sauce side down. Cut each sandwich in half to serve.

EACH SERVING: About 399 calories, 17 g protein, 36 g carbohydrate, 20 g total fat (9 g saturated), 4 g fiber, 40 mg cholesterol, 597mg sodium.

Salsa Verde

2 cups packed fresh flat-leaf parsley leaves (3 bunches)

¹/₃ cup olive oil

3 tablespoons capers, drained

3 tablespoons fresh lemon juice

1 teaspoon Dijon mustard

1 garlic clove, cut in half

¹/₄ teaspoon salt

¹/₈ teaspoon ground black pepper

In food processor with knife blade attached, or in blender, combine parsley, oil, capers, lemon juice, mustard, garlic, salt, and pepper; puree until almost smooth. If not using right away, cover and refrigerate up to 3 days. *Makes about ³/₄ cup.*

EACH TABLESPOON: About 58 calories, 0 g protein, 1 g carbohydrate, 6 g total fat (1 g saturated), 0 g fiber, 0 mg cholesterol, 128 mg sodium.

Tofu "Egg" Salad Sandwiches Ⓥ

PREP 15 minutes   **MAKES** 4 servings

> **1 package (16 ounces) firm or extrafirm tofu, drained**
>
> **1 medium stalk celery, chopped**
>
> **$1/2$ small red pepper, cored and chopped**
>
> **1 green onion, chopped**
>
> **$1/4$ cup light mayonnaise (such as from Kraft or Hellman's)**
>
> **$1/2$ teaspoon Dijon mustard**
>
> **$1/2$ teaspoon salt**
>
> **$1/8$ teaspoon turmeric**
>
> **8 slices whole-wheat bread**
>
> **tomato slices (optional)**
>
> **lettuce leaves (optional)**

1.   In medium bowl, with fork, mash tofu until it resembles scrambled eggs. Stir in celery, red pepper, green onion, mayonnaise, mustard, salt, and turmeric. Cover and refrigerate if not serving right away.

2.   Spread a quarter of the tofu mix on each of four bread slices and top with another slice of bread. Add a tomato slice and lettuce leaf to each sandwich, if you like. Cut in half and serve.

EACH SERVING: About 303 calories, 16 g protein, 34 g carbohydrate, 11 g total fat (2 g saturated), 6 g fiber, 5 mg cholesterol, 586 mg sodium.

Bacon, Lettuce, and Tomato Sandwiches with Basil Mayonnaise

PREP 10 minutes   **COOK** 10 minutes   **MAKES** 4 servings

12 slices reduced-sodium bacon (8 ounces)

$1/3$ cup light mayonnaise (such as from Kraft or Hellman's)

$1/2$ cup loosely packed fresh basil leaves, finely chopped

$1/2$ teaspoon freshly grated lemon peel

$1/8$ teaspoon coarsely ground black pepper

8 slices whole-wheat bread, toasted

2 large ripe tomatoes (12 ounces each), sliced $1/4$ inch thick

Boston lettuce leaves

1. In 12-inch skillet, cook bacon over medium heat until browned, 10 minutes. Transfer bacon to paper towels to drain.

2. Meanwhile, in small bowl, mix mayonnaise, basil, lemon peel, and pepper until blended; set aside.

3. Spread mayonnaise mixture on 4 bread slices. Top with bacon, tomato, lettuce, then remaining bread.

EACH SERVING: About 362 calories, 16 g protein, 33 g carbohydrate, 19 g total fat (5 g saturated), 6 g fiber, 33 mg cholesterol, 727 mg sodium.

Chicken Cakes with "Roasted" Tomato Salsa

PREP 25 minutes **MAKES** 8 cakes or 4 servings

1 cup loosely packed fresh cilantro leaves

3 medium plum tomatoes (12 ounces)

1 teaspoon hot pepper sauce with chipotle, or 1 teaspoon adobo puree (see Note)

$1/4$ teaspoon salt

1 small zucchini (6 ounces), cut into 1-inch chunks

2 cups (1-inch chunks) skinless rotisserie chicken, light or dark meat (10 ounces)

$1/3$ cup plain dried bread crumbs

$1/4$ cup light mayonnaise (such as from Kraft or Hellman's)

1 tablespoon olive oil

2 large whole-wheat hamburger buns or Kaiser rolls (about 170 calories each, preferably 100% whole-wheat; if you can't find 100% whole-wheat, look for a bread that combines whole-wheat and white flours, such as Arnold Select Wheat Sandwich Rolls), split in half

1. Prepare salsa: In food processor with knife blade attached, pulse cilantro until coarsely chopped. Remove $1/4$ cup loosely packed chopped cilantro; reserve. Place tomatoes directly on clean gas or electric burner over high heat. With tongs, turn tomatoes frequently as skins burst and blacken, 2 to 3 minutes. Transfer tomatoes, as they are done, to food processor bowl with cilantro. Add hot pepper sauce and salt. Pulse 4 to 6 times or just until chunky. With rubber spatula, scrape salsa from food processor bowl into small serving bowl. It's OK if some salsa remains in processor bowl. *Makes about $1^1/2$ cups.*

2. To same food processor bowl, add zucchini. Pulse 5 to 6 times or until coarsely chopped. Add chicken, bread crumbs, mayonnaise, and reserved $1/4$ cup cilantro. Pulse 5 to 6 times or just until well combined (chicken should be chunky). Shape mixture by scant $1/2$ cups into eight 4-inch round patties.

3. In nonstick 12-inch skillet, heat oil over medium heat until very hot. Add chicken cakes; cook, turning once, until golden on both sides, 8 to 10 minutes. Serve 2 chicken cakes on top of each bun half with a heaping $1/3$ cup tomato salsa to make a total of 4 open-face sandwiches.

EACH SERVING (2 CAKES WITH SALSA AND HALF BUN): About 307 calories, 22 g protein, 23 g carbohydrate, 15 g total fat (3 g saturated), 3 g fiber, 58 mg cholesterol, 499 mg sodium.

NOTE: Adobo puree is the thick, vinegary sauce canned with chipolte chiles. Canned chipotle chiles are available in Latin markets and in the ethnic-foods section of some supermarkets.

Super Salsa

Anything that's mainly tomatoes is good for you: pizza sauce, spaghetti sauce, tomato paste, fresh tomato salad—and salsa. Whether you make your own, like the roasted tomato salsa in this recipe, or pick up a jar of store-bought (preferably with no more than 150 mg sodium per 2 tablespoons), you're getting a powerful antioxidant called lycopene. Linked to reduced risk of prostate cancer in men, and possibly reduced risk of heart disease in both men and women, lycopene also gives tomatoes their red color. A tip: Eat your tomato-y food with some fat and your body will absorb more lycopene. So, in this recipe, the mayo and olive oil enhance lycopene absorption; in pizza, fat in the cheese does the trick.

Portobello Burgers ⓥ

PREP 15 minutes plus marinating **GRILL** 20 minutes **MAKES** 4 servings

$1/4$ **cup reduced-sodium vegetable broth (preferably fewer than 350 sodium mg per cup, such as Health Valley Fat-Free)**

2 tablespoons olive oil

2 teaspoons balsamic vinegar

1 teaspoon chopped fresh thyme leaves

$1/4$ **teaspoon salt**

$1/4$ **teaspoon coarsely ground black pepper**

4 medium (4 ounces each) portobello mushrooms, stems removed

1 lemon

$1/3$ **cup light mayonnaise (such as from Kraft)**

1 small green onion, minced

4 ounces part-skim mozzarella, in 4 slices

4 large (4-inch) whole-wheat buns (about 170 calories each, preferably 100% whole-wheat; if you can't find 100% whole-wheat, look for a bread that combines whole-wheat and white flours, such as Arnold Select Wheat Sandwich Rolls)

1 bunch arugula, trimmed

1. In glass baking dish just large enough to hold mushrooms in a single layer, mix broth, oil, vinegar, thyme, $1/8$ teaspoon salt, and $1/8$ teaspoon pepper. Add mushrooms, turning to coat. Let stand, turning occasionally, 30 minutes.

2. Prepare charcoal fire or preheat grill for uncovered direct grilling over medium heat.

3. Meanwhile, from lemon, grate $1/2$ teaspoon peel and squeeze $1/2$ teaspoon juice. In small bowl, stir lemon peel and juice, mayonnaise, green onion, and remaining $1/8$ teaspoon salt and $1/8$ teaspoon pepper.

4. Place mushrooms on hot grill rack and grill, turning occasionally and brushing with remaining marinade, until mushrooms are browned and cooked through, 8 to 10 minutes per side. In final 4 minutes of cooking, top each mushroom with 1 ounce (1 slice) mozzarella and let it melt.

5. Cut each bun horizontally in half. Spread cut sides of buns with mayonnaise mixture; top with arugula leaves. Place a warm mushroom on each bottom half; replace top halves to serve.

EACH SERVING: About 371 calories, 15 g protein, 41 g carbohydrate, 18 g total fat (5 g saturated), 7 g fiber, 25 mg cholesterol, 703 mg sodium.

Steak Sandwiches with Grilled Onions

PREP 15 minutes plus marinating **GRILL** 12 minutes **MAKES** 4 servings

$^{1}/_{4}$ **cup reduced-sodium soy sauce (such as Kikkoman or La Choy Lite)**

$^{1}/_{4}$ **cup balsamic vinegar**

1 tablespoon brown sugar

1 teaspoon fresh thyme leaves

$^{1}/_{4}$ **teaspoon ground pepper**

1 beef flank steak (1$^{1}/_{4}$ pounds), trimmed of fat

1 medium red onion (8 ounces), cut into 4 thick slices

4 (6- to 7-inch) whole-wheat pita breads (about 150 calories each), toasted on grill if you like

2 ripe medium tomatoes, sliced

1 bunch arugula, trimmed

1. In large self-sealing plastic bag, mix soy sauce, vinegar, sugar, thyme, and pepper. Add steak to marinade, turning to coat. Seal bag, pressing out excess air. Place bag on plate; marinate 15 minutes at room temperature or 1 hour in the refrigerator, turning over several times.

2. Meanwhile, for easier handling, insert 1 long metal skewer horizontally through onion slices; set aside. Prepare charcoal fire or preheat gas grill for covered direct grilling over medium heat.

3. Remove steak from marinade; pour marinade into 1-quart saucepan. Heat marinade over high heat to boiling; boil 2 minutes.

4. Place steak and onion slices on hot grill rack. Cover grill and cook steak and onion until onions are browned and tender and meat is medium-rare, 12 to 15 minutes, brushing both with marinade occasionally and turning both over once. Transfer steak to cutting board; separate onion into rings.

5. Thinly slice steak diagonally across the grain. Open about a quarter of each pita around the edges. Stuff a quarter of the onion rings and steak into each pita. Drizzle any juices from board over onion and steak. Top with tomatoes and arugula.

EACH SERVING: About 416 calories, 42 g protein, 41 g carbohydrate, 8 g total fat (3 g saturated), 6 g fiber, 2 mg cholesterol, 477 mg sodium.

Cranberry Bean Soup ⓥ

PREP 40 minutes   **COOK** 45 minutes   **MAKES** about 9 cups or 4 servings

- **4 teaspoons olive oil**
- **1 medium butternut squash (2 pounds), peeled and cut into ¾-inch pieces**
- **1 medium onion, chopped**
- **2 garlic cloves, minced**
- **1 jalapeño chile, seeded and minced**
- **1 teaspoon ground cumin**
- **1 can (13¾ to 14½ ounces) reduced-sodium vegetable broth (preferably fewer than 350 mg sodium per cup, such as Health Valley Fat Free)**
- **2 medium tomatoes, chopped**
- **1½ pounds fresh cranberry beans, shelled, or 2 cups fresh or frozen lima beans**
- **1¼ cups loosely packed fresh basil leaves, chopped**
- **1 teaspoon sugar**
- **½ teaspoon salt**
- **2¼ cups water**
- **2 cups corn kernels cut from cobs (about 4 ears), or 2 cups frozen or canned no-salt-added corn (such as Del Monte or Green Giant Niblets)**

1. In 5-quart Dutch oven, heat 2 teaspoons oil over medium heat until hot. Add squash and onion and cook, stirring occasionally, until golden, about 10 minutes. Transfer squash mixture to bowl.

2. In same Dutch oven, heat remaining 2 teaspoons olive oil over medium heat; add garlic, jalapeño, and cumin and cook, stirring, 1 minute. Stir in squash mixture, broth, tomatoes, beans, ¼ cup basil, sugar, salt, and water; heat to boiling over high heat. Reduce heat to low; cover and simmer, stirring occasionally, until beans are tender, about 30 minutes.

3. Stir in corn; heat to boiling over high heat. Reduce heat to low; cover and simmer 5 minutes longer. Stir in remaining basil.

EACH SERVING: About 408 calories, 17 g protein, 81 g carbohydrate, 7 g total fat (1 g saturated), 13 g fiber, 0 mg cholesterol, 555 mg sodium.

Pasta e Fagioli ⓥ

PREP 5 minutes   **COOK** 25 minutes   **MAKES** about 8 cups or 4 servings

- 1 tablespoon olive oil
- 1 small onion, sliced
- 1 large stalk celery, sliced
- 1 can (14^1/$_2$ ounces) reduced-sodium vegetable broth (preferably less than 350 mg sodium per cup, such as Health Valley Fat Free)
- 2 cups water
- 2 cans (15 ounces each) white kidney (cannellini) beans (preferably fewer than 140 mg sodium per ^{1}/$_2$ cup, such as Eden Organic Cannellini or Westbrae Great Northern Beans), rinsed and drained
- 1^1/$_2$ cups (14 ounces) diced tomatoes (preferably less than 30 mg sodium per ^{1}/$_2$ cup, such as Pomi Chopped Tomatoes)
- 2 garlic cloves, crushed with garlic press
- 1 teaspoon sugar
- ^{1}/$_4$ teaspoon salt
- ^{1}/$_4$ teaspoon ground black pepper
- 1 cup tubettini or ditalini pasta (preferably whole-wheat)
- 1 package (10 ounces) frozen chopped spinach

1. In 5- to 6-quart Dutch oven, heat oil over medium heat until hot. Add onion and celery and cook, stirring occasionally, until vegetables are tender, about 10 minutes.

2. Meanwhile, in 2-quart saucepan, heat broth and water to boiling over high heat.

3. Add beans, tomatoes, garlic, sugar, salt, and pepper to onion mixture; heat to boiling over high heat. Add broth mixture and pasta; heat to boiling. Reduce heat to medium and cook 5 minutes. Add frozen spinach; cook, stirring frequently to separate spinach, 3 to 4 minutes longer.

EACH SERVING: About 352 calories, 17 g protein, 59 g carbohydrate, 6 g total fat (1 g saturated), 14 g fiber, 0 mg cholesterol, 430 mg sodium.

Chicken Soup with Latin Flavors

PREP 15 minutes   **COOK** 10 minutes   **MAKES** about 8 cups or 4 servings

1 tablespoon canola or olive oil

2 garlic cloves, chopped

2 medium carrots, chopped

2 medium stalks celery, chopped

1 medium onion, chopped

$^1/_2$ jalapeño chile with seeds, thinly sliced

1 teaspoon ground cumin

4 cups reduced-sodium chicken broth (preferably less than 100 mg
sodium per cup, such as Campbell's Low Sodium or Shelton's Organic
Fat Free/Low Sodium)

$1^1/_2$ cups water

1 cup corn kernels cut from cobs (about 2 ears), or 1 cup no-salt-added
frozen or canned corn (such as Del Monte or Green Giant Niblets)

2 tablespoons fresh lime juice

2 cups ($^1/_2$-inch pieces) skinless rotisserie chicken, light or dark meat
(10 ounces)

$^1/_2$ cup loosely packed fresh cilantro leaves, coarsely chopped

2 plum tomatoes, cut into $^1/_2$-inch pieces

1 ripe medium avocado, pitted, peeled, and cut into $^1/_2$-inch pieces

lime wedges

tortilla chips (such as Guiltless Gourmet Unsalted Yellow Corn), optional

1.   In 5- to 6-quart saucepot, heat oil over low heat until hot. Add garlic, carrots, celery, onion, and jalapeño; cook, covered, stirring frequently, until vegetables are tender, 8 to 10 minutes. Add cumin and cook, stirring, 30 seconds. Add broth and water to vegetable mixture; cover saucepot and heat to boiling over high heat.

2.   Stir corn kernels, lime juice, chicken, and cilantro into broth mixture in saucepot; heat to boiling over high heat. Remove saucepot from heat; stir in chopped tomatoes.

3.   Ladle soup into 4 warm large soup bowls; sprinkle with avocado pieces. Serve with lime wedges to squeeze over soup. Accompany with tortilla chips to crush into soup if you like.

EACH SERVING: About 365 calories, 25 g protein, 32 g carbohydrate, 17 g total fat (3 g saturated), 8 g fiber, 53 mg cholesterol, 245 mg sodium.

Chicken Soup with
Latin Flavors

Tomato and Cheese Pie

Tomato and Cheese Pie ⓥ

PREP 20 minutes   **BAKE** 30 minutes   **MAKES** 4 servings

> **1 container (15 ounces) part-skim ricotta cheese**
>
> **4 large eggs**
>
> **$1/4$ cup freshly grated Parmesan cheese**
>
> **$1/2$ teaspoon salt plus additional for sprinkling**
>
> **$1/8$ teaspoon coarsely ground black pepper plus additional for sprinkling**
>
> **$1/4$ cup low-fat milk (1%)**
>
> **1 tablespoon cornstarch**
>
> **1 cup packed fresh basil leaves, chopped**
>
> **1 pound ripe tomatoes (3 medium), thinly sliced**

1. Preheat oven to 375°F. In large bowl, with wire whisk or fork, beat ricotta, eggs, Parmesan, salt, and pepper until blended.

2. In cup, with fork, stir milk and cornstarch until blended; whisk into cheese mixture. Stir in basil. Pour mixture into 9-inch glass or ceramic pie plate. Arrange tomatoes on top, overlapping if necessary. Sprinkle tomatoes with salt and pepper.

3. Bake pie until lightly browned around edge and center is puffed, 30 to 35 minutes.

EACH SERVING: About 284 calories, 23 g protein, 14 g carbohydrate, 16 g total fat (8 g saturated), 2 g fiber, 251 mg cholesterol, 602 mg sodium.

Onion, Spinach, and Pecorino Frittata Ⓥ

PREP 6 minutes   **COOK/BAKE** 25 minutes   **MAKES** 4 servings

2 tablespoons olive oil

1 large sweet onion, quartered and thinly sliced

1 bag (5 to 6 ounces) baby spinach

8 large eggs

¹/₄ cup water

¹/₄ cup freshly grated Pecorino Romano cheese

¹/₄ teaspoon salt

¹/₄ teaspoon coarsely ground pepper

1. Preheat oven to 425°F. In nonstick oven-safe 12-inch skillet (if skillet is not oven-safe, wrap handle with double layer of foil), heat oil over medium heat until hot. Add onion and cook, stirring occasionally, until soft and golden brown, 10 minutes. Stir in spinach and cook, stirring constantly, just until wilted, 1 minute. Spread onion mixture evenly in skillet; remove skillet from heat.

2. In medium bowl, whisk eggs, water, Romano, salt, and pepper until blended. Carefully pour egg mixture into skillet over onion mixture; do not stir. Return to medium-high heat and cook until egg mixture begins to set around the edge, 2 to 3 minutes.

3. Place skillet in oven; bake until frittata is golden and set, 8 to 10 minutes. Slide frittata out of skillet onto cutting board. Cut into wedges to serve.

EACH SERVING: About 267 calories, 17 g protein, 9 g carbohydrate, 19 g total fat (5 g saturated), 2 g fiber, 427 mg cholesterol, 423 mg sodium.

Onion, Spinach, and Pecorino Frittata

Middle-Eastern Garbanzo Beans and Macaroni

Middle-Eastern Garbanzo Beans and Macaroni Ⓥ

PREP 10 minutes **COOK** 35 minutes **MAKES** about 8 cups or 6 servings

- **14 ounces whole-wheat macaroni twists, elbow macaroni, or other short, tubular pasta**
- **1 tablespoon olive oil**
- **1 tablespoon butter or margarine**
- **1 large onion (12 ounces), cut into $1/4$-inch pieces**
- **2 garlic cloves, crushed with garlic press**
- **1 teaspoon salt**
- **1 teaspoon ground cumin**
- **$3/4$ teaspoon ground coriander**
- **$1/4$ teaspoon ground allspice**
- **$1/4$ teaspoon coarsely ground black pepper**
- **1 can (28 ounces) low sodium crushed tomatoes**
- **$2^1/2$ cups ($1^1/2$ [15-ounce] cans) garbanzo beans (preferably fewer than 140 mg sodium per $1/2$ cup, such as Eden Organic or Goya Low Sodium Chickpeas), rinsed and drained**
- **$1/4$ cup loosely packed fresh parsley leaves, chopped**

1. In large saucepot, cook pasta as label directs.

2. Meanwhile, in nonstick 12-inch skillet, heat oil with butter over medium heat until hot and melted. Add onion and cook, stirring occasionally, until tender and golden, about 20 minutes. Stir in garlic, salt, cumin, coriander, allspice, and pepper; cook 1 minute.

3. Add tomatoes and garbanzo beans to skillet; heat to boiling over medium-high heat. Reduce heat to medium-low; simmer, stirring occasionally, 5 minutes.

4. Drain pasta; return to saucepot. Add garbanzo-bean mixture to pasta and toss; heat through. Toss with chopped parsley just before serving.

EACH SERVING: About 420 calories, 16 g protein, 74 g carbohydrate, 8 g total fat (1 g saturated), 13 g fiber, 0 mg cholesterol, 417 mg sodium.

Greens and Ricotta Pie (V)

PREP 30 minutes   BAKE 40 minutes   MAKES 6 servings

1 large head Swiss chard (1³⁄₄ pounds)

1 tablespoon olive oil

1 bunch green onions, cut into ¹⁄₄-inch-thick pieces

¹⁄₄ teaspoon coarsely ground black pepper

4 large eggs

1 container (15 ounces) part-skim ricotta cheese

³⁄₄ cup low-fat milk (1%)

¹⁄₂ cup freshly grated Parmesan cheese

2 tablespoons cornstarch

1. Preheat oven to 350°F. Grease 9¹⁄₂-inch deep-dish glass pie plate.

2. Trim off 2 inches from Swiss-chard stems; discard ends. Separate stems from leaves; thinly slice stems and coarsely chop leaves.

3. In nonstick 12-inch skillet, heat oil over medium-high heat until hot. Add sliced stems and cook, stirring frequently, until tender and lightly browned, about 4 minutes. Add green onions and pepper and cook 1 minute. Gradually add chopped leaves and cook, stirring, until leaves have wilted and excess moisture has evaporated, about 5 minutes.

4. In large bowl, with wire whisk, beat eggs, ricotta, milk, Parmesan, and cornstarch. Stir in Swiss-chard mixture.

5. Place prepared pie plate on foil-lined cookie sheet to catch any overflow. Pour mixture into pie plate. Bake pie until knife inserted 2 inches from center comes out clean, about 40 minutes.

EACH SERVING: About 248 calories, 18 g protein, 13 g carbohydrate, 14 g fat (6 g saturated), 2 g fiber, 172 mg cholesterol, 441 mg sodium.

Beef

Pepper-Crusted Filet Mignon

PREP 15 minutes plus standing   **GRILL** 16 minutes   **MAKES** 4 servings

- **1 tablespoon whole black peppercorns**
- **1 teaspoon whole fennel seeds**
- **4 beef tenderloin steaks (filet mignon), $3/4$ inch thick (4 ounces each)**
- **3 medium peppers (red, yellow, and/or orange)**
- **1 tablespoon minced fresh parsley leaves**
- **1 teaspoon olive oil**
- **$3/4$ teaspoon salt**

1. Prepare charcoal fire or preheat gas grill for covered direct grilling over medium-high heat.

2. Meanwhile, on cutting board, with rolling pin, crush peppercorns and fennel seeds. With hands, pat spice mixture around edges of steaks. Cover and refrigerate steaks until ready to cook. (Can be prepared up to 1 day ahead.)

3. Cut each pepper lengthwise in half; discard stems and seeds. With hand, flatten each pepper half.

4. Place peppers, skin side down, on hot grill rack. Cover grill and cook until skins are charred and blistered, 8 to 10 minutes. Transfer peppers to bowl; cover with plate and let steam at room temperature 15 minutes or until cool enough to handle. Reset grill temperature to medium.

5. Remove peppers from bowl. Peel off skins and discard. Cut peppers lengthwise into $1/4$-inch-wide strips. Return peppers to same bowl and toss with parsley, oil, and $1/4$ teaspoon salt.

6. Sprinkle steaks with remaining $1/2$ teaspoon salt. Place steaks on hot grill rack. Cover grill and cook steaks 4 to 5 minutes, turning once, per side for medium-rare or until desired doneness. Serve steaks topped with peppers.

EACH SERVING: About 210 calories, 26 g protein, 6 g carbohydrate, 9 g total fat (3 g saturated), 2 g fiber, 76 mg cholesterol, 357 mg sodium.

Skirt Steak with Chimichurri Sauce

Skirt Steak with Chimichurri Sauce

PREP 15 minutes plus standing   **GRILL** 6 minutes   **MAKES** 4 servings

Chimichurri Sauce

1 garlic clove, chopped

$1/4$ teaspoon salt

1 cup loosely packed fresh Italian parsley leaves, chopped

1 cup loosely packed fresh cilantro leaves, chopped

2 tablespoons olive oil

1 tablespoon red wine vinegar

$1/4$ teaspoon crushed red pepper

Steak

1 beef skirt steak* ($1^{1}/4$ pounds), trimmed of fat

$1/4$ teaspoon salt

$1/8$ teaspoon coarsely ground black pepper

1.   Prepare Chimichurri Sauce: On cutting board, with side of chef's knife, mash garlic with salt to a smooth paste. In small bowl, stir garlic mixture with parsley, cilantro, oil, vinegar, and crushed red pepper until mixed. (Or, in mini food processor or blender, blend all sauce ingredients until mixed.) *Makes about $1/4$ cup.*

2.   Prepare charcoal fire or preheat gas grill for covered direct grilling over medium heat.

3.   Sprinkle steak with salt and pepper; place on hot grill rack. Cover grill and cook steak about 3 minutes per side, turning once, for medium-rare.

4.   Transfer steak to cutting board; let stand 10 minutes to set juices for easier slicing. Thinly slice steak crosswise against the grain. Serve with Chimichurri Sauce.

EACH SERVING STEAK WITH 1 TABLESPOON SAUCE: About 302 calories, 31 g protein, 2 g carbohydrate, 18 g total fat (5 g saturated), 1 g fiber, 67 mg cholesterol, 363 mg sodium.

*Skirt steak, also called fajitas meat or Philadelphia steak, is a long, flat piece of meat from the plate, the area next to the flank. It can be very tough if not quickly grilled or broiled, or slowly braised. If you can't find skirt, use flank steak and grill 12 to 16 minutes.

Steak with Mushroom Sauce

PREP 10 minutes   **COOK** 20 minutes   **MAKES** 4 servings

4 beef tenderloin steaks (filet mignon), $^3/_4$ inch thick (4 ounces each)

$^1/_2$ teaspoon salt

$^1/_4$ teaspoon ground black pepper

1 tablespoon olive oil

1 large shallot, minced ($^1/_4$ cup)

1 package (10 ounces) sliced white mushrooms

1 package (4 ounces) assorted sliced wild mushrooms (gourmet blend)

$^1/_4$ cup port wine

$^1/_4$ cup water

1. Sprinkle steaks on both sides with $^1/_4$ teaspoon salt and $^1/_8$ teaspoon pepper. Heat a nonstick 12-inch skillet over medium-high heat until very hot. Add steaks and cook 4 to 5 minutes per side, turning once, for medium-rare or until desired doneness. Transfer steaks to platter; keep warm.

2. To drippings in skillet, add oil and shallot; cook 1 minute, stirring often. Add mushrooms and remaining $^1/_4$ teaspoon salt and $^1/_8$ teaspoon pepper; cook, stirring frequently, until liquid evaporates and mushroom mixture is golden, 8 to 10 minutes. Add port and water; cook 30 seconds, stirring constantly. Spoon mushroom sauce over steaks.

EACH SERVING: About 258 calories, 27 g protein, 9 g carbohydrate, 10 g total fat (3 g saturated), 1 g fiber, 67 mg cholesterol, 347 mg sodium.

Steak with Mushroom Sauce

Beef and Barley with Mushrooms

PREP 25 minutes   **COOK** 50 minutes   **MAKES** 4 servings

3 cups boiling water

1 package ($\frac{1}{2}$ ounce) dried porcini mushrooms ($\frac{1}{2}$ cup)

1 beef top round steak, $\frac{3}{4}$ inch thick (12 ounces), trimmed of fat

1 teaspoon olive oil

2 teaspoons reduced-sodium soy sauce (such as La Choy Lite)

1 package (8 ounces) sliced white mushrooms

2 medium carrots, each cut lengthwise in half, then crosswise into $\frac{1}{4}$-inch-thick slices

1 medium onion, finely chopped

$\frac{1}{4}$ teaspoon dried thyme

$\frac{1}{4}$ teaspoon salt

$\frac{1}{4}$ teaspoon ground black pepper

$1\frac{1}{2}$ cups pearl barley

1 can (14 to $14\frac{1}{2}$ ounces) reduced-sodium chicken broth (preferably fewer than 100 mg sodium per cup, such as Campbell's Low Sodium or Shelton's Organic Fat Free/Low Sodium)

$\frac{1}{2}$ cup loosely packed fresh parsley leaves (stems removed)

1.   Into medium bowl, pour boiling water over porcini; let stand 10 minutes.

2.   Meanwhile, cut steak lengthwise in half. With knife held in a slanted position, almost parallel to cutting surface, slice each half of steak crosswise into $\frac{1}{8}$-inch-thick slices.

3.   In deep nonstick 12-inch skillet, heat oil over medium-high heat until very hot. Add half of steak slices and cook, stirring constantly, until steak just loses its pink color, 2 minutes. Transfer steak to medium bowl; repeat with remaining steak. Toss steak with soy sauce; set aside.

4.   To same skillet, over medium-high heat, add white mushrooms, carrots, onion, thyme, salt, and pepper; cook, stirring occasionally, until vegetables are tender-crisp, 10 minutes.

5.   While vegetables are cooking, with slotted spoon, remove porcini from soaking liquid; reserve liquid. Rinse porcini to remove any sand; coarsely chop. Strain soaking liquid through sieve lined with paper towel into medium bowl.

6.   Add barley, broth, porcini, and soaking liquid to vegetables in skillet; heat mixture to boiling over medium-high heat. Reduce heat to medium-low;

cover and simmer, stirring occasionally, until barley and vegetables are tender and most of liquid has evaporated, 35 to 40 minutes. Stir in steak mixture and parsley; heat through.

EACH SERVING: About 439 calories, 31 g protein, 69 g carbohydrate, 5 g total fat (1 saturated), 14 g fiber, 49 mg cholesterol, 344 mg sodium.

NOTE: We've chosen top round steak because it is a very lean cut, but it must be thinly sliced across the grain—otherwise it may be tough.

Move Over Oat Bran, Barley's Coming!

Oat bran and oatmeal are famous cholesterol-reducers, and while their fame is well-deserved—research clearly shows that oats work—another grain should share the limelight because barley also helps bring down LDL, the "bad" cholesterol. No surprise, because both oats and barley are rich in a type of fiber called beta-glucans, which work in a number of ways to give you better lab results (for instance, trapping cholesterol in their thick fiber web and carrying some of it out of the body before it can be absorbed). Both pearled (some of the outer layer removed) and unpearled barley are rich in beta-glucans, because they present throughout the entire grain, not just in the outside layer. Enjoy barley as part of a soup or main dish (as in this recipe), by itself as a side dish, and as the basis of a hot breakfast cereal (look for barley-based cereals in the health-food aisle).

Jamaican Beef with Sweet Potatoes and Greens

PREP 10 minutes   **COOK** 25 minutes   **MAKES** 4 servings

- **2 medium onions**
- **4 teaspoons canola oil**
- **1 garlic clove, crushed with garlic press**
- **1 can (14 to 14^1/$_2$ ounces) reduced-sodium chicken broth (preferably fewer than 100 mg sodium per cup, such as Campbell's Low Sodium or Shelton's Organic Fat Free/Low Sodium)**
- **^{1}/$_4$ cup water**
- **^{1}/$_2$ teaspoon salt**
- **1 large bunch kale (1^1/$_2$ pounds), stems and tough ribs removed**
- **4 small sweet potatoes (8 ounces each)**
- **^{1}/$_2$ large red pepper, cut into ^{1}/$_4$-inch dice**
- **^{3}/$_4$ pound lean (90%) ground beef**
- **^{1}/$_4$ cup bottled jerk sauce (preferably fewer than 270 mg of sodium per tablespoon, such as KC Masterpiece Caribbean Jerk Marinade)**

1. Thinly slice 1 onion; coarsely chop remaining onion.

2. In 5-quart saucepot, heat 2 teaspoons oil over medium-high heat. Add sliced onion and cook until golden, 3 minutes. Add garlic; cook 30 seconds. Add 1^1/$_4$ cups broth, water, and ^{1}/$_4$ teaspoon salt; heat to boiling. Add kale in batches. Cover; reduce heat to low and simmer until tender, 15 to 20 minutes.

3. Meanwhile, pierce potatoes; place on paper towel in microwave oven. Cook on High 8 to 12 minutes, turning potatoes over and rearranging halfway through cooking.

4. In 12-inch skillet, heat remaining 2 teaspoons oil over medium-high heat until hot. Add chopped onion and red pepper; cook until golden, 3 minutes. Stir in ground beef and cook, breaking up meat with side of spoon, until meat is no longer pink, about 5 minutes. Stir in jerk sauce, remaining broth, and ^{1}/$_2$ teaspoon salt; simmer 2 minutes.

5. Cut potatoes open; serve with beef mixture and kale.

EACH SERVING: About 516 calories, 28 g protein, 74 g carbohydrate, 15 g total fat (4 g saturated), 9 g fiber, 57 mg cholesterol, 737 mg sodium.

Grilled Steak Caesar Salad

PREP 25 minutes plus standing   **GRILL** 10 minutes   **MAKES** 4 servings

$^1/_2$ **loaf whole-grain crusty bread (4 ounces), cut into $^3/_4$-inch cubes (3 cups)**

5 tablespoons olive oil

4 anchovy fillets, drained

1 garlic clove, crushed with garlic press

$^1/_4$ **cup grated Parmesan cheese**

3 tablespoons fresh lemon juice (from 1 to 2 lemons)

1 teaspoon Worcestershire sauce

$^1/_2$ **teaspoon dry mustard**

$^1/_2$ **teaspoon salt**

$^1/_4$ **teaspoon coarsely ground black pepper**

2 boneless beef top loin (shell) steaks, 1 inch thick (8 ounces each), trimmed of fat

2 medium heads romaine lettuce, cut crosswise into $^1/_2$-inch slices (10 cups)

1. Preheat oven to 350°F. In a $15^1/_2$" by $10^1/_2$" jelly-roll pan, toss bread cubes with 1 tablespoon oil. Toast bread in oven, stirring occasionally, until golden brown, 15 to 20 minutes. Cool croutons in pan on wire rack.

2. Meanwhile, prepare dressing: In medium bowl, mash anchovies with garlic to form paste. With wire whisk, mix in Parmesan, lemon juice, Worcestershire, mustard, $^1/_4$ teaspoon salt, and $^1/_8$ teaspoon pepper. Gradually whisk in remaining 4 tablespoons oil until well blended.

3. Heat ridged grill pan over medium heat until very hot. Place steaks in pan; sprinkle with remaining $^1/_4$ teaspoon salt and $^1/_8$ teaspoon pepper. Cook steaks 5 to 6 minutes per side, turning once, for medium-rare or until desired doneness. Transfer steaks to cutting board; let stand 10 minutes for easier slicing.

4. To serve, thinly slice steaks diagonally against the grain. In large serving bowl, toss steak slices with romaine, croutons, and dressing.

EACH SERVING: About 469 calories, 34 g protein, 22 g carbohydrate, 27 g total fat (6 g saturated), 4 g fiber, 79 mg cholesterol, 764 mg sodium.

Tuscan Steak and Beans

Tuscan Steak and Beans

PREP 5 minutes   **COOK** 15 minutes   **MAKES** 4 servings

- **1 teaspoon olive oil**
- **2 boneless beef top loin (strip) steaks, ³⁄₄ inch thick (10 ounces each), trimmed of fat**
- **¹⁄₂ teaspoon salt**
- **¹⁄₂ teaspoon coarsely ground pepper**
- **1 medium onion, sliced**
- **¹⁄₃ cup balsamic vinegar**
- **2 tablespoons water**
- **2 teaspoons chopped fresh rosemary**
- **1 pint grape or cherry tomatoes**
- **1 can (15 ounces) white kidney (cannellini) beans (preferably fewer than 140 mg sodium per ¹⁄₂ cup, such as Eden Organic Cannellini or Westbrae Great Northern Beans), rinsed and drained**

1. In 10-inch skillet, heat oil over medium-high heat until very hot but not smoking. Sprinkle steaks with salt and pepper. Add steaks to skillet and cook 4 to 5 minutes per side, turning once, for medium-rare or until desired doneness. Transfer steaks to cutting board; keep warm.

2. Reduce heat to medium. Add onion to drippings in skillet and cook, stirring, until browned and tender, 5 minutes. Add vinegar, water, and rosemary, stirring until browned bits are loosened from bottom of skillet. Stir in tomatoes and beans; cook, stirring occasionally, until heated through, 2 minutes.

3. Thinly slice steaks and serve with tomato-and-bean mixture.

EACH SERVING: About 339 calories, 36 g protein, 21 g carbohydrate, 10 g total fat (3 g saturated), 6 g fiber, 84 mg cholesterol, 417 mg sodium.

No-Bake Tamale Pie

PREP 15 minutes **COOK** 15 minutes **MAKES** 4 servings

4 teaspoons canola oil

1 small onion, chopped

2 garlic cloves, crushed with garlic press

1 pound lean (90%) ground beef

2 teaspoons chili powder

1 teaspoon ground cumin

1 log (16 ounces) precooked polenta, cut crosswise into 8 slices

1 jar (16 ounces) medium-hot salsa (fewer than 140 mg sodium per 2 tablespoons)

1 cup frozen corn kernels

1/2 cup loosely packed fresh cilantro leaves, chopped

1. In nonstick 12-inch skillet, heat 2 teaspoons oil over medium-high heat. Add onion and cook until golden, 3 minutes. Stir in garlic; cook 30 seconds. Stir in ground beef and cook, breaking up meat with side of spoon, until meat is no longer pink, about 5 minutes. Add chili powder and cumin; cook 1 minute.

2. In nonstick 10-inch skillet, heat remaining 2 teaspoons oil over medium-high heat. Add polenta and cook until golden on both sides and heated through, 10 minutes.

3. While polenta cooks, add salsa and frozen corn to meat mixture; cook 3 to 5 minutes to blend flavors. Stir in cilantro.

4. Spoon meat mixture into deep-dish pie plate or shallow $1^1/_2$-quart casserole. Arrange polenta on top.

EACH SERVING: About 433 calories, 28 g protein, 43 g carbohydrate, 17 g total fat (5 g saturated), 6 g fiber, 74 mg cholesterol, 948 mg sodium.

No-Bake Tamale Pie

Steak and Pepper Fajitas

PREP 15 minutes   **COOK** 20 minutes   **MAKES** 6 servings

3 tablespoons fresh lime juice

3 tablespoons fresh orange juice

$^1/_2$ teaspoon dried oregano, crumbled

pinch crushed red pepper

$^3/_4$ teaspoon salt

1 beef flank steak ($1^3/_4$ pounds), trimmed of fat

1 tablespoon olive oil

1 large (12 ounces) or 2 medium onions, cut into $^1/_2$-inch-wide slices

1 large red pepper, cut into $^1/_2$-inch-wide strips

1 large yellow pepper, cut into $^1/_2$-inch-wide strips

1 large green pepper, cut into $^1/_2$-inch-wide strips

2 garlic cloves, thinly sliced

6 burrito-size flour tortillas, preferably whole-wheat (175 calories each)

6 tablespoons reduced-fat sour cream, at room temperature

6 tablespoons shredded Monterey Jack cheese, at room temperature

12 tablespoons salsa (fewer than 140 mg sodium per 2 tablespoons)

1. In medium bowl, combine lime and orange juices, oregano, crushed red pepper, and $^1/_2$ teaspoon salt. Add steak to bowl, turning to coat.

2. In nonstick 12-inch skillet, heat oil over medium heat until hot. Add onion and cook, covered, stirring frequently, until onion is tender, 5 minutes. Add red, yellow, and green peppers, garlic, and remaining $^1/_4$ teaspoon salt; cook, covered, stirring frequently, until peppers are tender, 7 to 8 minutes.

3. Meanwhile, heat ridged grill pan or heavy skillet over medium-high heat until very hot but not smoking. Remove steak from bowl; discard marinade. Place steak in grill pan and cook 6 to 8 minutes per side, turning once, for medium-rare or until desired doneness.

4. Transfer steak to cutting board. Thinly slice steak diagonally against the grain and wrap in tortillas with pepper mixture. Either top the steak and peppers in each tortilla with 1 tablespoon sour cream, 1 tablespoon cheese, and 2 tablespoons salsa before rolling, or serve the accompaniments on each plate.

EACH SERVING WITH SOUR CREAM, CHEESE, AND SALSA: About 489 calories, 38 g protein, 44 g carbohydrate, 19 g total fat, (6 g saturated), 8 g fiber, 67 mg cholesterol, 771 mg sodium.

Thai Beef Salad

PREP 30 minutes plus marinating   **GRILL** 10 minutes   **MAKES** 4 servings

> **2 tablespoons Asian fish sauce (nuoc nam)**
>
> **$2^1/_2$ teaspoons sugar**
>
> **1 beef top round steak, $^3/_4$ inch thick (1 pound), trimmed of fat**
>
> **2 limes**
>
> **3 tablespoons canola oil**
>
> **$^1/_4$ teaspoon crushed red pepper**
>
> **$^1/_4$ teaspoon coarsely ground black pepper**
>
> **2 bunches watercress, trimmed**
>
> **1 cup loosely packed fresh mint leaves**
>
> **1 cup loosely packed fresh cilantro leaves**
>
> **1 bunch radishes, each cut in half and thinly sliced**
>
> **$^1/_2$ small red onion, thinly sliced**

1. In 8- or 9-inch square glass baking dish, stir 1 tablespoon fish sauce and 1 teaspoon sugar. Add steak, turning to coat; marinate 15 minutes at room temperature or 1 hour in refrigerator, turning occasionally.

2. Prepare charcoal fire or preheat gas grill for covered direct grilling over medium heat.

3. Meanwhile, from limes, with vegetable peeler, remove peel in 2" by $^3/_4$" strips. With sharp knife, remove any white pith from peel and cut enough peel crosswise into matchstick-thin strips to equal 1 tablespoon. From limes, squeeze 3 tablespoons juice. In small bowl, whisk lime juice, oil, crushed red pepper, black pepper, and remaining 1 tablespoon fish sauce and $1^1/_2$ teaspoons sugar until blended; set dressing aside.

4. In large bowl, toss watercress, mint, cilantro, radishes, onion, and lime peel; cover and refrigerate until ready to serve.

5. Place steak on hot grill rack. Cover grill and cook steak 5 to 8 minutes per side, turning once, for medium-rare or until desired doneness. Transfer steak to cutting board; let stand 10 minutes to set juices for easier slicing. Cut steak diagonally into thin strips.

6. Add steak and dressing to watercress mixture and toss until well coated.

EACH SERVING: About 295 calories, 29 g protein, 15 g carbohydrate, 14 g total fat (2 g saturated), 5 g fiber, 58 mg cholesterol, 401 mg sodium.

Tangerine Beef Stir-Fry

PREP 20 minutes **COOK** 15 minutes **MAKES** 4 servings

2 to 3 tangerines (1$^{1}/_{2}$ pounds)

$^{1}/_{4}$ cup dry sherry

2 tablespoons hoisin sauce

2 tablespoon cornstarch

2 tablespoons soy sauce

**1 beef flank steak (1 pound), trimmed of fat and cut crosswise into
$^{1}/_{8}$-inch-thick slices**

5 teaspoons canola oil

1 bag (12 ounces) broccoli florets

1 medium red pepper, thinly sliced

1 tablespoon grated peeled fresh ginger

1. From 1 tangerine, with vegetable peeler, remove peel. With small knife, remove any white pith from peel; slice peel very thinly and set aside. Squeeze $^{1}/_{2}$ cup juice from tangerines. Combine juice, sherry, and hoisin sauce in a small bowl; set aside. In medium bowl, stir to combine cornstarch and soy sauce. Add steak and stir to coat; set aside.

2. In nonstick 12-inch skillet, heat 1 teaspoon oil over medium-high heat until very hot. Add broccoli, red pepper, ginger, and tangerine peel and cook, stirring, until vegetables are tender-crisp, 3 minutes. Transfer to large bowl.

3. In same skillet, heat 2 teaspoons oil over medium-high heat; add half of beef and cook, stirring, until lightly browned, 2 minutes. Transfer to bowl with broccoli mixture. Repeat with remaining 2 teaspoons oil and remaining beef.

4. Add juice mixture to skillet and heat to boiling; boil 1 minute. Return vegetables and beef to skillet; heat through.

EACH SERVING: About 368 calories, 30 g protein, 31 g carbohydrate, 14 g total fat (4 g saturated), 3 g fiber, 48 mg cholesterol, 500 mg sodium.

Tangerine
Beef Stir-Fry

Glazed Pork with Pear Chutney

Glazed Pork with Pear Chutney

PREP 10 minutes   **BROIL** 20 minutes   **MAKES** 4 servings

> **¹/₄ cup packed light brown sugar**
>
> **1 tablespoon cider vinegar**
>
> **1 teaspoon Dijon mustard**
>
> **2 pork tenderloins (12 ounces each)**
>
> **¹/₄ teaspoon salt**
>
> **¹/₄ teaspoon ground black pepper**
>
> **Pear Chutney (below)**

1. Preheat broiler. In small bowl, mix brown sugar, vinegar, and mustard; set aside. Rub tenderloins with salt and pepper; place on rack in broiling pan. With broiling pan 5 to 7 inches from source of heat, broil tenderloins 8 minutes. Brush with some brown-sugar glaze and broil 2 minutes longer. Turn tenderloins and broil 8 minutes. Brush with remaining brown-sugar glaze and broil until tenderloins are still slightly pink in center (internal temperature of meat should be 155°F. on meat thermometer), 2 minutes longer. When done, let pork stand for 5 minutes, as internal temperature will rise to 160°F.

2. Meanwhile, prepare Pear Chutney.

3. Place pork tenderloins on cutting board. Holding knife at an angle, thinly slice tenderloins. Spoon warm chutney over pork slices to serve.

Pear Chutney

Discard all but ¹/₂ cup syrup from *1 can (28 ounces) pear halves in heavy syrup;* cut pears into ¹/₂-inch chunks. In 2-quart saucepan, heat *¹/₃ cup sweet red peppers,* chopped, *¹/₄ cup dark raisins, 2 teaspoons cider vinegar, 1 teaspoon light brown sugar, ¹/₄ teaspoon salt, ¹/₈ teaspoon coarsely ground black pepper,* and the ¹/₂ cup pear syrup to boiling over high heat. Reduce heat to medium and cook 5 minutes. Reduce heat to low; stir in pears and *1 chopped green onion;* cook, covered, 5 minutes longer. *Makes about 2¹/₂ cups chutney.*

EACH SERVING PORK WITH HEAPING ¹/₂ CUP CHUTNEY: About 407 calories, 32 g protein, 59 g carbohydrate, 6 g total fat (2 g saturated), 5 g fiber, 98 mg cholesterol, 539 mg sodium.

Tarragon Pork Tenderloins with Grilled Grapes

PREP 12 minutes   **GRILL** 18 minutes   **MAKES** 8 servings

- $^1/_2$ **small shallot, cut in half**
- **3 tablespoons chopped fresh tarragon leaves or 1 teaspoon dried**
- **2 tablespoons Dijon mustard**
- $^1/_2$ **teaspoon ground black pepper**
- $^1/_2$ **teaspoon salt**
- **2 whole pork tenderloins (1 pound each)**
- **1 large bunch seedless red grapes (1$^1/_2$ pounds)**

1. Prepare charcoal fire or preheat outdoor gas grill for covered direct grilling over medium heat.

2. Meanwhile, press shallot through garlic press into cup; stir in tarragon, mustard, pepper, and salt. Spread tarragon mixture all over tenderloins.

3. Place tenderloins on hot grill rack. Cover grill and cook, turning occasionally, until temperature on meat thermometer inserted in center of tenderloins reaches 155°F., 18 to 20 minutes. When done, let pork stand for 5 minutes, as internal temperature will rise to 160°F.

4. After tenderloins have cooked 15 minutes, add the bunch of grapes to same grill rack and cook, turning occasionally, until grapes soften slightly and brown in spots, 4 to 5 minutes.

5. Place tenderloins on cutting board. Place grapes on large platter; with kitchen shears, cut into 8 clusters. To serve, holding knife at an angle, thinly slice tenderloins; transfer to platter with grapes.

EACH SERVING: About 208 calories, 27 g protein, 15 g carbohydrate, 5 g total fat (2 g saturated), 1 g fiber, 73 mg cholesterol, 171 mg sodium.

Tarragon Pork Tenderloins with Grilled Grapes

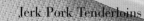
Jerk Pork Tenderloins

Jerk Pork Tenderloins

PREP 15 minutes plus marinating   **GRILL** 18 minutes   **MAKES** 8 servings

> 1 bunch green onions, cut into 1-inch pieces
>
> 3 bay leaves, broken into pieces
>
> 3 garlic cloves, peeled
>
> 2 jalapeño chiles, seeds and membrane discarded, cut up
>
> 2 tablespoons distilled white vinegar
>
> 1 tablespoon dried thyme
>
> 2 teaspoons ground allspice
>
> 1 teaspoon salt
>
> $^1/_2$ teaspoon coarsely ground black pepper
>
> 2 whole pork tenderloins (1 pound each)
>
> 1 large or 2 small ripe pineapples

1. In food processor with knife blade attached, blend green onions, bay leaves, garlic, jalapeños, vinegar, thyme, allspice, salt, and pepper to a thick paste.

2. On large plate, rub tenderloins all over with jerk paste; cover and refrigerate 1 hour or overnight.

3. Prepare charcoal fire or preheat gas grill for covered direct grilling over medium heat.

4. Meanwhile, with sharp knife, cut pineapple lengthwise through crown to stem end into 8 wedges, leaving on leafy crown; or cut 2 small pineapples in the same way into 4 wedges each.

5. Place tenderloins on hot grill rack. Cover grill and cook, turning once, until browned on the outside and still slightly pink in the center (internal temperature of meat should be 155°F. on meat thermometer), 18 to 22 minutes. When done, let pork stand for 5 minutes, as internal temperature will rise to 160°F. While tenderloins are cooking, add pineapple wedges, cut sides down, to same grill; cook, turning once, until golden brown and heated through, 5 to 8 minutes.

6. Transfer pineapple to platter. Transfer tenderloins to cutting board and thinly slice. Serve sliced tenderloins with pineapple wedges.

EACH SERVING: About 172 calories, 23 g protein, 11 g carbohydrate, 4 g total fat (1 g saturated), 1 g fiber, 70 mg cholesterol, 347 mg sodium.

Dijon-Fennel Pork Tenderloin with Sweet Potato Fries

PREP 15 minutes   **ROAST** 25 minutes   **MAKES** 4 servings

Sweet Potato Fries

nonstick cooking spray

2 to 3 large sweet potatoes (1$^1/_2$ pounds)

$^1/_4$ teaspoon salt

Dijon-Fennel Pork

1 tablespoon Dijon mustard

2 teaspoons fennel seeds, crushed

1 garlic clove, crushed with garlic press

$^1/_2$ teaspoon dried thyme

$^1/_4$ teaspoon salt

$^1/_2$ teaspoon ground black pepper

1 whole pork tenderloin (1 pound)

1. Prepare Sweet-Potato Fries: Preheat oven to 475°F. Spray 15$^1/_2$" by 10 $^1/_2$" jelly-roll pan or large cookie sheet with nonstick cooking spray.

2. Scrub potatoes well but do not peel. Slice each potato lengthwise in half. Place each potato half cut side down; cut lengthwise into $^1/_4$-inch-thick slices. Place potatoes in jelly-roll pan; sprinkle with salt and lightly coat with nonstick cooking spray.

3. Prepare Dijon-Fennel Pork: In small bowl, mix mustard, fennel, garlic, thyme, salt, and pepper. Rub pork with mixture. Place pork on rack in small (14" by 10") roasting pan.

4. Place potatoes and pork on 2 oven racks, and roast until pork is still slightly pink in the center (internal temperature of meat should be 155°F. on meat thermometer) and potatoes are tender and lightly browned, about 25 minutes. When done, let pork stand for 5 minutes, as internal temperature will rise to 160°F. Transfer pork to cutting board; holding knife at an angle, thinly slice. Transfer potatoes to serving bowl.

EACH SERVING: About 297 calories, 27 g protein, 36 g carbohydrates, 4 g total fat (1 g saturated), 6 g fiber, 74 mg cholesterol, 500 mg sodium.

Chorizo and Bean Burritos

PREP 15 minutes   **COOK** 10 minutes   **MAKES** 6 servings

> 2 cans (15 to 16 ounces each) pinto beans (preferably fewer than 140 mg sodium per $1/2$ cup, such as Eden Organic or Goya Low Sodium)
>
> 1 teaspoon canola oil
>
> 1 small onion, chopped
>
> 2 teaspoons chili powder
>
> $1/4$ teaspoon ground cumin
>
> 8 ounces fully-cooked chorizo, sliced
>
> 6 (9-inch) tortillas, preferably whole-wheat (120 to 140 calories each), warmed
>
> 1 cup shredded reduced-fat Cheddar cheese (such as Cabot 50% Light)
>
> $1/2$ cup packed fresh cilantro leaves
>
> 1 large ripe tomato, chopped
>
> 2 cups lettuce, shredded

1. In food processor with knife blade attached, pulse undrained beans until coarsely chopped.

2. In nonstick 10-inch skillet, heat oil over medium heat. Add onion and cook, stirring occasionally, until lightly browned, 3 to 4 minutes. Stir in chili powder, cumin, and chorizo; cook 2 minutes. Add beans and cook, stirring frequently, 2 minutes.

3. Place tortillas on work surface. Spoon equal amounts of bean mixture, Cheddar, cilantro, tomato, and lettuce across center of each tortilla. Fold sides of tortilla over filling.

EACH SERVING: About 488 calories, 26 g protein, 50 g carbohydrate, 22 g total fat (8 g saturated), 13 g fiber, 4 mg cholesterol, 1,126 mg sodium.

Pork Chops with Tomatoes and Arugula

PREP 10 minutes   **COOK** 5 minutes   **MAKES** 4 servings

$1/3$ **cup plain dried bread crumbs**

$1/4$ **cup grated Romano cheese**

$3/4$ **teaspoon salt**

1 large egg

4 boneless pork loin chops, $1/2$ inch thick (4 ounces each), trimmed of fat

3 tablespoons olive oil

$1^1/2$ tablespoons fresh lemon juice

10 ounces baby arugula (two 5-ounce bags or one larger bag)

1 small red onion, thinly sliced

2 large ripe tomatoes (12 ounces each), coarsely chopped

1. On waxed paper, combine bread crumbs, Romano, and $1/4$ teaspoon salt. In pie plate, with fork, beat egg. Dip 1 chop in egg, then in bread-crumb mixture to coat. Repeat with remaining chops.

2. In nonstick 12-inch skillet, heat 1 tablespoon oil over medium-high heat. Add chops and cook, turning once, until browned, 5 to 6 minutes.

3. Meanwhile, in medium bowl, combine lemon juice and remaining 2 tablespoons oil and $1/2$ teaspoon salt. Add arugula, onion, and tomatoes and toss.

4. Transfer chops to 4 dinner plates; top with salad.

EACH SERVING: About 364 calories, 31 g protein, 15 g carbohydrate, 20 g total fat (5 g saturated), 3 g fiber, 67 mg cholesterol, 676 mg sodium.

Pork Chops with Tomatoes and Arugula

Pork, Cabbage, and Apple Sauté

Pork, Cabbage, and Apple Sauté

PREP 15 minutes   **COOK** 40 minutes   **MAKES** 4 servings

- 1 teaspoon olive oil
- 4 bone-in pork loin chops, $3/4$ inch thick (6 ounces each), trimmed of fat
- $3/4$ teaspoon salt
- $1/4$ teaspoon ground black pepper
- 1 onion, thinly sliced
- 1 bag (16 ounces) shredded cabbage mix for coleslaw
- 2 large Golden Delicious apples (8 ounces each), cored and cut into $1/2$-inch-thick slices
- 12 ounces red potatoes, cut into 1-inch pieces
- $3/4$ cup apple cider
- $1/4$ teaspoon dried thyme
- 1 tablespoon cider vinegar

1. In nonstick 12-inch skillet, heat oil over medium-high heat until very hot. Add pork chops; sprinkle with $1/4$ teaspoon salt and $1/8$ teaspoon pepper. Cook, turning once, until golden on the outside and still slightly pink on the inside, 8 minutes. Transfer chops to plate; keep warm.

2. Add onion to skillet and cook over medium heat, covered, stirring occasionally, until tender and golden, 8 to 10 minutes. Stir in cabbage mix and cook until wilted, 5 minutes. Add apples, potatoes, apple cider, thyme, and remaining $1/2$ teaspoon salt and $1/8$ teaspoon pepper; heat to boiling. Reduce heat to medium-low and simmer, covered, until potatoes are tender, 15 minutes.

3. Stir in vinegar. Tuck chops into cabbage mixture and heat through.

EACH SERVING: About 325 calories, 24 g protein, 44 g carbohydrate, 7 g total fat (2 g saturated), 7 g fiber, 59 mg cholesterol, 513 mg sodium.

Brazilian Pork

PREP 15 minutes   **COOK** 15 minutes   **MAKES** 4 servings

4 boneless pork loin chops, $^3/_4$ inch thick (5 ounces each), trimmed of fat

$^1/_2$ teaspoon ground cumin

$^1/_2$ teaspoon ground coriander

$^1/_4$ teaspoon dried thyme

$^1/_8$ teaspoon ground allspice

$^1/_2$ teaspoon salt

1 teaspoon olive oil

1 medium onion, chopped

3 garlic cloves, crushed with garlic press

1 can (15 ounces) black beans (preferably less than 140 mg sodium per $^1/_2$ cup, such as Eden Organic or Goya Low Sodium), rinsed and drained

$^1/_2$ cup reduced-sodium chicken broth (preferably less than 100 mg sodium per cup, such as Campbell's Low Sodium or Shelton's Organic Fat Free/Low Sodium)

1 tablespoon fresh lime juice

$^1/_4$ teaspoon coarsely ground black pepper

$^1/_4$ cup packed fresh cilantro, chopped

fresh orange wedges (optional)

1. Pat pork chops dry with paper towels. In cup, mix cumin, coriander, thyme, allspice, and $^1/_4$ teaspoon salt. Rub spice mixture on both sides of pork chops.

2. Heat nonstick 12-inch skillet over medium heat until hot. Add pork chops and cook 4 minutes; turn chops over and cook until lightly browned on the outside and still slightly pink on the inside, 3 to 4 minutes longer. Transfer pork to platter; cover with foil to keep warm.

3. In same skillet, heat oil over medium heat. Add onion and cook, stirring frequently, until golden, about 5 minutes. Add garlic and cook, stirring, 1 minute longer. Stir in beans, broth, lime juice, pepper, and remaining $^1/_4$ teaspoon salt; heat through.

4. To serve, spoon bean mixture over pork; sprinkle with cilantro. Serve with orange wedges if you like.

EACH SERVING: About 300 calories, 37 g protein, 20 g carbohydrate, 7 g total fat (2 g saturated), 8 g fiber, 90 mg cholesterol, 490 mg sodium.

Brazilian Pork

Couscous with Ham and Tomatoes

Couscous with Ham and Tomatoes

PREP 15 minutes   **COOK** 5 minutes   **MAKES** 4 servings

- 1$\frac{1}{2}$ cups water
- 1 cup plain couscous (Moroccan pasta), preferably whole-wheat (such as from Fantastic Foods or Casbah)
- $\frac{1}{2}$ teaspoon salt
- 8 ounces deli ham in 1 piece ($\frac{1}{2}$ inch thick), cut into $\frac{1}{2}$-inch pieces
- 4 ripe plum tomatoes (1 pound), coarsely chopped
- 12 large basil leaves, thinly sliced
- 2 green onions, thinly sliced
- 1 can (15 ounces) garbanzo beans (preferably fewer than 140 mg sodium per $\frac{1}{2}$ cup, such as Eden Organic or Goya Low Sodium Chickpeas), rinsed and drained
- $\frac{1}{4}$ cup chopped pimiento-stuffed olives (salad olives)
- 1 tablespoon extravirgin olive oil
- 1 tablespoon fresh lemon juice

1. In covered 2-quart saucepan, heat water to boiling over high heat. Remove saucepan from heat. Stir in couscous and salt; cover and let stand 5 minutes.

2. Fluff couscous with fork and transfer to large serving bowl. Stir in ham, tomatoes, basil, green onions, beans, olives, oil, and lemon juice.

EACH SERVING: About 427 calories, 24 g protein, 66 g carbohydrate, 8 g total fat (1 g saturated), 12 g fiber, 27 mg cholesterol, 984 mg sodium.

Chicken-Spinach Salad with Warm Mushroom-Onion Vinaigrette

PREP 10 minutes   **COOK** 15 minutes   **MAKES** 4 servings

- **3 tablespoons olive oil**
- **1 large red onion, cut in half and thinly sliced**
- **$1/2$ teaspoon salt**
- **$1/4$ teaspoon coarsely ground pepper**
- **2 packages (4 ounces each) assorted sliced wild mushrooms (gourmet blend)**
- **$1/3$ cup cider vinegar**
- **1 tablespoon sugar**
- **2 bags (5 to 6 ounces each) baby spinach**
- **2 cups ($1/2$-inch pieces) skinless rotisserie chicken, light or dark meat, (10 ounces)**

1. In nonstick 12-inch skillet, heat 1 tablespoon oil over medium-high heat until hot. Add onion, salt, and pepper and cook, stirring occasionally, until onion is tender and golden, 10 minutes. Add mushrooms and cook until mushrooms are browned and liquid evaporates, 5 minutes.

2. Stir vinegar, sugar, and remaining 2 tablespoons oil into mushroom mixture. Heat to boiling; boil 30 seconds, stirring.

3. In large serving bowl, toss spinach and chicken with warm dressing until salad is evenly coated. Serve immediately.

EACH SERVING: About 286 calories, 24 g protein, 13 g carbohydrate, 16 g total fat (3 g saturated), 3 g fiber, 62 mg cholesterol, 419 mg sodium.

Warm Chicken and Apple Salad

PREP 15 minutes   COOK 20 minutes   MAKES 4 servings

1 cup apple cider

2 tablespoons fresh lemon juice

2 teaspoons cornstarch

3 tablespoons margarine or butter

1 pound skinless, boneless chicken-breast halves, cut into 1-inch chunks

³/₄ teaspoon salt

3 medium celery stalks, cut into 1-inch chunks

1 small onion, chopped

2 large Granny Smith apples, cored and cut into 1-inch chunks

2 cups seedless red grapes (¹/₂ pound), each cut in half

1 bag (5 to 6 ounces) baby spinach

¹/₂ cup celery leaves, chopped

¹/₂ cup walnuts, toasted

1.   In small bowl, blend cider, lemon juice, and cornstarch; set aside.

2.   In nonstick 12-inch skillet, melt 1 tablespoon margarine over medium-high heat. Add chicken and ¹/₂ teaspoon salt; cook, stirring frequently (stir-frying), just until lightly browned and chicken loses its pink color throughout, 6 to 8 minutes. With slotted spoon, transfer chicken to large bowl; keep warm.

3.   In same skillet, melt 1 tablespoon margarine over medium heat. Add celery, onion, and remaining ¹/₄ teaspoon salt; stir-fry until vegetables are tender and lightly browned, 6 to 8 minutes. Transfer to bowl with chicken. To same skillet, add apples and grapes and stir-fry until apples are tender-crisp, 5 minutes. Transfer to bowl with chicken.

4.   Stir cider mixture and add to skillet; heat to boiling over medium-high heat, stirring. Boil 1 minute. Remove skillet from heat; stir in remaining 1 tablespoon margarine. Pour cider dressing over chicken mixture; toss to coat.

5.   Divide spinach among 4 dinner plates; top with chicken mixture and sprinkle with celery leaves and nuts.

EACH SERVING: About 426 calories, 30 g protein, 44 g carbohydrate, 16 g total fat (2 g saturated), 6 g fiber, 66 mg cholesterol, 572 mg sodium.

Chicken and Prosciutto Roll-Ups

PREP 15 minutes   **COOK** 15 minutes   **MAKES** 4 servings

4 medium skinless, boneless chicken-breast halves (1¹/₄ pounds)

4 ounces Fontina cheese, cut into 4 slices

4 large slices prosciutto (2 to 2¹/₂ ounces)

12 large fresh basil leaves

1 bag (6 ounces) baby spinach

1. Holding knife parallel to work surface, cut a horizontal pocket in thickest part of each chicken breast. Insert 1 slice of cheese in each pocket.

2. Arrange prosciutto slices on work surface; top each with 3 basil leaves. Place a breast over each set of basil leaves; wrap with prosciutto to cover pocket. Secure with toothpicks.

3. Heat nonstick 12-inch skillet over medium heat until hot. Add chicken to skillet; cover and cook 10 minutes. Uncover; turn chicken over and cook until chicken just loses its pink color throughout, 3 to 5 minutes longer.

4. When chicken is done, place spinach in same skillet with chicken. Cook, uncovered, stirring constantly, until leaves wilt, 1 minute.

5. To serve, remove toothpicks from chicken. Arrange spinach on 4 dinner plates; top with chicken.

EACH SERVING: About 295 calories, 44 g protein, 2 g carbohydrate, 12 g total fat (6 g saturated), 1 g fiber, 123 mg cholesterol, 630 mg sodium.

Chicken and Prosciutto Roll-Ups

Glazed Rotisserie Chicken Four Ways

PREP 5 minutes   **MICROWAVE** 1 minute   **MAKES** 4 servings

Choice of 4 glazes (below)
1 (2- to 2¹/₂-pound) warm rotisserie chicken, skin removed

Prepare choice of glaze as recipe directs. Place whole chicken on platter; use pastry brush to coat all over with hot glaze. Cut chicken into pieces or slice to serve.

Apricot-Ginger Glaze

In microwave-safe small bowl, stir *2 tablespoons apricot jam, 2 tablespoons prepared horseradish,* and *¹/₂ teaspoon ground ginger.* Cook, uncovered, in microwave oven on High, stirring once, 30 seconds.

EACH SERVING CHICKEN WITH GLAZE: About 365 calories, 38 g protein, 8 g carbohydrate, 19 g total fat (5 g saturated), 0 g fiber, 152 mg cholesterol, 125 mg sodium.

Hoisin and Five-Spice Glaze

In microwave-safe small bowl, stir *¹/₄ cup hoisin sauce, 2 tablespoons reduced-sodium soy sauce,* and *1 teaspoon Chinese five-spice powder.* Cook, uncovered, in microwave oven on High, stirring once, 30 seconds.

EACH SERVING CHICKEN WITH GLAZE: About 375 calories, 39 g protein, 8 g carbohydrate, 19 g total fat (5 g saturated), 1 g fiber, 152 mg cholesterol, 860 mg sodium.

Moroccan-Spiced Glaze

In microwave-safe small bowl, stir *3 tablespoons honey, 1 tablespoon fresh lemon juice, ¹/₂ teaspoon ground cinnamon,* and *¹/₂ teaspoon ground cumin* until blended. Cook, uncovered, in microwave oven on High, stirring once, 1 minute.

EACH SERVING CHICKEN WITH GLAZE: About 380 calories, 38 g protein, 14 g carbohydrate, 19 g total fat (5 g saturated), 0 g fiber, 152 mg cholesterol, 115 mg sodium.

Honey-Mustard Glaze

In microwave-safe small bowl, stir *2 tablespoons Dijon mustard with seeds, 2 tablespoons honey,* and *¹/₂ teaspoon dried thyme (or 2 teaspoons minced fresh thyme leaves)*. Cook, uncovered, in microwave oven on High, stirring once, 30 seconds.

EACH SERVING CHICKEN WITH GLAZE: About 375 calories, 39 g protein, 10 g carbohydrate, 19 g total fat (5 g saturated), 0 g fiber, 152 mg cholesterol, 155 mg sodium.

Chicken Breasts with Cranberry-Balsamic Sauce and Brussels Sprouts

Chicken Breasts with Cranberry-Balsamic Sauce and Brussels Sprouts

PREP 20 minutes   **ROAST** 15 minutes   **MAKES** 4 servings

> 1 container (10 ounces) fresh Brussels sprouts
>
> 1 tablespoon plus 1 teaspoon olive oil
>
> $1/2$ teaspoon salt
>
> $1/4$ teaspoon ground black pepper
>
> 2 tablespoons all-purpose flour
>
> 4 skinless, boneless chicken-breast halves ($1^{1/4}$ pounds)
>
> 2 cups cranberries
>
> $1/4$ cup sugar
>
> $1/4$ cup balsamic vinegar
>
> $3/4$ cup water

1. Preheat oven to 450°F. Trim Brussels sprouts; cut lengthwise into thin slices. In $15^{1/2}$" by $10^{1/2}$" jelly-roll pan, toss sprouts with 1 tablespoon oil, $1/4$ teaspoon salt, and $1/8$ teaspoon pepper to coat. Spread evenly in pan; roast until tender and browned at edges, 15 to 20 minutes.

2. Meanwhile, in nonstick 12-inch skillet, heat remaining 1 teaspoon oil over medium-high heat until hot. On waxed paper, combine flour and remaining $1/4$ teaspoon salt and $1/8$ teaspoon pepper; use to coat chicken.

3. Add chicken to skillet and cook 6 minutes. Reduce heat to medium; turn chicken over and cook until chicken loses its pink color throughout, 6 to 8 minutes longer. Transfer chicken to platter; keep warm.

4. To skillet, add cranberries, sugar, vinegar, and water; heat to boiling over medium-high heat. Cook until sauce thickens slightly, about 5 minutes. Serve chicken with sauce and Brussels sprouts.

EACH SERVING: About 321 calories, 36 g protein, 28 g carbohydrate, 12 g total fat (1 g saturated), 5 g fiber, 82 mg cholesterol, 402 mg sodium.

TIP: When it's peak season for cranberries, buy extra and freeze in their original bag for use year-round. Don't thaw to use; just rinse with cold water and drain well.

Arroz con Pollo

PREP 15 minutes   **COOK** 35 minutes   **MAKES** 6 servings

> 1 teaspoon canola oil
>
> 6 small chicken thighs, (1¹/₂ pounds) skin and fat removed
>
> ³/₄ teaspoon salt
>
> ¹/₄ teaspoon ground black pepper
>
> 1 medium onion, finely chopped
>
> 1 medium green pepper, cut into 1-inch pieces
>
> 1 lemon
>
> 1¹/₂ cups 30-minute brown rice (such as Uncle Ben's Whole Grain Brown Rice)
>
> 1 can (14 to 14¹/₂ ounces) reduced-sodium chicken broth (preferably fewer than 100 mg sodium per cup, such as Campbell's Low Sodium or Shelton's Organic Fat Free/Low Sodium)
>
> 1¹/₄ cups water
>
> 1 large garlic clove, crushed with garlic press
>
> ¹/₈ teaspoon ground red pepper (cayenne)
>
> 1 package (10 ounces) frozen peas
>
> ¹/₃ cup drained chopped pimiento-stuffed olives (salad olives)

1. In nonstick 12-inch skillet, heat oil over medium heat until hot. Add chicken and sprinkle with ¹/₄ teaspoon salt and black pepper. Add onion and green pepper. Cook until chicken is browned and vegetables are tender, about 10 minutes, turning chicken over once and stirring vegetable mixture occasionally.

2. Meanwhile, with vegetable peeler, remove 3-inch strip peel from lemon. Cut lemon into wedges; reserve.

3. Stir lemon peel, rice, broth, water, garlic, ground red pepper, and remaining ¹/₂ teaspoon salt into mixture in skillet; heat to boiling over high heat. Reduce heat to low; cover and simmer 30 minutes. Stir in frozen peas; cover and cook 5 minutes. Remove skillet from heat; stir in olives. Serve with lemon wedges to squeeze over each serving.

EACH SERVING: About 323 calories, 21 g protein, 46 g carbohydrates, 6 g total fat (1 g saturated), 4 g fiber, 58 mg cholesterol, 510 mg sodium.

Arroz con Pollo

Quick Chicken Mole

Quick Chicken Mole

PREP 5 minutes   **COOK** 10 minutes   **MAKES** 4 servings

2 teaspoons olive oil

1 medium onion, chopped

2 garlic cloves, crushed with garlic press

2 teaspoons chili powder

2 teaspoons unsweetened cocoa

$1/_4$ teaspoon ground cinnamon

$1^1/_4$ cups reduced-sodium chicken broth (preferably fewer than 100 mg sodium per cup, such as Campbell's Low Sodium or Shelton's Organic Fat Free/Low Sodium)

1 tablespoon creamy peanut butter

1 tablespoon tomato paste

$1/_4$ cup golden or dark raisins

1 (2- to $2^1/_2$-pound) rotisserie chicken, cut into 8 pieces, skin removed

$1/_4$ cup loosely packed fresh cilantro leaves, chopped

lime wedges

1. In nonstick 12-inch skillet, heat oil over medium heat until hot. Add onion and cook, stirring occasionally, 5 minutes. Add garlic, chili powder, cocoa, and cinnamon; cook, stirring constantly, 1 minute.

2. Stir in broth, peanut butter, and tomato paste. Add raisins; heat to boiling. Add chicken pieces to skillet. Reduce heat to medium-low; cover and simmer about 5 minutes (10 minutes if chicken has been refrigerated) to blend flavors, turning chicken pieces over halfway through cooking to coat all sides with sauce.

3. Sprinkle chicken with cilantro. Serve with lime wedges.

EACH SERVING: About 319 calories, 35 g protein, 15 g carbohydrate, 13 g total fat (3 g saturated), 2 g fiber, 97 mg cholesterol, 199 mg sodium.

Smoky Almond Chicken

PREP 10 minutes **BAKE** 15 minutes **MAKES** 4 servings

$1/2$ **cup salted smoked almonds**

1 slice firm white bread, torn into pieces

$1/4$ **teaspoon ground black pepper**

$1/4$ **cup reduced-fat sour cream**

$1/2$ **cup barbecue sauce (preferably fewer than 260 mg sodium per 2 tablespoons, such as Sweet Baby Ray's)**

4 small skinless, boneless chicken-breast halves (1 pound)

1. Preheat oven to 400°F. In food processor with knife blade attached, pulse almonds, bread, and pepper until coarsely chopped; transfer to waxed paper. In pie plate, mix sour cream with 1 tablespoon barbecue sauce.

2. Dip chicken into sour-cream mixture, then into almond mixture to coat, firmly pressing so mixture adheres; arrange on cookie sheet.

3. Bake until chicken loses its pink color throughout, 12 to 15 minutes. Serve with remaining sauce.

EACH SERVING: About 311 calories, 32 g protein, 12 g carbohydrate, 15 g total fat (2 g saturated), 2 g fiber, 74 mg cholesterol, 502 mg sodium.

Smoky Almond Chicken

Grilled Summer Squash and Chicken

Grilled Summer Squash and Chicken

PREP 15 minutes plus marinating   **GRILL** 10 minutes   **MAKES** 4 servings

1 lemon

1 tablespoon olive oil

$^1/_2$ teaspoon salt

$^1/_4$ teaspoon coarsely ground black pepper

4 medium skinless, boneless chicken thighs (1$^1/_4$ pounds)

4 medium yellow summer squash and/or zucchini (6 ounces each), each cut lengthwise into 4 wedges

$^1/_4$ cup snipped fresh chives

grilled lemon slices

1. From lemon, grate 1 tablespoon peel and squeeze 3 tablespoons juice. In medium bowl, whisk together lemon peel and juice, oil, salt, and pepper; transfer 2 tablespoons to cup and set aside.

2. Add chicken to bowl with lemon-juice marinade; cover and let stand 15 minutes at room temperature or 30 minutes in the refrigerator.

3. Meanwhile, prepare charcoal fire or preheat gas grill for covered direct grilling over medium heat.

4. Discard chicken marinade. Place chicken and squash on hot grill rack. Cover grill and cook chicken and squash until juices run clear when thickest part of thigh is pierced with tip of knife and squash is tender and browned, 10 to 12 minutes, turning chicken and squash over once and removing pieces as they are done.

5. Transfer chicken and squash to cutting board. Cut chicken into 1-inch-wide strips; cut each squash wedge crosswise in half.

6. To serve, on large platter, toss squash with reserved lemon-juice marinade, then toss with chicken and sprinkle with chives. Serve with grilled lemon slices.

EACH SERVING: About 208 calories, 30 g protein, 6 g carbohydrate, 7 g total fat (2 g saturated), 2 g fiber, 118 mg cholesterol, 235 mg sodium.

Jerk Rice and Beans

PREP 30 minutes   **COOK** 5 minutes   **MAKES** 6 servings

2 tablespoons olive oil

2 tablespoons Worcestershire sauce

2 tablespoons cider vinegar

2 teaspoons grated fresh ginger

1 teaspoon dried thyme

$^1/_2$ teaspoon freshly ground black pepper

$^1/_2$ teaspoon ground allspice

$^1/_2$ teaspoon hot pepper flakes

$1^1/_2$ pounds boneless, skinless chicken breasts, cut crosswise into thin strips

8 green onions, sliced

1 red bell pepper, thinly sliced

2 cans (15 ounces each) Eden Organic (Caribbean Black Beans) Rice & Beans

2 large ripe mangos, peeled, pitted, and diced

1. In a bowl, combine 1 teaspoon olive oil, Worcestershire, vinegar, ginger, thyme, pepper, allspice, and hot pepper flakes. Add chicken and toss to combine; let stand 5 minutes.

2. In a large nonstick skillet, heat remaining oil over medium-high heat. Add chicken, green onions, and bell pepper. Cook, stirring constantly, until chicken is no longer pink throughout, 1 to 2 minutes. Stir in rice and beans and cook until hot, about 2 minutes.

3. Divide mixture among 6 dinner plates. Top each serving with a spoonful of mango chunks.

EACH SERVING: About 367 calories, 32 g protein, 44 g carbohydrate, 7 g total fat (1 g saturated), 7 g fiber, 66 mg cholesterol, 244 mg sodium.

Chicken Breasts with Cumin, Coriander, and Lime

(Pictured on cover)

PREP 10 minutes   **GRILL** 10 minutes   **MAKES** 4 servings

- **3 tablespoons fresh lime juice**
- **2 tablespoons olive oil**
- **1 teaspoon ground cumin**
- **1 teaspoon ground coriander**
- **1 teaspoon sugar**
- **1 teaspoon salt**
- **$^1/_8$ teaspoon ground red pepper (cayenne)**
- **4 medium skinless, boneless chicken breast halves ($1^1/_4$ pounds)**
- **1 tablespoon chopped fresh cilantro leaves**

1. Prepare grill. In large bowl, combine lime juice, oil, cumin, coriander, sugar, salt, and ground red pepper. Add chicken, turning to coat.

2. Arrange chicken on grill over medium heat and grill 5 to 6 minutes per side, brushing with any remaining cumin mixture halfway through cooking, until chicken loses its pink color throughout.

3. Transfer chicken to warm platter and sprinkle with cilantro.

EACH SERVING: About 225 calories, 33g protein, 2g carbohydrate, 9g total fat (1g saturated), 2 g fiber, 82 mg cholesterol, 676mg sodium.

Cashew Chicken Stir-Fry

PREP 25 minutes   **COOK** 45 minutes   **MAKES** 4 servings

- **1 cup brown Texmati or basmati rice (such as from Lundberg or Kohinoor)**
- **$^1/_2$ cup reduced-sodium chicken broth (preferably fewer than 100 mg sodium per cup, such as Campbell's Low Sodium or Shelton's Organic Fat Free/Low Sodium)**
- **$^1/_4$ cup dry sherry**
- **2 tablespoons reduced-sodium soy sauce (such as Kikkoman or La Choy Lite)**
- **1 tablespoon cornstarch**
- **1 tablespoon grated peeled fresh ginger**
- **1 teaspoon brown sugar**
- **$^1/_4$ teaspoon salt**
- **2 tablespoons canola oil**
- **8 ounces asparagus, trimmed and cut into 2-inch pieces**
- **4 ounces snow peas, strings removed and each cut in half**
- **2 large carrots, cut into 2" by $^1/_8$" matchstick-thin strips**
- **1 bunch green onions, cut into 2-inch pieces**
- **$^1/_3$ cup unsalted cashews**
- **1 pound skinless, boneless chicken-breast halves, thinly sliced crosswise**

1. Prepare rice as label directs.

2. Meanwhile, in small bowl, whisk broth, sherry, soy sauce, cornstarch, ginger, sugar, and salt; set aside.

3. In nonstick 12-inch skillet, heat 1 tablespoon oil over medium-high heat until hot. Add asparagus and snow peas and cook, stirring frequently (stir-frying), until tender-crisp, 4 minutes. Transfer vegetables to large bowl. To same skillet, add carrots, green onions, and cashews; stir-fry 3 minutes. Transfer to bowl with asparagus.

4. In same skillet, heat remaining 1 tablespoon oil. Add half of chicken and stir-fry just until chicken loses its pink color throughout, 2 to 3 minutes. With slotted spoon, transfer chicken to bowl with vegetables. Repeat with remaining chicken.

5. Stir broth mixture and add to skillet; heat to boiling, stirring. Boil 1 minute. Return vegetables and chicken to skillet; heat through. Serve with rice.

EACH SERVING: About 504 calories, 36 g protein, 55 g carbohydrate, 15 g total fat (2 g saturated), 6 g fiber, 66 mg cholesterol, 550 mg sodium.

Thai Chicken Saté with Pickled Cucumbers

PREP 45 minutes   **GRILL** 5 minutes   **MAKES** 4 servings

12 (12-inch) bamboo skewers

1 English (seedless) cucumber, thinly sliced crosswise

1$\frac{1}{2}$ teaspoons salt

1 tablespoon Thai green curry paste (such as from Roland)

$\frac{1}{4}$ cup plus $\frac{1}{3}$ cup well-stirred unsweetened coconut milk (not cream of coconut)

4 medium skinless, boneless chicken-breast halves (1$\frac{1}{4}$ pounds), each cut diagonally into 6 strips

$\frac{1}{4}$ cup creamy peanut butter

2 teaspoons reduced-sodium soy sauce (such as Kikkoman or La Choy Lite)

1 teaspoon packed dark brown sugar

$\frac{1}{8}$ teaspoon ground red pepper (cayenne)

1 tablespoon hot water

$\frac{1}{4}$ cup rice vinegar

3 tablespoons granulated sugar

2 medium shallots, thinly sliced

1 jalapeño chile, seeds and membrane discarded, minced

1.   Soak skewers in water to cover for 30 minutes. Drain before using.

2.   While skewers are soaking, in medium bowl, toss cucumber with salt; let stand 30 minutes at room temperature. In another medium bowl, stir curry paste and $\frac{1}{4}$ cup coconut milk until combined. Add chicken and turn to coat. Marinate 15 minutes at room temperature, stirring occasionally.

3.   Prepare charcoal fire or preheat gas grill for covered direct grilling over medium heat.

4.   Meanwhile, prepare peanut sauce: In small bowl, with wire whisk, mix peanut butter, soy sauce, brown sugar, ground red pepper, remaining $\frac{1}{3}$ cup coconut milk, and hot water until blended and smooth. Transfer sauce to serving bowl. *Makes about $\frac{2}{3}$ cup.*

5.   Drain cucumber, discarding liquid in bowl. Pat cucumber dry with paper towels. Return cucumber to bowl; stir in vinegar, granulated sugar, shallots, and jalapeño; refrigerate until ready to serve.

Thai Chicken Saté with Pickled Cucumbers

6.   Thread 2 chicken strips on each skewer, accordion-style; discard marinade. Place skewers on hot grill rack. Cover grill and cook, turning skewers over once, just until chicken loses its pink color throughout, 5 to 8 minutes.

7.   Arrange skewers on platter. Serve with peanut sauce and pickled cucumbers.

EACH SERVING WITHOUT PEANUT SAUCE: About 252 calories, 34 g protein, 20 g carbohydrate, 4 g total fat (52 g saturated), 1 g fiber, 82 mg cholesterol, 734 mg sodium.

EACH SERVING WITH 2 TABLESPOONS PEANUT SAUCE: About 373 calories, 38 g protein, 28 g carbohydrate, 13 g total fat (6 g saturated), 1 g fiber, 82 mg cholesterol, 986 mg sodium.

EACH TABLESPOON PEANUT SAUCE: About 60 calories, 2 g protein, 4 g carbohydrate, 4 g total fat (2 g saturated), 0 g fiber, 0 mg cholesterol, 126 mg sodium.

Spiced Grilled Turkey Breast with Peach Salsa

Spiced Grilled Turkey Breast with Peach Salsa

PREP 35 minutes plus brining and standing   **GRILL** 25 minutes   **MAKES** 12 servings

Brined Turkey

3/4 **cup sugar**

1/4 **cup kosher salt**

2 **tablespoons cracked black pepper**

2 **tablespoons ground ginger**

1 **tablespoon ground cinnamon**

1 **whole boneless turkey breast (4 pounds), skin removed and breast cut in half**

4 **garlic cloves, crushed with side of chef's knife**

Honey Glaze

2 **tablespoons honey**

2 **tablespoons Dijon mustard**

1 **chipotle chile in adobo, minced**

1 **teaspoon balsamic vinegar**

Peach Salsa

3 **pounds ripe peaches, peeled, pitted, and cut into** 1/2**-inch dice**

1 **green onion, finely chopped**

2 **tablespoons fresh lime juice**

1 **small hot red pepper (such as cayenne), seeded and minced**

1/2 **teaspoon salt**

1. Prepare Brined Turkey: In 2-quart saucepan, heat sugar, salt, pepper, ginger, cinnamon, and *1 cup water* to boiling over high heat. Reduce heat to low; simmer 2 minutes. Remove saucepan from heat; stir in *3 cups ice water*.

2. Place turkey breast in large self-sealing plastic bag; add brine and garlic. Seal bag, pressing out excess air. Place bag in bowl and refrigerate 24 hours, turning over occasionally.

3. Prepare charcoal fire or gas grill for covered direct grilling over medium heat.

4. While grill heats, prepare Honey Glaze: In small bowl, stir honey, mustard, chipotle, and vinegar until blended; set aside.

5.   Remove turkey from bag; discard brine and garlic. With paper towels, pat turkey dry and brush off most of pepper. With long-handled basting brush, oil grill rack. Place turkey on hot rack. Cover grill and cook turkey, turning over once, 20 minutes. Brush turkey with glaze and cook, brushing and turning frequently, 5 to 10 minutes longer (depending on thickness of breast), until temperature on meat thermometer inserted into thickest part of breast reaches 165°F. (Internal temperature will rise 5°F. upon standing.) Place turkey on cutting board and let rest 10 minutes to set juices for easier slicing.

6.   While turkey rests, prepare Peach Salsa: In medium bowl, stir peaches, green onion, lime juice, hot red pepper, and salt until mixed. *Makes about 4 cups.*

7.   Serve turkey hot, or cover and refrigerate to serve cold. Arrange sliced turkey and salsa on platter.

EACH SERVING TURKEY: About 172 calories, 35 g protein, 3 g carbohydrate, 1 g total fat (0 g saturated), 0 g fiber, 89 mg cholesterol, 394 mg sodium.

EACH 1/3 CUP SALSA: About 46 calories, 1 g protein, 11 g carbohydrate, 0 g total fat, 2 g fiber, 0 mg cholesterol, 97 mg sodium.

Turkey Cutlets Three Ways

Here, turkey cutlets are the basis for your choice of three delicious meals: Turkey with Warm Arugula Salad, Curried Turkey with Apricot Raisin Sauce, and Lemon Turkey.

Turkey Cutlets

PREP 15 minutes   **COOK** 5 minutes   **MAKES** 4 servings

> **4 large turkey cutlets (1 pound)**
> **$1/4$ teaspoon salt**
> **$1/4$ teaspoon coarsely ground black pepper**
> **1 tablespoon olive oil**

If necessary, with meat mallet or between two sheets of plastic wrap or waxed paper with rolling pin, pound cutlets to uniform $1/4$-inch thickness. Rub cutlets with salt and pepper (and other seasonings if directed in variations). In nonstick 12-inch skillet, heat oil over medium-high heat until hot. Add cutlets; cook, turning once, until golden, about 4 minutes. Transfer to platter; cover with foil to keep warm. Proceed with one of the variations that follow.

> **TIP**: Thinly sliced chicken breasts or pork tenderloin can be substituted for turkey cutlets. Either would be delicious with any of the 3 toppings.

Turkey with Warm Arugula Salad

> **Turkey Cutlets (above)**
> **4 large plum tomatoes (12 ounces), cut into $1/2$-inch pieces**
> **1 green onion, thinly sliced**
> **2 tablespoons grated Parmesan cheese**
> **1 tablespoon red wine vinegar**
> **1 tablespoon olive oil**
> **$1/4$ teaspoon salt**
> **$1/4$ teaspoon coarsely ground black pepper**
> **2 bunches arugula (8 ounces total), coarsely chopped**

Turkey Cutlets Three Ways

Prepare turkey cutlets as directed. To skillet in which turkey was cooked, add tomatoes and cook 1 minute. Remove skillet from heat; set aside. In medium bowl, with fork, mix green onion, Parmesan, vinegar, oil, salt, and pepper. Add arugula, and gently toss to mix well. To serve, top turkey cutlets with arugula mixture; spoon warm tomatoes over greens.

EACH SERVING: About 224 calories, 26 g protein, 7 g carbohydrate, 11 g total fat (2 g saturated), 3 g fiber, 52 mg cholesterol, 576 mg sodium.

Curried Turkey with Apricot Raisin Sauce

Turkey Cutlets (page 209)

1 teaspoon curry powder

$^1/_2$ teaspoon ground cumin

$^3/_4$ cup reduced-sodium chicken broth (preferably fewer than 100 mg sodium per cup, such as Campbell's Low Sodium or Shelton's Organic Fat Free/Low Sodium)

1 teaspoon cornstarch

$^1/_4$ cup apricot preserves

$^1/_4$ cup golden raisins

1 teaspoon distilled white vinegar

1. Prepare turkey cutlets as directed, mixing the curry powder and cumin with the salt and pepper and rubbing 1 side of each turkey cutlet with the curry mixture before cooking.

2. In cup, whisk broth with cornstarch. To skillet in which turkey was cooked, add apricot preserves, raisins, vinegar, and broth mixture; boil 2 minutes. To serve, spoon apricot sauce over turkey cutlets.

EACH SERVING: About 228 calories, 23 g protein, 21 g carbohydrate, 6 g total fat (1 g saturated), 1 g fiber, 50 mg cholesterol, 392 mg sodium.

Lemon Turkey

Turkey Cutlets (page 209)

2 medium lemons

³/₄ cup reduced-sodium chicken broth (preferably fewer than 100 mg sodium per cup, such as Campbell's Low Sodium or Shelton's Organic Fat Free/Low Sodium)

1¹/₂ teaspoons cornstarch

1 garlic clove, crushed with garlic press

2 tablespoons chopped fresh parsley leaves

1. Prepare turkey cutlets as directed.

2. Thinly slice 1 lemon. From other lemon, grate ¹/₂ teaspoon peel and squeeze 2 tablespoons juice. In cup, whisk broth with cornstarch. To skillet in which turkey was cooked, add garlic, lemon peel, lemon juice, and half of the lemon slices; cook 30 seconds. Add broth mixture and boil 1 minute. Stir in parsley.

3. To serve, pour sauce over turkey cutlets. Garnish with remaining lemon slices.

EACH SERVING: About 153 calories, 22 g protein, 2 g carbohydrate, 6 g total fat (1 g saturated), 0 g fiber, 50 mg cholesterol, 380 mg sodium.

Turkey Cutlets, Indian Style

PREP 15 minutes **GRILL** 4 minutes **MAKES** 6 servings

2 large limes

¹/₃ cup plain low-fat yogurt

1 tablespoon canola oil

2 teaspoons minced peeled fresh ginger

1 teaspoon ground cumin

1 teaspoon ground coriander

1 teaspoon salt

1 garlic clove, crushed with garlic press

6 turkey cutlets (1¹/₂ pounds)

1. Prepare charcoal fire or preheat gas grill for covered direct grilling over medium heat.

2. Meanwhile, from 1 lime, grate 1 teaspoon peel and squeeze 1 tablespoon juice. Cut remaining lime into wedges; reserve for squeezing juice over cooked cutlets. In large bowl, mix lime peel and juice, yogurt, oil, ginger, cumin, coriander, salt, and garlic until blended.

3. Just before grilling, add turkey cutlets to yogurt mixture in bowl, stirring to coat cutlets. (Do not let cutlets marinate in yogurt mixture more than 15 minutes; their texture will become mealy.)

4. Place cutlets on hot grill rack. Cover grill and cook, turning once, until cutlets just lose their pink color throughout, 4 to 5 minutes. Serve with lime wedges.

EACH SERVING: About 127 calories, 22 g protein, 1 g carbohydrate, 4 g total fat (1 g saturated), 0 g fiber, 50 mg cholesterol, 411 mg sodium.

Greek Turkey Cutlets with Lentil Pilaf

PREP 15 minutes   **COOK** 35 minutes   **MAKES** 4 servings

1 box (6.75 ounces) Near East Rice Pilaf with Lentils

2 tablespoons olive oil

¼ cup finely chopped red onion

2 tablespoons fresh lemon juice

1 garlic clove, finely chopped

4 large turkey cutlets (1 pound)

1 tablespoon chopped fresh oregano (or ½ teaspoon dried)

¼ teaspoon salt

⅛ teaspoon ground black pepper

2 cups baby arugula leaves

¼ cup reduced-fat crumbled feta cheese

1. Prepare pilaf mix according to package directions, using 1 tablespoon of the olive oil.

2. Meanwhile, prepare dressing: In small bowl, whisk remaining 1 tablespoon oil, red onion, lemon juice, and garlic.

3. Lightly grease grill pan and set over medium-high heat. With meat mallet or between two sheets of plastic wrap or waxed paper with rolling pin, pound turkey cutlets to ½-inch thickness. Sprinkle oregano, salt, and pepper on cutlets. Grill turkey until it loses its pink color throughout, about 2 minutes per side. Transfer cutlets to warm dish.

4. Transfer pilaf mix to large bowl; stir in dressing. Add arugula; mix well. Spoon pilaf on platter; top with turkey cutlets and sprinkle with cheese.

EACH SERVING: About 365 calories, 33 g protein, 34 g carbohydrate, 12 g total fat (3 g saturated), 8 g fiber, 58 mg cholesterol, 889 mg sodium.

Broccoli-Shrimp Curry

PREP 10 minutes   **COOK** 15 minutes   **MAKES** 4 servings

- 1 package (10 ounces) plain couscous (Moroccan pasta), preferably whole-wheat (such as from Fantastic Foods or Casbah)
- 2 teaspoons canola oil
- 2 garlic cloves, thinly sliced
- 1 tablespoon grated peeled fresh ginger
- 2 teaspoons curry powder
- 3 green onions, cut into 1½-inch pieces
- 1 bag (12 ounces) broccoli florets
- ½ teaspoon salt
- 2 tablespoons water
- 1 can (13½ ounces) unsweetened light coconut milk (not cream of coconut; such as from A Taste of Thai, Thai Kitchen, or Trader Joe's), well-stirred
- 1 teaspoon grated fresh lemon peel
- 1 pound cooked cleaned large shrimp

1. Prepare couscous as label directs.

2. Meanwhile, in nonstick 12-inch skillet, heat oil over medium-high heat until hot. Add garlic, ginger, and curry powder; cook, stirring, 1 minute. Add green onions, broccoli, salt, and water; cover and cook, stirring occasionally, until broccoli is tender-crisp, 4 to 5 minutes.

3. Stir in coconut milk and lemon peel; heat to boiling. Stir in shrimp and cook 1 minute more to heat through. Serve shrimp curry with couscous.

EACH SERVING: About 500 calories, 35 g protein, 63 g carbohydrate, 12 g total fat (5 g saturated), 6 g fiber, 172 mg cholesterol, 504 mg sodium.

Sesame Shrimp and Asparagus

Sesame Shrimp and Asparagus

PREP 10 minutes   **COOK** 45 minutes   **MAKES** 4 servings

- 1¼ cups brown basmati rice
- 2 tablespoons olive oil
- 1½ teaspoons Asian sesame oil
- ⅛ teaspoon salt
- 2 pounds asparagus, trimmed
- 3 tablespoons reduced-sodium soy sauce (such as Kikkoman or La Choy Lite)
- 2 teaspoons seasoned rice vinegar
- 1 large green onion, chopped
- 1 pound large shrimp, shelled and deveined
- ⅛ teaspoon crushed red pepper

1. Preheat oven to 450°F. Prepare rice as label directs.

2. Meanwhile, in cup, combine 1 tablespoon olive oil, 1 teaspoon sesame oil, and salt. In jelly-roll pan, toss asparagus with oil mixture; roast until tender, 10 to 12 minutes.

3. In small bowl, whisk soy sauce, vinegar, green onion, and remaining ½ teaspoon sesame oil; set aside dressing.

4. In nonstick 12-inch skillet, heat remaining 1 tablespoon olive oil over medium-high heat until very hot. Add shrimp; sprinkle with crushed red pepper and cook, stirring frequently, until opaque throughout, 3 minutes.

5. Arrange shrimp, asparagus, and rice on 4 plates; drizzle with dressing.

EACH SERVING: About 467 calories, 34 g protein, 57 g carbohydrate, 12 g total fat (2 g saturated), 7 g fiber, 172 mg cholesterol, 708 mg sodium.

Shrimp Saté with Cucumber Salad

PREP 45 minutes plus marinating   **GRILL** 5 minutes   **MAKES** 4 servings

about 8 (7-inch) bamboo skewers

1 tablespoon canola oil

6 tablespoons fresh lime juice (from 3 to 4 limes)

3 tablespoons minced cilantro

$^1/_2$ teaspoon salt

$^1/_2$ teaspoon crushed red pepper

1 pound large shrimp, shelled and deveined

2 small cucumbers (8 ounces each)

2 tablespoons sugar

1 tablespoon snipped fresh chives

2 tablespoons slivered fresh basil leaves

3 tablespoons chopped roasted salted peanuts

1. Prepare charcoal fire or gas grill for direct grilling over medium heat.

2. Soak skewers in water to cover for 30 minutes. Drain before using.

3. While skewers soak, in medium bowl, whisk together oil, 3 tablespoons lime juice, 2 tablespoons cilantro, $^1/_4$ teaspoon salt, and $^1/_4$ teaspoon crushed red pepper. Stir in shrimp and marinate at room temperature 15 minutes.

4. Meanwhile, prepare Cucumber Salad: Cut each unpeeled cucumber lengthwise in half. With spoon, scoop out seeds. Thinly slice cucumber halves crosswise. In another medium bowl, with rubber spatula, stir cucumbers, sugar, chives, 1 tablespoon basil, remaining 3 tablespoons lime juice, 1 tablespoon cilantro, $^1/_4$ teaspoon salt, and $^1/_4$ teaspoon crushed red pepper. Set aside. *Makes about 3 cups.*

5. Thread about 4 shrimp on each skewer. With long-handled basting brush, lightly oil grill rack. Place skewers on hot rack. Cook shrimp, turning over once, just until opaque throughout, 4 to 5 minutes.

6. Spoon cucumber salad onto 4 dinner plates; sprinkle with peanuts. Arrange skewers with shrimp over salad. Sprinkle with remaining 1 tablespoon basil.

EACH SERVING: About 194 calories, 22 g protein, 13 g carbohydrate, 6 g total fat (1 g saturated), 1 g fiber, 146 mg cholesterol, 235 mg sodium.

Shrimp and Scallop Kabobs

PREP 35 minutes   **GRILL** 6 minutes   **MAKES** 6 servings

- **12 ounces large sea scallops (or large bay scallops)**
- **1 pound large shrimp, shelled and deveined, leaving tail part of shell on if you like**
- **3 tablespoons reduced-sodium soy sauce (such as Kikkoman or La Choy Lite)**
- **3 tablespoons seasoned rice vinegar**
- **1 tablespoon Asian sesame oil**
- **2 tablespoons grated peeled fresh ginger**
- **2 garlic cloves, crushed with garlic press**
- **1 tablespoon brown sugar**
- **1 bunch green onions, cut on diagonal into 3-inch pieces**
- **12 cherry tomatoes**
- **6 long metal skewers**

1. Prepare charcoal fire or preheat gas grill for covered direct grilling over medium heat.

2. Pull off and discard tough crescent-shaped muscle from each scallop. Pat scallops and shrimp dry with paper towels. In large bowl, combine soy sauce, vinegar, sesame oil, ginger, garlic, and brown sugar. Add shrimp and scallops, tossing to coat.

3. Alternately thread shrimp, scallops, green-onion pieces, and cherry tomatoes onto skewers. Place skewers on hot grill rack and cook, turning skewers occasionally, until shrimp and scallops are just opaque throughout, 6 to 8 minutes.

EACH SERVING: About 149 calories, 24 g protein, 6 g carbohydrate, 3 g total fat (0 g saturated), 1 g fiber, 122 mg cholesterol, 332 mg sodium.

Grilled Shrimp with Black Bean Salad

PREP 15 minutes   **GRILL** 3 minutes   **MAKES** 4 servings

- 2 limes
- 2 cans (15 ounces each) black beans (preferably fewer than 140 mg sodium per $1/2$ cup, such as Eden Organic or Goya Low Sodium), rinsed and drained
- 2 ripe plum tomatoes (8 ounces), chopped
- 2 green onions, thinly sliced
- 1 small yellow pepper, seeded and chopped
- 1 jalapeño chile, finely chopped
- $1/2$ cup loosely packed fresh cilantro leaves, chopped
- 1 tablespoon olive oil
- $3/4$ teaspoon salt
- 1 pound large shrimp, shelled and deveined

1.   Prepare charcoal fire or preheat gas grill for uncovered direct grilling over medium-high heat.

2.   Meanwhile, prepare Black Bean Salad: From 1 lime, grate $1/2$ teaspoon peel and squeeze 2 tablespoons juice. Cut remaining lime into wedges and reserve for squeezing over shrimp. In large bowl, stir lime juice and $1/4$ teaspoon lime peel with beans, tomatoes, green onions, pepper, jalapeño, cilantro, oil, and $1/2$ teaspoon salt. Set aside at room temperature. *Makes about 5 cups*.

3.   In medium bowl, toss shrimp with remaining $1/4$ teaspoon lime peel and $1/4$ teaspoon salt. Place shrimp on hot grill rack and cook, turning once, just until opaque throughout, 3 to 4 minutes.

4.   Stir about half of shrimp into bean salad; top with remaining shrimp. Serve with lime wedges.

EACH SERVING: About 337 calories, 34 g protein, 38 g carbohydrate, 5 g total fat (1 g saturated), 12 g fiber, 155 mg cholesterol, 533 mg sodium.

Shrimp and Grains Paella

PREP 10 minutes   **COOK** 30 minutes   **MAKES** 4 servings

1 box (6.25 ounces) Near East Whole Grain Blends Brown Rice Pilaf

1 tablespoon plus 2 teaspoons olive oil

1 teaspoon turmeric

1 small red pepper, diced

³/₄ pound large shrimp, shelled and deveined

1 garlic clove, finely chopped

¹/₈ teaspoon red pepper flakes

1 cup canned black beans (preferably fewer than 140 mg sodium per ¹/₂ cup, such as Eden Organic or Goya Low Sodium), rinsed and drained

1 cup frozen peas, thawed

lemon wedges

1. Prepare pilaf mix according to package directions, using 1 tablespoon of the olive oil and adding the turmeric.

2. Meanwhile, in nonstick large skillet, heat remaining 2 teaspoons oil over medium-high heat. Add red pepper and cook, stirring frequently, until crisp-tender, 1 to 2 minutes. Add shrimp and cook, stirring constantly, until just opaque throughout, about 1 minute Add garlic and pepper flakes and cook, stirring constantly, until fragrant, 30 seconds. Remove from heat; stir in beans and peas. Cover and keep warm.

3. Transfer pilaf mix to large serving bowl; stir in shrimp mixture. Serve with lemon wedges.

EACH SERVING: About 388 calories, 26 g protein, 48 g carbohydrate, 8 g total fat (1 g saturated), 7 g fiber, 129 mg cholesterol, 776 mg sodium.

Seafood with Zesty Tomatoes and Wine

PREP 15 minutes   **COOK** 15 minutes   **MAKES** 4 servings

- **1 tablespoon olive oil**
- **1 small onion, chopped**
- **2 large garlic cloves, crushed with garlic press**
- **$^1/_4$ teaspoon crushed red pepper**
- **1 jar (14 to 16 ounces) marinara sauce (preferably fewer than 450 mg sodium per $^1/_2$ cup)**
- **$^3/_4$ cup dry white wine**
- **$^3/_4$ pound monkfish, dark membrane removed, cut into 2-inch pieces**
- **2 pounds medium mussels, scrubbed and debearded**
- **$^1/_2$ pound large shrimp, shelled and deveined**
- **1 tablespoon chopped fresh parsley leaves**

1. In 5-quart Dutch oven, heat oil over medium heat. Add onion; cover and cook, stirring, until golden brown and tender, 5 minutes. Add garlic and crushed red pepper and cook, uncovered, 30 seconds. Stir in marinara sauce and wine; cook 3 minutes.

2. Increase heat to medium-high. Stir in monkfish; cover and cook 2 minutes. Stir in mussels; cover and cook 2 minutes. Stir in shrimp; cover and cook until mussels open, monkfish is tender, and shrimp are opaque. Discard any unopened mussels.

3. Sprinkle with parsley to serve.

EACH SERVING: About 317 calories, 38 g protein, 13 g carbohydrate, 10 g total fat (1 g saturated), 0 g fiber, 136 mg cholesterol, 744 mg sodium.

Seafood with Zesty Tomatoes and Wine

Salmon Patties with Broccoli Slaw

PREP 25 minutes   **COOK** 5 minutes   **MAKES** 4 servings

- **1 can (14.75 to 15 ounces) salmon, picked over**
- **1 green onion, thinly sliced**
- **1 celery stalk, chopped**
- **¼ cup horseradish sauce**
- **4 tablespoons plain dried bread crumbs**
- **2 teaspoons canola oil**
- **1 bag (12 ounces) broccoli slaw (such as Mann's Broccoli Cole Slaw)**
- **3 tablespoons light mayonnaise (such as from Kraft or Hellman's)**
- **2 tablespoons cider vinegar**
- **1 teaspoon dry mustard**
- **4 hamburger buns (about 200 calories each, preferably 100% whole-wheat buns) split and toasted**
- **4 iceberg lettuce leaves**
- **2 small tomatoes, sliced**

1. In medium bowl, with fork, gently combine salmon, green onion, celery, horseradish sauce, and 2 tablespoons bread crumbs.

2. In nonstick 10-inch skillet, heat oil over medium-high heat until hot. Shape salmon mixture into four 3½-inch round patties. On waxed paper, coat patties with remaining 2 tablespoons bread crumbs.

3. Add patties to skillet; cook, turning once, until golden and heated through, 5 to 6 minutes.

4. While patties are cooking, prepare Broccoli Slaw: In medium bowl, toss broccoli slaw, mayonnaise, vinegar, and mustard until well coated.

5. Place patties on buns with lettuce and tomatoes. Serve with slaw.

EACH SERVING WITH SLAW: About 482 calories, 32 g protein, 50 g carbohydrate, 17 g total fat (5 g saturated), 7 g fiber, 58 mg cholesterol, 1,071 mg sodium.

Salmon Fillets with Tomato Jam

PREP 15 minutes   **COOK/BAKE** 15 minutes   **MAKES** 4 servings

4 pieces salmon fillet (6 ounces each), skin removed

3 teaspoons olive oil

$^1/_8$ teaspoon salt

$^1/_8$ teaspoon ground black pepper

1 medium onion, chopped

2 large garlic cloves, crushed with garlic press

$^1/_2$ teaspoon dried basil

$^1/_4$ teaspoon dried oregano

1 tablespoon sugar

$^1/_4$ cup red wine vinegar

1 cup marinara sauce (preferably with fewer than 450 mg sodium per $^1/_2$ cup)

$^1/_2$ teaspoon grated fresh orange peel

orange slices for garnish

1. Preheat oven to 400°F. Grease 13" by 9" glass baking dish.

2. With tweezers, remove bones from salmon. Arrange salmon in prepared dish; rub with 1 teaspoon oil and sprinkle with salt and pepper. Bake salmon until just opaque throughout, 15 to 20 minutes.

3. Meanwhile, prepare Tomato Jam: In nonstick 10-inch skillet, heat remaining 2 teaspoons oil over medium heat. Add onion; cook, stirring occasionally, until lightly browned, 3 minutes. Stir in garlic, basil, and oregano; cook 20 seconds. Add sugar; cook until sugar begins to caramelize, about 1 minute. Add vinegar; boil until almost evaporated, 1 minute. Stir in marinara sauce and orange peel; cook until sauce has a jamlike consistency, 5 minutes.

4. Serve salmon with tomato jam. Garnish with orange slices.

EACH SERVING: About 394 calories, 35 g protein, 10 g carbohydrate, 23 g total fat (4 g saturated), 0 g fiber, 100 mg cholesterol, 349 mg sodium.

Provençal Salmon with Tomato-Olive Relish

PREP 25 minutes   **GRILL** 8 minutes   **MAKES** 4 servings

Tomato-Olive Relish

1 lemon

$^{1}/_{2}$ cup green olives, pitted and coarsely chopped

1 medium tomato, cut into $^{1}/_{4}$-inch dice

1 tablespoon minced red onion

Provençal Salmon

1 tablespoon fennel seeds, crushed

2 teaspoons herbes de Provence

1 teaspoon grated fresh orange peel

$^{3}/_{4}$ teaspoon salt

4 salmon steaks, $^{3}/_{4}$ inch thick (6 ounces each)

1. Prepare Tomato-Olive Relish: From lemon, grate $^{1}/_{2}$ teaspoon peel and squeeze 1 tablespoon juice. In medium bowl, toss lemon peel and juice with olives, tomato, and red onion. Cover and refrigerate relish up to 1 day if not serving right away. *Makes about 1$^{1}/_{4}$ cups.*

2. Prepare charcoal fire or preheat gas grill for covered direct grilling over medium heat.

3. Prepare salmon: In cup, mix fennel, herbes de Provence, orange peel, and salt. Coat both sides of salmon with herb mixture.

4. With long-handled basting brush, lightly oil grill rack. Place salmon on hot rack. Cook salmon until just opaque throughout, 8 to 10 minutes, carefully turning salmon over once with wide metal spatula. Serve salmon with relish.

EACH SERVING SALMON: About 283 calories, 30 g protein, 0 g carbohydrate, 17 g total fat (3 g saturated), 0 g fiber, 86 mg cholesterol, 288 mg sodium.

EACH HEAPING $^{1}/_{4}$ CUP RELISH: About 27 calories, 1 g protein, 2 g carbohydrate, 2 g total fat (0 g saturated), 1 g fiber, 0 mg cholesterol, 401 mg sodium.

Salmon Steaks with Nectarine Salad

PREP 20 minutes   **GRILL** 8 minutes   **MAKES** 4 servings

1 tablespoon brown sugar

2 teaspoons canola oil

1 teaspoon ground coriander

1$\frac{1}{2}$ teaspoons fresh thyme leaves

1$\frac{1}{4}$ teaspoons salt

$\frac{1}{4}$ teaspoon coarsely ground pepper

4 salmon steaks, $\frac{3}{4}$ inch thick (6 ounces each)

3 ripe nectarines (1 pound), pitted, each cut into quarters and thinly sliced crosswise

2 kirby cucumbers (4 ounces each), each cut lengthwise in half and thinly sliced crosswise

1 green onion, thinly sliced

1 tablespoon fresh lemon juice

1. Prepare charcoal fire or preheat gas grill for covered direct grilling over medium heat.

2. Meanwhile, in cup, combine sugar, oil, coriander, 1 teaspoon thyme, $\frac{3}{4}$ teaspoon salt, and $\frac{1}{8}$ teaspoon pepper. Use to rub on both sides of salmon steaks.

3. Prepare Nectarine Salad: In medium bowl, stir nectarines, cucumbers, green onion, lemon juice, remaining $\frac{1}{2}$ teaspoon thyme, $\frac{1}{2}$ teaspoon salt, and $\frac{1}{8}$ teaspoon pepper. *Makes about 4 $\frac{1}{2}$ cups.*

4. With long-handled basting brush, lightly oil grill rack. Place salmon on hot rack. Cover grill and cook salmon, turning once, just until opaque throughout, about 8 minutes. Serve with salad.

EACH SERVING: About 364 calories, 33 g protein, 15 g carbohydrate, 19 g total fat (4 g saturated), 2 g fiber, 89 mg cholesterol, 264 mg sodium.

Grilled Sea Bass

Grilled Sea Bass

PREP 10 minutes plus marinating   **GRILL** 12 minutes   **MAKES** 4 servings

2 lemons

3 tablespoons olive oil

1 tablespoon chopped fresh oregano leaves, plus 2 large oregano sprigs

1 teaspoon ground coriander

1¼ teaspoons salt

2 whole sea bass (1½ pounds each), cleaned and scaled

¼ teaspoon ground black pepper

1. Prepare charcoal fire or preheat gas grill for covered direct grilling over medium heat.

2. Meanwhile, from 1 lemon, grate 1 tablespoon peel and squeeze 2 tablespoons juice. In small bowl, stir lemon juice and peel, oil, chopped oregano, coriander, and ¼ teaspoon salt. Cut half of remaining lemon into slices, other half into wedges.

3. Rinse fish and pat dry with paper towels. Make 3 slashes in both sides of each fish. Sprinkle inside and out with pepper and remaining 1 teaspoon salt. Place lemon slices and oregano sprigs inside fish cavities. Place fish in 13" by 9" glass baking dish. Rub half of oil mixture over outsides of fish; reserve remaining oil mixture to drizzle over cooked fish. Let marinate at room temperature 15 minutes.

4. With long-handled basting brush, lightly oil grill rack; place fish on hot rack. Cover grill and cook fish, turning once, until just opaque throughout when knife is inserted in back bone, 12 to 14 minutes.

5. To serve, place fish on cutting board. Working with 1 fish at a time, with knife, cut along backbone from head to tail. Slide wide metal spatula or cake server under front section of top fillet and lift off from backbone; transfer to platter. Gently pull out backbone and rib bones from bottom fillet and discard. Transfer bottom fillet to platter. Repeat with second fish. Drizzle fillets with the remaining oil mixture. Serve with lemon wedges.

EACH SERVING: About 267 calories, 42 g protein, 1 g carbohydrate, 10 g total fat (2 g saturated), 0 g fiber, 93 mg cholesterol, 591 mg sodium.

Cod with Peppers and Onions

PREP 15 minutes **COOK** 20 minutes **MAKES** 2 servings

scant 1 cup (about 3¹/₂ ounces) whole-wheat small shell pasta (see Note)

1 tablespoon olive oil

1 small onion, thinly sliced

¹/₂ small red pepper, thinly sliced

¹/₂ small yellow pepper, thinly sliced

1 garlic clove, finely chopped

¹/₄ teaspoon fennel seeds, crushed (optional)

1 can (14¹/₂ ounces) diced tomatoes (preferably fewer than 30 mg sodium per ¹/₂ cup, such as Pomi Chopped Tomatoes)

2 cod fillets or other mild white fish, ³/₄ inch thick (6 ounces each)

¹/₄ teaspoon salt

pinch coarsely ground black pepper

1. In large saucepot, cook pasta as label directs.

2. Meanwhile, in nonstick 12-inch skillet, heat oil over medium-high heat until hot. Add onion, red and yellow peppers, garlic, and fennel (if using); cook, stirring frequently, until vegetables are tender, 5 minutes.

3. Stir in tomatoes with their juice; heat to boiling. Reduce heat to low and simmer 5 minutes.

4. Place cod fillets on top of tomato mixture in skillet. Sprinkle cod with salt and pepper. Cover skillet and simmer, occasionally spooning sauce over cod, until fish is just opaque throughout, 8 to 10 minutes.

5. To serve, drain pasta; spoon into two bowls. Top with cod and sauce.

EACH SERVING: About 439 calories, 39 g protein, 48 g carbohydrate, 10 g total fat (1 g saturated), 11 g fiber, 73 mg cholesterol, 402 mg sodium.

NOTE: If you can't find small whole-wheat shells, then use 1¹/₃ cups whole-wheat penne or other medium-size whole-wheat short pasta or 3¹/₂ ounces of whole-wheat spaghetti (about one-fifth of the package).

Spinach and Flounder Bake

PREP 5 minutes   **BAKE** 20 minutes   **MAKES** 4 servings

1 package (4.9 to 5.25 ounces) dehydrated au gratin potatoes (see Note)

$1/2$ cup skim milk

3 tablespoons margarine

1 package (10 ounces) frozen chopped spinach

$1/4$ cup plain dried bread crumbs

4 flounder or scrod fillets (6 ounces each)

$1/8$ teaspoon salt

$1/8$ teaspoon ground black pepper

1. Preheat oven to 450°F. In shallow 2-quart glass or ceramic baking dish, prepare potatoes with the milk and 2 tablespoons margarine as label directs, but bake only 15 minutes.

2. Meanwhile, in microwave-safe small bowl, heat frozen spinach in microwave oven on High just until spinach is mostly thawed but still cool enough to handle, $1^1/2$ to 2 minutes. Squeeze spinach to remove excess water. In microwave-safe cup, melt remaining 1 tablespoon margarine in microwave oven on High about 30 seconds, swirling once. Stir in bread crumbs.

3. After potatoes have baked 15 minutes, top with spinach, and place flounder over spinach. Sprinkle with salt, pepper, and bread-crumb mixture. Bake until fish is just opaque throughout, 5 to 10 minutes longer, depending on thickness of fish.

EACH SERVING: About 388 calories, 40 g protein, 38 g carbohydrate, 10 g total fat (3 g saturated), 4 g fiber, 82 mg cholesterol, 1,142 mg sodium.

NOTE: Because of the au gratin mix, this dish is high in sodium, but convenient and nutrient-rich enough to have on occasion. Balance your day out with lower-sodium meals for breakfast and lunch.

Asian Flounder Bake

PREP 5 minutes   **BAKE** 15 minutes   **MAKES** 4 servings

3 tablespoons reduced-sodium soy sauce (such as Kikkoman or La Choy Lite)

2 tablespoons dry sherry

1 teaspoon sugar

1 teaspoon grated peeled fresh ginger

1 teaspoon Asian sesame oil

1 bag (10 ounces) shredded carrots

1 bag (5 to 6 ounces) baby spinach

4 flounder or sole fillets (5 ounces each)

1 green onion, thinly sliced

1 tablespoon sesame seeds, toasted (optional)

1. Preheat oven to 450°F. In 1-cup liquid measure, combine soy sauce, sherry, sugar, ginger, and sesame oil.

2. In bottom of 13" by 9" ceramic or glass baking dish, spread carrots evenly. Place spinach over carrots, then top with flounder. Pour soy-sauce mixture evenly over flounder.

3. Bake until fish is just opaque throughout, 12 to 14 minutes. To serve, sprinkle with green onion and top with sesame seeds, if using.

EACH SERVING: About 198 calories, 30 g protein, 11 g carbohydrate, 3 g total fat (1 g saturated), 3 g fiber, 68 mg cholesterol, 612 mg sodium.

Asian Tuna Burgers

PREP 20 minutes   **GRILL** 5 minutes   **MAKES** 4 servings

1 tuna steak (1 pound)

1 green onion, thinly sliced

2 tablespoons reduced-sodium soy sauce (such as Kikkoman or La Choy Lite)

1 teaspoon grated peeled fresh ginger

¹/₄ teaspoon coarsely ground pepper

¹/₄ cup plain dried bread crumbs

2 tablespoons sesame seeds

nonstick cooking spray

pickled ginger (optional)

1. Prepare charcoal fire or preheat gas grill for covered direct grilling over medium heat.

2. Meanwhile, with chef's knife, finely chop tuna (see Note). Place tuna in medium bowl; with fork, lightly mix in green onion, soy sauce, ginger, and pepper until combined. Shape tuna mixture into four 3-inch round patties (mixture will be very soft and moist).

3. On waxed paper, combine bread crumbs and sesame seeds. With hands, carefully press patties, one at a time, into bread-crumb mixture, turning to coat both sides. Spray both sides of patties with nonstick spray.

4. Place patties on hot grill rack. Cover the grill and cook patties, turning once, until browned on the outside and still slightly pink in the center for medium-rare, 5 to 6 minutes. (If you prefer well-done, cook 2 to 3 minutes longer.) Serve with pickled ginger if you like.

EACH SERVING: About 218 calories, 29 g protein, 7 g carbohydrate, 8 g total fat (2 g saturated), 1 g fiber, 45 mg cholesterol, 374 mg sodium.

NOTE: Chop fish by hand for a light texture; using a food processor will make the patties dense and dry.

Thai Snapper

PREP 20 minutes   **GRILL** 6 minutes   **MAKES** 4 servings

3 tablespoons fresh lime juice

1 tablespoon Asian fish sauce (such as from Thai Kitchen or Taste of Thai)

1 tablespoon olive oil

1 teaspoon grated peeled fresh ginger

1/2 teaspoon sugar

1 small garlic clove, minced

4 red snapper fillets (6 ounces each)

1 large carrot, cut into 2$\frac{1}{4}$-inch-long matchstick-thin strips

1 large green onion, thinly sliced

1/4 cup packed fresh cilantro leaves

1.   Prepare charcoal fire or preheat gas grill for covered direct grilling over medium heat.

2.   Meanwhile, in small bowl, mix lime juice, fish sauce, oil, ginger, sugar, and garlic. From roll of foil, cut four 16" by 12" sheets. Fold each sheet crosswise in half and open up again.

3.   Just before grilling, assemble packets: Place 1 red snapper fillet, skin side down, on half of each piece of foil. Top with carrot, green onion, then cilantro leaves. Spoon lime-juice mixture over snapper and vegetables. Fold other half of foil over fish; fold and crimp foil edges all around to create 4 sealed packets.

4.   Place packets on hot grill rack. Cover grill and cook 6 to 8 minutes, depending on thickness of snapper. Do not turn packets over.

5.   Before serving, with kitchen shears, cut an X in top of each packet to let steam escape, then carefully pull back foil to open. When packets are open, check that fish is just opaque throughout.

EACH SERVING: About 223 calories, 36 g protein, 5 g carbohydrate, 6 g total fat (1 g saturated), 1 g fiber, 63 mg cholesterol, 296 mg sodium.

Lentil-Sausage Stew

PREP 10 minutes   **COOK** 15 minutes   **MAKES** about 7 cups or 4 servings

- **1 bunch red Swiss chard (1 pound), well rinsed**
- **12 ounces hot or sweet Italian turkey sausage links (with less than 7 g fat per 2$\frac{1}{2}$ ounces, such as from Shady Brook Farms or Honeysuckle White), casings removed**
- **2 small yellow summer squashes (6 ounces each), halved and cut crosswise into $\frac{1}{4}$-inch slices**
- **1 can (15 ounces) lentil soup (preferably fewer than 450 mg sodium per cup, such as Health Valley Organic No Salt Added)**
- **1 cup water**
- **2 small ripe plum tomatoes, chopped**

1. Cut Swiss chard stems into $\frac{1}{4}$-inch pieces; cut leaves into 1-inch slices.

2. In 6-quart saucepot, cook sausages and chard stems over medium-high heat, breaking up sausages with side of spoon, until sausages are browned and stems are tender-crisp, 10 minutes.

3. Increase heat to high. Add chard leaves, squashes, soup, and water; cover and cook until squashes are tender, 5 minutes. Top with tomatoes to serve.

EACH SERVING: About 226 calories, 22 g protein, 18 g carbohydrate, 1 g total fat (2 g saturated), 6 g fiber, 59 mg cholesterol, 1,155 mg sodium (980 mg sodium if you use no-salt-added lentil soup).

Southwest Chicken Stew

PREP 25 minutes **COOK** 30 minutes **MAKES** 4 servings

1 teaspoon olive oil

6 large chicken thighs (2 pounds), skin and fat removed

1 medium onion, chopped

2 jalapeño chiles, seeded and minced

2 garlic cloves, crushed with garlic press

³/₄ teaspoon ground cumin

¹/₂ teaspoon dried oregano

1 pound medium red potatoes, cut into 1¹/₂-inch pieces

1 can (15 ounces) white kidney (cannellini) beans (preferably fewer than 140 mg sodium per ¹/₂ cup, such as Eden Foods Organic Cannellini or Westbrae Great Northern Beans), rinsed and drained

1 can (15¹/₄ ounces) no-salt-added whole kernel corn (such as Del Monte Fresh Cut Sweet Corn Whole Kernel No Salt Added), drained

1 can (14 to 14¹/₂ ounces) reduced-sodium chicken broth (preferably fewer than 100 mg sodium per cup, such as Campbell's Low Sodium or Shelton's Organic Fat Free/Low Sodium)

¹/₂ teaspoon salt

¹/₄ cup crushed baked tortilla chips (such as Guiltless Gourmet Unsalted Yellow Corn)

¹/₂ cup loosely packed fresh cilantro leaves, chopped

1. In deep nonstick 12-inch skillet, heat oil over medium-high heat until hot. Add chicken and cook, turning once, until browned, 6 to 8 minutes. Transfer chicken to plate.

2. To same skillet, add onion, jalapeños, garlic, cumin, and oregano; cook over medium heat, covered, stirring occasionally, until onion is golden, about 5 minutes.

3. Return chicken thighs to skillet. Add potatoes, beans, corn, broth, and salt; heat mixture to boiling. Reduce heat to medium-low; simmer, covered, stirring occasionally, until potatoes are fork-tender and chicken loses its pink color throughout, 15 minutes.

4. Stir in tortilla chips and cook, uncovered, until mixture thickens slightly, about 2 minutes. Add cilantro just before serving.

EACH SERVING: About 483 calories, 38 g protein, 48 g carbohydrate, 15 g total fat (4 g saturated), 10 g fiber, 101 mg cholesterol, 731 mg sodium.

Southwest Chicken Stew

Moroccan-Style Chicken Stew

PREP 10 minutes   **COOK** 20 minutes   **MAKES** about 8 cups or 6 servings

> 1 tablespoon olive oil
>
> 1 medium onion, chopped
>
> 1 tablespoon all-purpose flour
>
> 1 teaspoon ground coriander
>
> 1 teaspoon ground cumin
>
> 1/2 teaspoon salt
>
> 1/4 teaspoon ground red pepper (cayenne)
>
> 1/4 teaspoon ground cinnamon
>
> 1 1/2 pounds skinless, boneless chicken thighs, cut into 2-inch chunks
>
> 2 garlic cloves, crushed with garlic press
>
> 2 cans (14 1/2 ounces each) whole tomatoes (preferably fewer than 35 mg sodium per 1/2 cup, such as Hunt's Whole Tomatoes No Salt Added), 2 tomatoes coarsely matched
>
> 1 can (15 ounces) garbanzo beans (preferably fewer than 140 mg sodium per 1/2 cup, such as Eden Organic or Goya Low Sodium Chickpeas), rinsed and drained
>
> 1/3 cup dark seedless raisins
>
> 1/4 cup chopped pimiento-stuffed olives (salad olives)
>
> 1 cup water
>
> 1/2 cup loosely packed fresh cilantro leaves

1. In nonstick 5- to 6-quart Dutch oven, heat oil over medium heat until hot. Add onion and cook, stirring, until light golden, 5 minutes.

2. Meanwhile, in pie plate, mix flour with coriander, cumin, salt, ground red pepper, and cinnamon. Toss chicken with flour mixture to coat evenly.

3. Add chicken to Dutch oven and cook, turning once, until lightly browned, 7 minutes. Add garlic and cook 1 minute.

4. Stir in tomatoes, beans, raisins, olives, and water. Simmer, breaking up tomatoes with side of spoon, until chicken is no longer pink throughout, 5 minutes. Garnish with cilantro.

EACH SERVING: About 284 calories, 28 g protein, 28 g carbohydrate, 8 g total fat (2 g saturated), 6 g fiber, 94 mg cholesterol, 505 mg sodium.

Jambalaya

PREP 25 minutes   **COOK** 12 minutes   **MAKES** about 11 cups or 6 servings

2 teaspoons olive oil

2 small onions, chopped

2 celery stalks, chopped

1 red pepper, chopped

8 ounces turkey kielbasa (with fewer than than 90 calories and 540 mg sodium per 2 ounces, such as from Hillshire Farms), cut into $^1/_2$-inch pieces

1 pound boneless skinless chicken breast, cut into bite-sized pieces

1$^1/_2$ cups (14 ounces) diced tomatoes (preferably fewer than 30 mg sodium per $^1/_2$ cup, such as Pomi Chopped Tomatoes)

2 cans (15 ounces each) Eden Organic (Cajun Small Red Beans) Rice & Beans

1. In a large nonstick skillet, heat oil over medium-high heat. Add onions, celery, red pepper, and kielbasa. Cook, stirring occasionally, until vegetables soften and brown lightly, 6 minutes.

2. Add chicken and tomatoes; cook, stirring frequently, until chicken is no longer pink throughout, about 2 minutes.

3. Stir in rice and beans; cook until hot, about 2 minutes.

EACH SERVING: About 309 calories, 28 g protein, 34 g carbohydrate, 7 g total fat (2 g saturated), 8 g fiber, 71 mg cholesterol, 538 mg sodium.

Barley-Vegetable Stew ⓥ

PREP 25 minutes   **COOK** 15 minutes   **MAKES** about 9 cups or 4 servings

> **1 cup quick-cooking barley**
>
> **1 tablespoon olive oil**
>
> **1 package (20 ounces) peeled butternut squash, cut into $1/2$-inch dice (4 cups)**
>
> **2 medium celery stalks, cut into $1/2$-inch dice**
>
> **1 medium onion, chopped**
>
> **1 jar (14 to 16 ounces) marinara sauce (preferably fewer than 450 mg sodium per $1/2$ cup)**
>
> **1 package (9 to 10 ounces) frozen cut green beans**
>
> **1 cup reduced-sodium chicken broth (preferably fewer than 100 mg sodium cup, such as Campbell's Low Sodium or Shelton's Organic Fat Free/Low Sodium)**
>
> **$1/2$ teaspoon salt**
>
> **$1/4$ teaspoon ground black pepper**
>
> **$1/2$ cup loosely packed fresh parsley leaves, chopped**
>
> **$1/2$ teaspoon fresh grated lemon peel**
>
> **1 small garlic clove, minced**

1. Cook barley as label directs.

2. Meanwhile, in nonstick 12-inch skillet, heat oil over medium-high heat. Add squash, celery, and onion; cook, covered, stirring occasionally, until lightly browned, 10 minutes. Stir in marinara sauce, frozen beans, broth, salt, and pepper. Simmer, uncovered, until slightly thickened, 4 minutes.

3. In small bowl, combine parsley, lemon peel, and garlic.

4. Drain liquid from barley, if any. Stir barley into vegetables. Sprinkle with parsley mixture to serve.

EACH SERVING: About 370 calories, 11 g protein, 72 g carbohydrate, 7 g total fat (1 g saturated), 14 g fiber, 1 mg cholesterol, 725 mg sodium.

Vegetarian Lentil Stew ⓥ

PREP 10 minutes   **COOK** 20 minutes   **MAKES** about 6¼ cups or 4 servings

2 teaspoons olive oil

2 teaspoons grated peeled fresh ginger

2 garlic cloves, crushed with garlic press

2 teaspoons curry powder

1 package (1 pound) cut-up peeled butternut squash (about 4 cups), cut into bite-size pieces

1 large apple, unpeeled, cored, and cut into 1-inch chunks

1 can (19 ounces) lentil soup (preferably fewer than 450 mg sodium per cup, such as Progresso 99% Fat Free)

1 cup boiling water

1 bag (10 ounces) spinach

1. In 4-quart saucepan, heat oil over medium heat until hot. Add ginger, garlic, and curry powder, and cook, stirring, 30 seconds. Add squash, apple, soup, and boiling water; cover and heat to boiling over high heat. Reduce heat to medium; cook, covered, stirring occasionally, until squash is just tender, 5 minutes longer.

2. In batches, gently add as many spinach leaves as possible to lentil mixture, stirring to wilt spinach. Cover and simmer on low 5 minutes to blend flavors.

EACH SERVING: About 191 calories, 8 g protein, 36 g carbohydrate, 4 g total fat (1 g saturated), 9 g fiber, 0 mg cholesterol, 309 mg sodium.

Sweet Potato Chili con Carne

PREP 15 minutes **COOK** 55 minutes **MAKES** about 11 cups or 6 servings

- **1 pound lean (85%) ground beef**
- **1 large onion, chopped**
- **4 large garlic cloves, crushed with garlic press**
- **2 tablespoons chili powder**
- **2 teaspoons ground cumin**
- **1 teaspoon salt**
- **$\frac{1}{2}$ teaspoon dried oregano, crumbled**
- **2 cans ($14\frac{1}{2}$ ounces each) whole tomatoes (preferably fewer than 35 mg sodium per $\frac{1}{2}$ cup, such as Hunt's Whole Tomatoes No Salt Added)**
- **3 tablespoons tomato paste**
- **2 medium sweet potatoes (14 ounces each), peeled and diced**
- **2 cups water**
- **1 can (15 ounces) black beans (preferably fewer than 140 mg sodium per $\frac{1}{2}$ cup, such as Eden Organic or Goya Low Sodium)**
- **1 medium zucchini (8 ounces), chopped**
- **1 tablespoon chipotle pepper sauce**

1. Heat 5- to 6-quart saucepot over high heat until hot. Add ground beef and onion and cook, stirring frequently, until browned, 6 minutes. Spoon off any fat. Reduce heat to medium. Add garlic, chili powder, cumin, salt, and oregano; cook, stirring, 1 minute.

2. Add tomatoes with their juice and tomato paste, stirring to break up tomatoes with side of spoon. Add sweet potatoes and water; heat to boiling over high heat. Reduce heat to low; cover and simmer, stirring occasionally, 30 minutes.

3. Add beans, zucchini, and pepper sauce to saucepot; heat to boiling over high heat. Reduce heat to low; simmer, uncovered, until zucchini is tender and chili thickens slightly, 15 minutes.

EACH SERVING: About 384 calories, 23 g protein, 47 g carbohydrate, 12 g total fat (5 g saturated), 12 g fiber, 51 mg cholesterol, 655 mg sodium.

Vegetarian Chili

Vegetarian Chili Ⓥ

PREP 30 minutes   **COOK** 50 minutes   **MAKES** about 10 cups or 6 servings

- 4 teaspoons olive oil
- 1 medium butternut squash (2 pounds), peeled and cut into ¾-inch pieces
- 3 medium carrots, peeled and cut into ¼-inch pieces
- 1 large onion (12 ounces), chopped
- 2 tablespoons chili powder
- 2 garlic cloves, crushed with garlic press
- 2 cans (14½ ounces each) plum tomatoes (preferably fewer than 35 g sodium per ½ cup, such as Hunt's Whole Tomatoes No Salt Added)
- 3 jalapeño chiles, seeded and minced
- 1 cup reduced-sodium vegetable broth (preferably fewer than 350 mg sodium per cup, such as Health Valley Fat-Free)
- 1 tablespoon sugar
- ½ teaspoon salt
- 2 cans (15 ounces each) black soybeans (such as Eden Organic), rinsed and drained, or 2 cans (15 ounces each) black beans
- 1 cup lightly packed fresh cilantro leaves, chopped
- plain nonfat yogurt (optional)

1. In nonstick 5-quart Dutch oven or saucepot, heat 2 teaspoons oil over medium-high heat until hot. Add squash and cook, stirring occasionally, until golden, 8 to 10 minutes. Transfer squash to bowl; set aside.

2. In same Dutch oven, heat remaining 2 teaspoons oil. Add carrots and onion and cook, stirring occasionally, until golden, about 10 minutes. Stir in chili powder and garlic; cook, stirring, 1 minute longer.

3. Add tomatoes with their juice, jalapeños, broth, sugar, and salt; heat to boiling over medium-high heat, stirring to break up tomatoes with side of spoon. Stir in soybeans and squash; heat to boiling over medium-high heat. Reduce heat to low; cover and simmer until squash is tender, about 30 minutes.

4. Remove Dutch oven from heat; stir in cilantro. Serve chili with yogurt, if you like.

EACH SERVING: About 303 calories, 16 g protein, 44 g carbohydrate, 10 g total fat (2 g saturated), 15 g fiber, 0 mg cholesterol, 359 mg sodium.

Black Bean and Sweet Potato Chili ⓥ

This hearty chili is great for cool autumn nights. Try with pinto, cannellini, kidney, or pink beans, or use a combination for a colorful entrée.

PREP 10 minutes   **COOK** 10 minutes   **MAKES** 10 cups or 4 servings

- **1 tablespoon olive oil**
- **1 medium onion, chopped**
- **2 garlic cloves, chopped**
- **2 medium sweet potatoes (12 ounces each), peeled and cut into $1/2$-inch dice**
- **1 jar (16 ounces) mild salsa (fewer than 140 mg sodium per 2 tablespoons)**
- **1 cup water**
- **1 tablespoon chili powder**
- **2 cans (15 ounces each) black beans (preferably fewer than 140 mg sodium per $1/2$ cup, such as Eden Organic or Goya Low Sodium)**
- **$1/2$ cup reduced-fat sour cream**
- **$1/4$ cup loosely packed fresh cilantro leaves, chopped**

1. In 4-quart saucepan, heat oil over medium-high heat. Add onion and garlic; cook, stirring occasionally, until soft, 4 minutes. Stir in sweet potatoes, salsa, water, and chili powder; heat to boiling. Reduce heat to medium-low and cook, stirring occasionally, until potatoes are fork-tender, 12 to 15 minutes. Add beans with their liquid and cook 3 minutes to blend flavors.

2. In small bowl, combine sour cream and cilantro. Serve chili with cilantro cream.

EACH SERVING: About 441 calories, 18 g protein, 77 g carbohydrate, 8 g total fat (3 g saturated), 19 g fiber, 16 mg cholesterol, 491 mg sodium.

Tofu and Black Bean Chili Ⓥ

PREP 15 minutes   **COOK** 25 minutes   **MAKES** about 5 cups or 4 servings

> **1 package (14 ounces) firm tofu, drained and cut into $1/2$-inch cubes**
>
> **4 teaspoons olive oil**
>
> **1 envelope (1.25 ounces) McCormick's 30% Less Sodium Chili Seasoning**
>
> **1 can (15 ounces) black beans (preferably fewer than 140 mg sodium per $1/2$ cup, such as Eden Organic or Goya Low Sodium), rinsed and drained**
>
> **$1 1/2$ cups (14 ounces) diced tomatoes (preferably less than 30 mg sodium per $1/2$ cup, such as Pomi Chopped Tomatoes)**
>
> **1 cup frozen corn**
>
> **$1 1/2$ cups reduced-sodium vegetable broth (preferably less than 350 mg sodium per cup, such as Health Valley Fat Free) or water**
>
> **$1/2$ cup plain low-fat yogurt**
>
> **chopped cilantro**

1. In medium bowl, place 3 layers paper towel; add tofu and cover with 3 more layers paper towel, pressing gently to extract liquid from tofu. Let tofu stand 10 minutes to drain.

2. In a large nonstick skillet, heat 2 teaspoons oil over medium heat. Add half of tofu to skillet and cook, turning occasionally, until browned, about 5 minutes. Transfer to a plate and repeat with remaining oil and tofu.

3. In a 5-quart Dutch oven, combine tofu, chili seasoning, beans, tomatoes, corn, and broth. Bring to a boil; reduce heat and simmer, stirring occasionally, 15 to 20 minutes. Serve in bowls with yogurt and cilantro.

EACH SERVING: About 327 calories, 20 g protein, 40 g carbohydrate, 10 g total fat (1 g saturated), 12 g fiber, 2 mg cholesterol, 473 mg sodium.

Terrific Tofu

Nutritionally, tofu's got a lot going for it. It's a virtually saturated fat–free protein source, and protein has been shown to help lower cholesterol. In addition, researchers are investigating whether compounds in tofu (and other soy foods) called isoflavones might help lower the risk of breast and prostate cancer. And, depending on how it's processed, tofu can be a rich source of calcium. As you're probably aware, calcium is critical for healthy bones, helps regulate blood pressure, and may help keep you slim (another area still being researched). But check the labels. Tofu can have as little as 20 mg of calcium or as much as 200 mg per 3-ounce serving. Look for "% daily value" of calcium and pick the higher source.

Red Bean and Collard Gumbo ⓥ

PREP 20 minutes   **COOK** 30 minutes   **MAKES** about 8 cups or 4 servings

$1/4$ cup all-purpose flour

1 tablespoon olive oil

1 medium onion, thinly sliced

1 medium red pepper, cut into $1/2$-inch pieces

1 large celery stalk, thinly sliced

2 garlic cloves, crushed with garlic press

$1/2$ **teaspoon salt**

$1/4$ **teaspoon ground red pepper (cayenne)**

$1/4$ **teaspoon dried thyme**

$1/4$ **teaspoon ground allspice**

1 can ($14 1/2$ ounces) reduced-sodium vegetable broth (preferably fewer than 350 mg sodium per cup, such as Health Valley Fat-Free)

3 cups water

1 bunch collard greens ($1 1/4$ pounds), tough stems trimmed and leaves coarsely chopped

2 cans (15 ounces each) small red beans (preferably fewer than 140 mg sodium per $1/2$ cup, such as Eden Organic or Goya Low Sodium), rinsed and drained

1. In dry nonstick 5- to 6-quart saucepot, toast flour over medium heat, stirring frequently, until pale golden, about 5 minutes. Transfer flour to medium bowl; set aside.

2. In same saucepot, heat oil over medium-high heat until hot. Add onion, red pepper, and celery and cook, stirring occasionally, until vegetables are tender-crisp, about 10 minutes. Add garlic, salt, ground red pepper, thyme, and allspice and cook, stirring, 2 minutes.

3. Whisk broth into toasted flour until blended. Stir broth mixture and water into vegetables in saucepot; heat to boiling over medium-high heat. Add collard greens, stirring until wilted; stir in beans. Heat gumbo to boiling. Reduce heat to medium-low; cover and simmer until greens are tender, about 10 minutes.

EACH SERVING: About 299 calories, 15 g protein, 50 g carbohydrate, 5 g total fat (1 g saturated), 15 g fiber, 0 mg cholesterol, 519 mg sodium.

Curried Vegetable Stew ⓥ

PREP 30 minutes   **COOK** 40 minutes   **MAKES** about 10 cups or 4 servings

- 1 tablespoon olive oil
- 1 medium onion, coarsely chopped
- 5 cups small cauliflower flowerets (1 small head cauliflower)
- 4 medium carrots, peeled and each cut lengthwise in half, then crosswise into $1/4$-inch-thick slices
- 1 tablespoon minced peeled fresh ginger
- 3 garlic cloves, crushed with garlic press
- 1 tablespoon curry powder
- 1 teaspoon ground cumin
- $3/4$ teaspoon salt
- $1/8$ to $1/4$ teaspoon ground red pepper (cayenne)
- 2 cans (15 ounces each) garbanzo beans (preferably fewer than 140 mg sodium per $1/2$ cup, such as Eden Organic or Goya Low Sodium Chickpeas), rinsed and drained
- $1 1/2$ cups ($14 1/2$ ounces) diced tomatoes (preferably fewer than 30 mg sodium per $1/2$ cup, such as Pomi Chopped Tomatoes)
- $1/4$ cup golden raisins
- $1/2$ cup water
- $1/2$ cup loosely packed fresh cilantro leaves, chopped

1. In nonstick 12-inch skillet, heat oil over medium heat until hot. Add onion and cook, stirring occasionally, 5 minutes. Increase heat to medium-high; add cauliflower and carrots and cook, stirring occasionally, until vegetables are lightly browned, about 10 minutes. Add ginger, garlic, curry powder, cumin, salt, and ground red pepper; cook, stirring, 1 minute.

2. Add garbanzo beans, tomatoes, raisins, and water; heat to boiling over high heat. Reduce heat to low; cover and simmer until vegetables are tender and sauce thickens slightly, 15 to 20 minutes. Stir in cilantro and serve.

EACH SERVING: About 326 calories, 15 g protein, 63 g carbohydrate, 5 g total fat (1 g saturated), 19 g fiber, 0 mg cholesterol, 741 mg sodium.

Pasta with No-Cook Tomato Sauce and Bocconcini ⓥ

PREP 20 minutes plus standing   **COOK** 15 minutes   **MAKES** 6 servings

2 pints cherry tomatoes, each cut in half

$1/_2$ cup loosely packed fresh flat-leaf parsley leaves, chopped

$1/_2$ cup loosely packed fresh basil leaves, thinly sliced

$1/_4$ cup olive oil

1 teaspoon salt

$1/_4$ teaspoon coarsely ground black pepper

1 garlic clove, crushed with garlic press

14 ounces whole-wheat penne or corkscrew pasta (5 cups dry)

12 ounces small mozzarella balls (*bocconcini*), each cut in half

1. In large serving bowl, stir cherry tomatoes, parsley, basil, oil, salt, pepper, and garlic. Let stand at room temperature at least 1 hour or up to 4 hours to blend flavors.

2. In large saucepot, cook pasta as label directs. Drain well.

3. Add pasta to tomato mixture and toss; and *bocconcini* and toss again.

EACH SERVING: About 500 calories, 19 g protein, 51 g carbohydrate, 24 g total fat (9 g saturated), 7 g fiber, 40 mg cholesterol, 560 mg sodium.

Pasta with Broccoli Rabe and Garbanzo Beans Ⓥ

PREP 20 minutes **COOK** 20 minutes **MAKES** 4 servings

> **12 ounces whole-wheat penne or ziti pasta (5 cups dry)**
>
> **2 bunches broccoli rabe (12 ounces each), tough stems trimmed**
>
> **2 tablespoons olive oil**
>
> **3 garlic cloves, crushed with side of chef's knife**
>
> **1/4 teaspoon crushed red pepper**
>
> **1 can (15 ounces) garbanzo beans (preferably fewer than 140 mg sodium per 1/2 cup, such as Eden Organic or Goya Low Sodium Chickpeas), rinsed and drained**
>
> **1/4 cup golden raisins**
>
> **1 teaspoon salt**

1. In large saucepot, cook pasta as label directs.

2. Meanwhile, in another large saucepot, heat 4 quarts water to boiling. Add broccoli rabe and cook until thickest parts of stems are tender, 3 to 5 minutes. Drain and cool slightly; cut into 2-inch pieces.

3. Wipe saucepot dry. Add oil and heat over medium-high heat until hot. Add garlic and crushed red pepper and cook, stirring, 1 minute. Add broccoli rabe, garbanzo beans, and raisins; cook, stirring frequently, until heated through, about 3 minutes. Remove saucepot from heat.

4. Drain pasta, reserving 2/3 cup pasta cooking water. Add pasta, reserved pasta water, and salt to broccoli rabe mixture; toss well.

EACH SERVING: About 528 calories, 21 g protein, 90 g carbohydrate, 10 g total fat (1 g saturated), 17 g fiber, 0 mg cholesterol, 735 mg sodium.

Tortellini with Zucchini and Radicchio Ⓥ

PREP 10 minutes   **COOK** 20 minutes   **MAKES** 4 servings

- **1 pound frozen or 2 packages (9 ounces each) fresh tortellini or mini ravioli (preferably fewer than 480 mg sodium and 350 calories per cup (such as Buitoni Herb Chicken Tortellini, Portabella Mushroom & Cheese Tortelloni, or Three Cheese Tortellini)**
- **2 tablespoons extravirgin olive oil**
- **2 garlic cloves, thinly sliced**
- **2 small zucchini (5 ounces each), sliced**
- **1 small head radicchio (8 ounces), cut lengthwise in half, then crosswise into 1-inch slices, or 4 cups shredded cabbage mix for coleslaw (half of 16-ounce bag)**
- **¹/₂ teaspoon salt**
- **¹/₈ teaspoon crushed red pepper**
- **1 cup grape or cherry tomatoes, each cut in half**
- **1 wedge Parmesan cheese at room temperature (optional)**

1. In large saucepot, cook pasta as label directs.

2. Meanwhile, in nonstick 12-inch skillet, heat oil over medium-high heat. Add garlic and cook, stirring, until golden, 1 minute. Add zucchini and cook until tender, 5 minutes. Stir in radicchio, salt, and crushed red pepper; cook, stirring frequently, until radicchio wilts and browns, 2 to 4 minutes.

3. Drain pasta. In serving bowl, toss pasta with radicchio mixture and tomatoes. If you like, with vegetable peeler, shave long, thin strips from wedge of Parmesan. Top pasta with Parmesan shavings to serve.

EACH SERVING: About 486 calories, 19 g protein, 67 g carbohydrate, 16 g total fat (6 g saturated), 4 g fiber, 54 mg cholesterol, 753 mg sodium.

Pasta with Ham and Tricolor Peppers

PREP 10 minutes **COOK** 15 minutes **MAKES** 6 servings

1 package (16 ounces) whole-wheat penne pasta

3 tablespoons olive oil

4 red, yellow, and/or orange peppers, thinly sliced

4 ounces lower-sodium deli ham (such as from Healthy Choice), cut into thin strips

2 garlic cloves, thinly sliced

$^1/_2$ teaspoon salt

$^1/_4$ teaspoon coarsely ground black pepper

$^1/_2$ cup loosely packed fresh basil leaves, thinly sliced

$^1/_2$ cup grated Parmesan cheese

1. In large saucepot, cook pasta as label directs.

2. Meanwhile, in 12-inch skillet, heat oil over medium heat. Add peppers and cook, covered, stirring occasionally, until very soft and lightly browned, about 10 minutes. Stir in ham, garlic, salt, and black pepper; cook 1 minute.

3. Drain pasta, reserving $^1/_2$ cup pasta cooking water. In large serving bowl, toss pasta with pepper mixture and reserved cooking water; top with basil and Parmesan. Toss to serve.

EACH SERVING: About 416 calories, 17 g protein, 60 g carbohydrate, 13 g total fat (3 g saturated), 8 g fiber, 16 mg cholesterol, 487 mg sodium.

Shrimp Fra Diavolo

PREP 5 minutes   **COOK** 15 minutes   **MAKES** 6 servings

- **1 package (16 ounces) thin whole-wheat spaghetti**
- **1 tablespoon olive oil**
- **1 medium onion, chopped**
- **2 garlic cloves, crushed with garlic press**
- **$1/_4$ teaspoon crushed red pepper**
- **2 cans (14 $1/_2$ ounces each) whole tomatoes (preferably fewer than 35 mg sodium per $1/_2$ cup, such as Hunt's Whole Tomatoes No Salt Added)**
- **$1/_2$ teaspoon salt**
- **1 pound large shrimp, shelled and deveined**
- **$1/_4$ cup loosely packed fresh parsley leaves, chopped**

1. In large saucepot, cook pasta as label directs.

2. Meanwhile, in nonstick 12-inch skillet, heat oil over medium heat. Add onion and cook, covered, stirring often, until tender and golden, 5 minutes. Add garlic and crushed red pepper; cook 1 minute.

3. Add tomatoes with their juice and salt; heat to boiling over medium-high heat, breaking up tomatoes with side of spoon. Reduce heat to medium and cook, covered, 5 minutes. Stir in shrimp and cook, covered, until shrimp turn opaque throughout, 5 minutes.

4. Drain pasta; return to saucepot. Add shrimp mixture; toss well to combine. Sprinkle with parsley.

EACH SERVING: About 406 calories, 26 g protein, 61 g carbohydrate, 6 g total fat (1 g saturated), 9 g fiber, 115 mg cholesterol, 131 mg sodium.

Fusilli with Ricotta and Fresh Tomato Sauce Ⓥ

PREP 5 minutes **COOK** 25 minutes **MAKES** 4 servings

12 ounces whole-wheat fusilli, penne, or other short pasta

1 tablespoon olive oil

1 garlic clove, crushed with garlic press

4 medium tomatoes (1 1/2 pounds), chopped

1/2 teaspoon salt

1/4 teaspoon coarsely ground black pepper

3/4 cup part-skim ricotta cheese

1/4 cup fresh grated Pecorino Romano or Parmesan cheese

1. In large saucepot, cook pasta as label directs.

2. Meanwhile, in nonstick 10-inch skillet, heat oil over medium heat until hot. Add garlic and cook, stirring, 1 minute. Stir in tomatoes, salt, and pepper and cook, stirring occasionally, until tomatoes break up slightly, about 5 minutes.

3. Drain pasta; transfer to warm serving bowl. Stir in ricotta and Romano. Pour tomato mixture on top; toss before serving.

EACH SERVING: About 456 calories, 20 g protein, 69 g carbohydrate, 12 g total fat (4 g saturated), 10 g fiber, 20 mg cholesterol, 452 mg sodium.

Macaroni and Cheese on the Light Side Ⓥ

PREP 20 minutes   **COOK** 20 minutes   **MAKES** 6 servings

- 1 package (16 ounces) whole-wheat cavatelli, macaroni, or other short, tubular pasta
- 2 tablespoons margarine or butter
- 3 tablespoons all-purpose flour
- 1/2 teaspoon salt
- 1/4 teaspoon ground black pepper
- 1/8 teaspoon ground nutmeg
- 3 1/2 cups low-fat milk (1%)
- 6 ounces (1 1/2 cups) shredded reduced-fat sharp Cheddar cheese (such as Cabot 50% Light)
- 1/3 cup grated Parmesan cheese
- 2 packages (10 ounces each) frozen mixed vegetables (see Note)

1. In large saucepot, cook pasta as label directs.

2. Meanwhile, in 3-quart saucepan, melt margarine over medium heat. With wire whisk, stir in flour, salt, pepper, and nutmeg; cook 1 minute, stirring constantly. Gradually whisk in milk and, stirring constantly, cook over medium-high heat until sauce boils and thickens slightly. Boil 1 minute, stirring.

3. Remove saucepan from heat; stir in Cheddar and Parmesan cheeses just until melted. Use immersion blender to blend mixture in saucepan until smooth. (Or, in blender at low speed, with center part of cover removed to allow steam to escape, blend sauce in small batches until smooth. Pour sauce into bowl after each batch.)

4. Place frozen vegetables in colander; drain pasta over vegetables. Return pasta mixture to saucepot; stir in cheese sauce and heat through.

EACH SERVING: About 522 calories, 28 g protein, 77 g carbohydrate, 13 g total fat (5 g saturated), 11 g fiber, 27 mg cholesterol, 358 mg sodium.

NOTE: You can substitute 2 cups leftover cooked vegetables for the frozen ones in this recipe.

Broccoli Pesto and Chicken Spaghetti

PREP 8 minutes **COOK** 12 minutes **MAKES** 6 servings

- **1 package (16 ounces) whole-wheat spaghetti or thin spaghetti**
- **1 bag (16 ounces) frozen chopped broccoli**
- **1 cup reduced-sodium vegetable broth (preferably fewer than 350 mg sodium per cup, such as Health Valley Fat-Free)**
- **¼ cup grated Parmesan cheese**
- **2 tablespoons olive oil**
- **1 small garlic clove, peeled**
- **¼ teaspoon salt**
- **4 cups cooked skinless chicken meat**
- **coarsely ground black pepper**

1. In large saucepot, cook pasta as label directs. In saucepan, prepare broccoli as label directs.

2. To make broccoli pesto, in food processor, with knife blade attached, puree cooked broccoli, broth, Parmesan, oil, garlic, and salt until smooth, stopping processor occasionally to scrape down side.

3. Drain pasta; transfer to warm serving bowl. Add broccoli pesto and chicken to pasta; toss well. Sprinkle with pepper and serve.

EACH SERVING: About 507 calories, 37 g protein, 57 g carbohydrate, 15 g total fat (3 g saturated), 9 g fiber, 73 mg cholesterol, 304 mg sodium.

Spaghetti Primavera ⓥ

PREP 20 minutes   **COOK** 30 minutes   **MAKES** 4 servings

4 tablespoons butter or zero trans-fat margarine

3 medium carrots, cut lengthwise into matchstick-thin strips

1 medium onion, chopped

2 garlic cloves, crushed with garlic press

12 ounces whole-wheat spaghetti

1 bag (16 ounces) broccoli flowerets

1 pound asparagus, cut diagonally into 1-inch pieces

$1/2$ teaspoon salt

$1/8$ to $1/4$ teaspoon crushed red pepper

$1/2$ cup water

1 cup loosely packed fresh basil leaves, chopped

$1/2$ cup grated Parmesan cheese

1. In nonstick 12-inch skillet, melt 2 tablespoons butter over medium heat. Add carrots and onion and cook, stirring occasionally, until tender and golden, about 10 minutes. Add garlic; cook, stirring, 1 minute.

2. Meanwhile, in large saucepot, cook pasta as label directs.

3. To carrot mixture in skillet, add broccoli, asparagus, salt, crushed red pepper, and water; heat to boiling over medium-high heat. Reduce heat to medium; cover and cook, stirring occasionally, until vegetables are tender, 6 to 10 minutes longer.

4. Drain pasta, reserving $3/4$ cup pasta water; return pasta to saucepot. Add basil, Parmesan, remaining 2 tablespoons butter, and reserved pasta water; toss well. Add vegetable mixture and gently toss to combine.

EACH SERVING: About 516 calories, 22 g protein, 78 g carbohydrate, 15 g total fat (4 g saturated), 15 g fiber, 11 mg cholesterol, 693 mg sodium.

Spaghetti with Mussels and Fresh Tomatoes

PREP 15 minutes   **COOK** 20 minutes   **MAKES** 6 servings

1 package (16 ounces) whole-wheat spaghetti

1 tablespoon olive oil

2 large garlic cloves, crushed with press

1/4 teaspoon crushed red pepper

1/2 cup dry white wine

1/2 teaspoon salt

3 pounds mussels, scrubbed and debearded

1 1/2 pounds plum tomatoes (6 medium), coarsely chopped

1. In large saucepot, cook pasta as label directs.

2. Meanwhile, in deep 12-inch skillet, heat oil over medium heat. Add garlic and crushed red pepper and cook, stirring constantly, until garlic begins to turn golden brown, 1 to 2 minutes. Add wine and salt; heat to boiling over high heat. Boil until wine is reduced to about $1/3$ cup, 2 minutes.

3. Add mussels and tomatoes; heat to boiling. Reduce heat to medium; cover and cook until mussels open, 5 to 6 minutes. Discard any unopened mussels.

4. Drain spaghetti; transfer to large serving bowl. Top spaghetti with mussel mixture.

EACH SERVING: About 447 calories, 29 g protein, 63 g carbohydrate, 9 g total fat (1 g saturated), 8 g fiber, 42 mg cholesterol, 568 mg sodium.

Thai Noodles with Cilantro and Basil

Thai Noodles with Cilantro and Basil

PREP 25 minutes   **COOK** 20 minutes   **MAKES** 4 servings

8 ounces soba noodles (such as from Eden Organic; see Note)

1 tablespoon canola oil

4 garlic cloves, thinly sliced

1 piece (3 inches) peeled fresh ginger, cut into thin slivers

1 medium onion, thinly sliced

3/4 pound lean (90%) ground beef

1/2 cup reduced-sodium chicken broth (preferably fewer than 100 mg
sodium per cup, such as Campbell's Low Sodium or Shelton's Organic
Fat Free Low Sodium)

3 tablespoons Asian fish sauce

1 teaspoon sugar

3/4 teaspoon crushed red pepper

1/4 cup chopped fresh cilantro

1/4 cup sliced fresh basil leaves

1 small cucumber, cut lengthwise in half and thinly sliced crosswise

1/2 cup bean sprouts

1/4 cup unsalted peanuts, chopped

1 lime, cut into wedges

1. In large bowl, pour *boiling water* over noodles to cover; let soak 15 minutes. Do not soak longer or noodles may become too soft.

2. Meanwhile, heat oil in 12-inch skillet over medium heat. Add garlic, ginger, and onion; cook, stirring occasionally, until golden, 8 to 10 minutes. Stir in beef; cook until meat is no longer pink, 5 minutes. Stir in broth, fish sauce, sugar, and crushed red pepper. Simmer, uncovered, 5 minutes to thicken slightly.

3. Drain noodles. Add noodles, cilantro, and basil to beef mixture, stirring to heat through. Spoon into 4 bowls; top with cucumber, bean sprouts, and peanuts. Serve with lime wedges.

EACH SERVING: About 484 calories, 29 g protein, 55 g carbohydrate, 17 g total fat (4 g saturated), 4 g fiber, 56 mg cholesterol, 599 mg sodium.

NOTE: Soba noodles, or Japanese buckwheat noodles, can be found in the Asian section of the supermarket, Asian markets, and many health food stores.

Roasted Vegetables with Arugula and Fusilli ⓥ

PREP 25 minutes **ROAST** 50 minutes **MAKES** 6 servings

> 1 package (20 ounces) peeled and precut butternut squash, cut into 1-inch pieces
>
> 4 garlic cloves, each cut in half
>
> 2 medium red onions, each cut into 8 wedges
>
> 2 medium red peppers, cut into $1/2$-inch-wide strips
>
> 2 tablespoons olive oil
>
> 1 teaspoon salt
>
> $1/4$ teaspoon coarsely ground black pepper
>
> 1 package (16 ounces) whole-wheat fusilli or corkscrew pasta
>
> 2 bunches arugula (4 ounces each), trimmed and coarsely chopped
>
> 2 tablespoons white or dark balsamic vinegar

1. Preheat oven to 450°F. In $15^{1}/_{2}$" by $10^{1}/_{2}$" jelly-roll pan, toss squash, garlic, onions, red peppers, oil, salt, and pepper until evenly mixed. Roast, stirring occasionally, until vegetables are tender and lightly golden, about 50 minutes.

2. Meanwhile, in large saucepot, cook pasta as label directs.

3. Drain pasta, reserving $1/2$ cup pasta water; return pasta to saucepot. Add roasted vegetables, arugula, vinegar, and reserved pasta water; toss until well mixed.

EACH SERVING: About 394 calories, 12 g protein, 72 g carbohydrate, 8 g total fat (1 g saturated), 11 g fiber, 0 mg cholesterol, 404 mg sodium.

Asian Rice Pilaf with Tofu ⓥ

PREP 10 minutes   **COOK** 20 minutes   **MAKES** 4 servings

1 box (6 ounces) Near East Rice Pilaf Mix

2 tablespoons olive oil

8 ounces extra-firm tofu, diced

1 tablespoon reduced-sodium soy sauce (such as Kikkoman or La Choy Lite)

1 garlic clove, finely chopped

1 teaspoon grated fresh ginger

2 carrots, diced

1 yellow bell pepper, diced

$1/2$ seedless cucumber, diced

2 green onions, thinly sliced

$1/4$ cup slivered almonds, toasted

1.   Prepare pilaf mix according to package directions using 1 tablespoon of the olive oil. Remove pan from heat. Stir in tofu; cover and let stand until heated through, 5 minutes.

2.   Meanwhile, in small bowl, whisk remaining 1 tablespoon oil, soy sauce, garlic, and ginger.

3.   Transfer pilaf and tofu mixture to large bowl; stir in dressing. Add carrots, bell pepper, cucumber, and green onions; mix well. Sprinkle with almonds.

EACH SERVING: About 312 calories, 10 g protein, 44 g carbohydrate, 12 g total fat (1 g saturated), 3 g fiber, 0 mg cholesterol, 785 mg sodium.

Couscous with Garbanzo Beans ⓥ

PREP 5 minutes   **COOK** 10 minutes   **MAKES** 4 servings

- **1 box (5.6 ounces) couscous (Moroccan pasta) with toasted pine nuts (such as from Near East)**
- **2 teaspoons plus 1 tablespoon olive oil**
- **1/3 cup dark seedless raisins**
- **1 medium zucchini (10 ounces), cut lengthwise in half, then crosswise into 1/2-inch-thick slices**
- **1 garlic clove, crushed with garlic press**
- **3/4 teaspoon ground cumin**
- **3/4 teaspoon ground coriander**
- **1/8 teaspoon ground red pepper (cayenne)**
- **2 cans (15 ounces each) garbanzo beans (preferably fewer than 140 mg sodium per 1/2 cup, such as Eden Organic or Goya Low Sodium Chickpeas), rinsed and drained**
- **1/2 cup chopped pimiento-stuffed olives (salad olives), drained**
- **1/4 cup water**

1.   Prepare couscous as label directs, using 2 teaspoons of the oil and adding the raisins to cooking water.

2.   Meanwhile, in nonstick 12-inch skillet, heat remaining 1 tablespoon oil over medium-high heat until hot. Add zucchini and cook, stirring occasionally, 5 minutes. Add garlic, cumin, coriander, and ground red pepper and cook, stirring, 30 seconds. Add beans, olives, and water and cook, stirring often, until heated through, about 5 minutes.

3.   Add cooked couscous to bean mixture and toss gently.

EACH SERVING: About 464 calories, 19 g protein, 72 g carbohydrate, 13 g total fat (1 g saturated), 11 g fiber, 0 mg cholesterol, 770 mg sodium.

Couscous with
Garbanzo Beans

Japanese Eggplant and Tofu Stir-Fry Ⓥ

PREP 25 minutes   **COOK** 20 minutes   **MAKES** 4 servings

- 1 pound firm tofu, drained and cut into 1-inch cubes
- 1 cup reduced-sodium vegetable broth (preferably fewer than 350 mg sodium per cup, such as Health Valley Fat-Free)
- $1/2$ cup plus $1/3$ cup water
- $1/4$ cup reduced-sodium soy sauce (such as Kikkoman or La Choy Lite)
- 2 tablespoons brown sugar
- 2 tablespoons cornstarch
- 2 tablespoons canola oil
- 4 medium Japanese eggplants (4 ounces each), cut diagonally into 2-inch-thick pieces
- 8 ounces shiitake mushrooms, stems removed and caps cut into quarters
- 1 tablespoon grated peeled fresh ginger
- 3 garlic cloves, crushed with garlic press
- 3 green onions, thinly sliced
- 2 heads baby bok choy (6 ounces each), cut crosswise into 1-inch slices

1. In medium bowl, place 3 layers paper towel; add tofu and cover with 3 more layers paper towel, pressing gently to extract liquid from tofu. Let tofu stand 10 minutes to drain.

2. Meanwhile, in small bowl, with fork, mix broth, $1/2$ cup water, soy sauce, sugar, and cornstarch until blended; set aside.

3. In deep nonstick 12-inch skillet or wok, heat 1 tablespoon oil over medium-high heat until hot. Add eggplant and remaining $1/3$ cup water; cover and cook, stirring occasionally, until eggplant is tender, 7 to 10 minutes. Transfer eggplant to small bowl; set aside.

4. Add remaining 1 tablespoon oil to skillet and heat until hot. Add mushrooms and tofu and cook, stirring frequently (stir-frying), until tofu is lightly browned, about 5 minutes. Stir in ginger, garlic, and half of green onions; stir-fry 1 minute. Add bok choy and stir-fry until vegetables are lightly browned, about 4 minutes longer.

5. Stir broth mixture to blend; add broth mixture and eggplant to tofu mixture. Heat to boiling over medium-high heat; reduce heat to low and simmer, stirring, 1 minute. Sprinkle with remaining green onions before serving.

EACH SERVING: About 273 calories, 17 g protein, 26 g carbohydrate, 12 g total fat (1 g saturated), 7 g fiber, 0 mg cholesterol, 705 mg sodium.

Bok Choy Is a Cancer-fighter

Bok choy, a type of cabbage, is a member of the super-nutritious cruciferous family. Cruciferous vegetables—which include other cabbages, arugula, broccoli, Brussels sprouts, cauliflower, kale, collard and mustard greens, rutabagas, and turnips—are rich in compounds such as indoles and sulforaphane that help prevent cancer. Bok choy is a staple in Chinese cooking, so ask for it next time you order Chinese. It's great stir-fried, with a little garlic, or as part of a stir-fry mix like the recipe above.

Falafel with Tahini Sauce Ⓥ

PREP 25 minutes   **COOK** 25 minutes   **MAKES** 4 servings

1 box (6 ounces) Near East Falafel Mix

1/4 cup tahini

2 tablespoons plain low-fat yogurt

2 tablespoons fresh lemon juice

2 tablespoons water

1/4 teaspoon ground cumin

6 (6- to 7-inch) whole-wheat pitas (about 150 calories each)

3 cups broccoli slaw (such as Mann's Broccoli Cole Slaw, use 3/4 of a 12 ounce package)

1. Prepare falafel mix according to package directions, making 12 patties. Bake (don't fry) according to package directions.

2. In a small bowl, combine tahini, yogurt, lemon juice, water, and cumin; whisk until smooth.

3. Cut pitas in half. Fill each half with a falafel and broccoli slaw; spoon tahini sauce over.

EACH SERVING: About 462 calories, 26 g protein, 77 g carbohydrate, 10 g total fat (1 g saturated), 16 g fiber, 0 mg cholesterol, 764 mg sodium.

Polenta with Spicy Eggplant Sauce

Polenta with Spicy Eggplant Sauce ⓥ

PREP 15 minutes **COOK** 25 minutes **MAKES** 4 servings

1 tablespoon olive oil

1 medium onion, finely chopped

2 small eggplants (1 pound each), cut into 1-inch pieces

1 garlic clove, crushed with garlic press

$^1/_4$ teaspoon crushed red pepper

3 cups (28 ounces) crushed tomatoes (preferably fewer than 35 mg sodium per $^1/_2$ cup, such as Pomi Chopped Tomatoes)

1 $^1/_4$ teaspoons salt

5 cups water

2 cups low-fat milk (1%)

1 $^1/_2$ cups yellow cornmeal

Parmesan-cheese wedge (optional)

1. In nonstick 12-inch skillet, heat oil over medium heat until hot. Add onion and cook, stirring occasionally, 5 minutes. Increase heat to medium-high; add eggplant and cook, stirring occasionally, until golden and tender, about 8 minutes. Add garlic and crushed red pepper and cook, stirring, 1 minute. Add tomatoes, $^1/_2$ teaspoon salt, and $^1/_2$ cup water; heat to boiling. Reduce heat to low; cover and simmer, stirring occasionally, 10 minutes.

2. Meanwhile, in deep 4-quart microwave-safe bowl or casserole, combine milk, cornmeal, and remaining $^3/_4$ teaspoon salt and 4 $^1/_2$ cups water. Cook in microwave oven on High until thickened, 15 to 20 minutes. After first 5 minutes of cooking, whisk vigorously until smooth (mixture will be lumpy at first), and twice more during remaining cooking time.

3. While polenta is cooking, with vegetable peeler, remove long, thin strips from Parmesan wedge for garnish, if you like.

4. To serve, spoon polenta into 4 bowls; top with eggplant sauce. Garnish each serving with some Parmesan strips if using.

EACH SERVING (WITHOUT PARMESAN): About 369 calories, 13 g protein, 69 g carbohydrate, 6 g total fat (1 g saturated), 17 g fiber, 6 mg cholesterol, 804 mg sodium.

Tex-Mex Wrap ⓥ

PREP 15 minutes   **COOK** 15 minutes   **MAKES** 4 servings

1 box (6 ounces) Near East Whole Grain Blends Wheat Pilaf Mix

1 can (15 ounces) reduced-sodium red kidney beans (preferably fewer than 140 mg per $^1/_2$ cup), rinsed and drained

2 tablespoons fresh lime juice

1 tablespoon olive oil

1 tablespoon minced seeded jalapeño chile

1 garlic clove, finely chopped

1 container (8 ounces) plain low-fat yogurt

$^1/_4$ cup chopped fresh cilantro

2 green onions, chopped

pinch ground cumin

pinch salt

2 plum tomatoes, diced

4 burrito-size flour tortillas (preferably whole-wheat), heated according to package directions

2 cups shredded iceberg lettuce

1. Prepare pilaf mix according to package directions. Remove pan from heat. Stir in beans; cover and let stand until heated through, 5 minutes.

2. Meanwhile, in small bowl, whisk lime juice, oil, jalapeño, and garlic. Combine yogurt, cilantro, green onions, cumin, and salt in another small bowl.

3. Transfer pilaf mix to a large bowl; stir in lime juice mixture. Add tomatoes; mix well.

4. Spoon 1 generous cup pilaf mixture in center of each tortilla; add $^1/_2$ cup lettuce. Fold bottom and sides of tortilla up and around filling. Serve with yogurt mixture.

EACH SERVING: About 456 calories, 22 g protein, 78 g carbohydrate, 9 g total fat (2 g saturated), 19 g fiber, 4 mg cholesterol, 665 mg sodium.

Picnic Potato Salad Ⓥ

PREP 5 minutes plus cooling   **COOK** 15 minutes   **MAKES** about 8 cups or 12 servings

3 pounds red-skin potatoes (12 medium), unpeeled, cut into 1-inch chunks

¹/₄ cup distilled white vinegar

1 tablespoon olive oil

2 teaspoons spicy brown mustard

1¹/₄ teaspoons salt

¹/₄ teaspoon coarsely ground black pepper

¹/₂ cup light mayonnaise (such as from Kraft or Hellman's)

¹/₃ cup whole milk

2 small celery stalks, thinly sliced

2 green onions, minced

1. In 5- to 6-quart saucepot, place potatoes and enough *water to cover;* heat to boiling over high heat. Reduce heat to low; cover and simmer until potatoes are fork-tender, 8 to 10 minutes.

2. Meanwhile, in large bowl, with wire whisk, mix vinegar, oil, mustard, salt, and pepper.

3. Drain potatoes. Add hot potatoes to bowl with vinaigrette; gently stir with rubber spatula until evenly coated and vinaigrette is absorbed. Cool 15 minutes.

4. In small bowl, with wire whisk, mix mayonnaise and milk until smooth. Add mayonnaise mixture, celery, and green onions to potatoes. Gently stir with rubber spatula until mixed. Serve warm or cover and refrigerate up to 1 day.

EACH SERVING: About 132 calories, 3 g protein, 20 g carbohydrate, 5 g total fat (1 g saturated), 2 g fiber, 4 mg cholesterol, 345 mg sodium.

Roasted Rosemary Potato Packets ⓥ

PREP 15 minutes **COOK** 30 minutes **MAKES** about 6 cups or 8 servings

> **2$^1/_2$ pounds red potatoes, unpeeled, cut into 1-inch chunks**
>
> **1 tablespoon olive oil**
>
> **1 tablespoon fresh rosemary leaves, chopped (or 1 teaspoon dried)**
>
> **1 teaspoon grated orange peel**
>
> **$^3/_4$ teaspoon salt**
>
> **$^1/_4$ teaspoon coarsely ground pepper**

1. Preheat oven to 450°F.

2. In large bowl, toss potatoes, oil, rosemary, orange peel, salt, and pepper until potatoes are evenly coated.

3. Place potato mixture in 14$^1/_2$" by 12$^1/_2$" extra-heavy-duty foil cooking bag (see Note); seal. (Or layer two 30" by 18" sheets heavy-duty foil to make a double thickness. Place potato mixture on center of stacked foil. Bring short ends of foil up and over potatoes; fold several times to seal well, then tightly fold remaining sides of foil.)

4. Place packet on large cookie sheet. Roast packets until potatoes are fork-tender, 30 minutes.

5. Before serving, with kitchen shears, cut an X in top of foil packet to let steam escape, then carefully pull back foil to open.

EACH SERVING: About 117 calories, 3 g protein, 23 g carbohydrate, 2 g total fat (0 g saturated), 2 g fiber, 0 mg cholesterol, 227 mg sodium.

NOTE: Look for foil cooking bags in your supermarket where foil and plastic wrap are sold.

Multi-Colored Slaw (v)

PREP 10 minutes plus chilling   **MAKES** about 12 cups or 12 servings

²/₃ **cup red wine vinegar**

¹/₄ **cup olive oil**

2 **tablespoons sugar**

2 **teaspoons salt**

¹/₂ **teaspoon celery seeds**

¹/₄ **teaspoon ground black pepper**

2 **bags (16 ounces each) shredded cabbage mix for coleslaw**

1 **bag (10 ounces) shredded red cabbage**

1. In large bowl, with fork, mix vinegar, oil, sugar, salt, celery seeds, and pepper until blended. Add cabbage mix and red cabbage; toss well to coat with dressing.

2. Cover and refrigerate coleslaw at least 1 hour or up to 1 day to allow flavors to blend.

EACH SERVING: About 76 calories, 1 g protein, 9 g carbohydrate, 5 g total fat (1 g saturated), 2 g fiber, 0 mg cholesterol, 408 mg sodium.

NOTE: To make just 1 serving, use *1 tablespoon vinegar, 1 teaspoon olive oil, ¹/₂ teaspoon sugar, dash celery seeds, dash pepper, 1 cup shredded cabbage mix,* and *1 cup shredded red cabbage.*

Tomato Salsa ⓥ

PREP 10 minutes   **MAKES** about 3 cups or 12 servings

1¹⁄₂ pounds tomatoes (4 medium), chopped

¹⁄₄ cup loosely packed fresh cilantro or parsley leaves, chopped

2 tablespoons fresh lime juice

¹⁄₂ teaspoon salt

¹⁄₈ teaspoon ground black pepper

In medium bowl, combine tomatoes, cilantro, lime juice, salt, and pepper until well mixed. Spoon into serving bowl; cover and refrigerate up to 2 hours if not serving right away.

EACH ¹⁄₄ CUP: About 11 calories, 1 g protein, 3 g carbohydrate, 0 g total fat, 1 g fiber, 0 mg cholesterol, 101 mg sodium.

Fire-Roasted Tomato Salsa Ⓥ

PREP 15 minutes   **GRILL** 8 minutes   **MAKES** about 3 cups or 12 servings

Grilled Plum Tomatoes (page 276)

1 large jalapeño chile

$1/4$ cup minced red onion

$1/3$ cup chopped fresh cilantro leaves

$1/4$ cup fresh lime juice

$3/4$ teaspoon salt

tortilla chips (such as Guiltless Gourmet Unsalted Yellow Corn)

1. Prepare Grilled Tomatoes.

2. While tomatoes are grilling, place whole jalapeño on same grill rack and cook over medium-high heat, turning occasionally, until skin is charred and blistered, 8 minutes. Transfer jalapeño to cutting board; cool until easy to handle.

3. Remove stem, skin, and seeds from jalapeño; discard. Finely chop jalapeño. Chop tomatoes.

4. In bowl, combine jalapeño, tomatoes with any juices, onion, cilantro, lime juice, and salt. If not serving right away, cover and refrigerated up to 3 hours. Serve with tortilla chips.

EACH $1/4$ CUP SALSA (WITHOUT CHIPS): About 24 calories, 1 g protein, 4 g carbohydrate, 1 g total fat (0 g saturated), 1 g fiber, 0 mg cholesterol, 179 mg sodium.

Grilled Plum Tomatoes Ⓥ

PREP 10 minutes **GRILL** 8 minutes **MAKES** 8 servings

2 pounds plum tomatoes (8 large), each cut lengthwise in half and cored

2 tablespoons olive oil

¹/₂ teaspoon salt

¹/₄ teaspoon ground black pepper

1. Prepare charcoal fire or gas grill for covered direct grilling over medium-high heat, or use your oven's broiler.

2. In large bowl, toss tomatoes with oil, salt, and pepper.

3. With long-handled basting brush, lightly oil grill rack. Place tomatoes on hot rack. Cover grill and cook tomatoes, turning once, until tomatoes begin to char and soften, 8 to 10 minutes.

EACH SERVING: About 32 calories, 1 g protein, 4 g carbohydrate, 2 g total fat (0 g saturated), 1 g fiber, 0 mg cholesterol, 50 mg sodium.

Grilled Eggplant, Peppers, Zucchini, and Summer Squash Ⓥ

PREP 15 minutes   **GRILL** 7 minutes   **MAKES** 8 servings

- **3 tablespoons olive oil**
- **2 tablespoons red wine vinegar**
- **$1/4$ teaspoon salt**
- **$1/4$ teaspoon coarsely ground black pepper**
- **$1/4$ cup loosely packed fresh basil leaves, coarsely chopped**
- **1 medium red pepper, cut lengthwise into quarters, stem and seeds discarded**
- **1 medium yellow pepper, cut lengthwise into quarters, stem and seeds discarded**
- **4 baby eggplants (5 ounces each), each cut lengthwise in half**
- **4 small zucchini and/or yellow summer squashes (6 ounces each), each cut lengthwise in half**

1. Prepare charcoal fire or preheat gas grill for covered direct grilling over medium-high heat.

2. Meanwhile, in cup, mix oil, vinegar, salt, pepper, and chopped basil.

3. Place red and yellow peppers, eggplants, and squashes on hot grill rack. Cover grill and cook vegetables until tender and browned, 7 to 10 minutes, turning and brushing with herb mixture occasionally and transferring vegetables to platter as they are done.

4. Drizzle vegetables with any remaining herb mixture.

EACH SERVING: About 86 calories, 2 g protein, 9 g carbohydrate, 5 g total fat (1 g saturated), 4 g fiber, 0 mg cholesterol, 83 mg sodium.

Mixed Summer Squash with Parsley and Lemon ⓥ

PREP 15 minutes   **COOK** 5 minutes   **MAKES** about 4 cups or 4 servings

4 small zucchini and/or yellow summer squashes (6 ounces each)

1 tablespoon zero-grams trans-fat margarine

$^1/_4$ teaspoon salt

$^1/_4$ teaspoon coarsely ground pepper

$^1/_4$ cup loosely packed fresh parsley leaves, chopped

$^1/_2$ teaspoon grated fresh lemon peel

1. Cut squashes diagonally into $^1/_4$-inch-wide slices, then cut slices crosswise into $^1/_4$-inch-wide strips.

2. In nonstick 12-inch skillet, melt margarine over medium-high heat. Add squashes, salt, and pepper and cook, stirring frequently, until squash is tender-crisp, 4 to 5 minutes. Stir in parsley and lemon peel.

EACH SERVING: About 42 calories, 2 g protein, 5 g carbohydrate, 2 g total fat (0 g saturated), 2 g fiber, 0 mg cholesterol, 162 mg sodium.

Butter vs. Margarine

After decades of hearing that margarine was healthier than butter, it turns out that most margarine is worse for you than butter. The problem is heart-unhealthy trans fat, formed when vegetable oils are partially hydrogenated (hardened) to form a solid spread.

So, why not just eat butter? Well, you can, if you limit yourself to 1 teaspoon per day on this plan, substituting butter for zero-grams trans-fat margarine. More than 1 teaspoon and you may get too much saturated fat, which is nearly as bad as trans fat in terms of heart disease. For instance, if you had a scrambled egg breakfast and used butter instead of zero-grams trans-fat margarine, you might accumulate 2 teaspoons at breakfast. Then, if you had butter with your whole-wheat dinner roll, there's another teaspoon, which might result in an intake of saturated fat that was too high. While most meals on this plan are low in saturated fat, a few contain enough that, paired with butter, your saturated fat level might exceed healthy standards.

If you really love butter, go ahead and stock it. But keep a tub of zero-grams trans-fat margarine on hand and make sure you have no more than 1 teaspoon of butter a day. Here's how to substitute zero-grams trans-fat margarine for butter in recipes other than those in this book: Use $^1/_3$ more zero-grams trans-fat margarine. For instance, if a recipe calls for 1 stick of butter, then substitute $1^1/_3$ sticks of zero-grams trans-fat margarine. (There's more water and less fat in zero-grams trans-fat margarine, so you have to use more.)

Acorn Squash with White Beans and Sage ⓥ

PREP 15 minutes   **COOK** 20 minutes   **MAKES** 4 servings

1 tablespoon olive oil

1 jumbo onion (1 pound), cut into $^1/_4$-inch dice

1 medium carrot, cut into $^1/_4$-inch dice

2 garlic cloves, finely chopped

1 can (15 to 19 ounces) white kidney (cannellini) beans (preferably fewer than 140 mg sodium per $^1/_2$ cup, such as Eden Organic Cannellini or Westbrae Great Northern Beans), rinsed and drained

$^3/_4$ cup reduced-sodium vegetable broth (preferably fewer than 350 mg sodium per cup, such as Health Valley Fat Free)

$^1/_4$ teaspoon salt

$^1/_4$ teaspoon coarsely ground black pepper

3 teaspoons chopped fresh sage leaves (or 1 teaspoon dried)

2 small acorn squashes (12 ounces each)

1 medium tomato, cut into $^1/_4$-inch dice

1. In nonstick 12-inch skillet, heat oil over medium-high heat until hot. Add onion, carrot, and garlic and cook, stirring occasionally, until vegetables are tender and golden, 15 minutes. Add beans, broth, salt, pepper, and 2 teaspoons sage and heat to boiling. Remove from heat; cover skillet and keep warm.

2. Meanwhile, cut each squash lengthwise in half and remove seeds and strings. Place squash halves in 3-quart microwave-safe baking dish. Cover and cook in microwave oven on High until squash is fork-tender, 6 to 8 minutes.

3. Place squash halves, cut sides up, on platter. Fill each half with bean mixture; sprinkle with diced tomato and remaining 1 teaspoon sage.

EACH SERVING: About 228 calories, 7 g protein, 43 g carbohydrate, 5 g total fat (1 g saturated), 8 g fiber, 0 mg cholesterol, 260 mg sodium.

Grilled Corn on the Cob with Molasses Butter Ⓥ

PREP 10 minutes   GRILL 10 minutes   MAKES 8 servings

2 tablespoons margarine or butter, softened

1 teaspoon light (mild) molasses (or honey)

¹/₂ teaspoon ground coriander

¹/₂ teaspoon salt

pinch ground red pepper (cayenne)

8 ears corn, husks and silks removed

1. Prepare charcoal fire or preheat gas grill for covered direct grilling over medium-high heat.

2. In small bowl, with fork, stir margarine, molasses, coriander, salt, and ground red pepper until well combined.

3. Place corn on hot grill rack. Cover grill and cook corn, turning frequently, until brown in spots, 10 to 15 minutes. Transfer corn to platter; spread each ear with molasses butter.

EACH SERVING: About 105 calories, 3 g protein, 18 g carbohydrate, 4 g total fat (1 g saturated), 3 g fiber, 0 mg cholesterol, 195 mg sodium.

Baby Spinach and Beet Salad ⓥ

PREP 20 minutes plus standing   **MAKES** 4 servings

> **3 medium beets (1 pound without tops), peeled and cut into matchstick-thin strips**
>
> **3 tablespoons seasoned rice vinegar**
>
> **2 teaspoons soy sauce**
>
> **$^1/_2$ teaspoon Asian sesame oil**
>
> **1 bag (5 to 6 ounces) baby spinach**
>
> **1 tablespoon sesame seeds, toasted**

1.   In medium bowl, stir uncooked beets, 1 tablespoon vinegar, 1 teaspoon soy sauce, and $^1/_4$ teaspoon sesame oil. Let stand at room temperature 15 minutes or up to 2 hours to blend flavors.

2.   Just before serving, in large salad bowl, toss spinach with remaining 2 tablespoons vinegar, 1 teaspoon soy sauce, and $^1/_4$ teaspoon sesame oil. Top spinach with beets and their marinade; sprinkle with sesame seeds.

EACH SERVING: About 92 calories, 4 g protein, 17 g carbohydrate, 2 g total fat (0 g saturated), 4 g fiber, 0 mg cholesterol, 389 mg sodium.

Vinaigrette Dressing ⓥ

If you're in too much of a hurry to make some of the oil-and-vinegar-based dressings in other recipes, you can substitute this vinaigrette. Make up a batch and it will last for a week.

PREP 5 minutes   **MAKES** $^1/_4$ cup or 4 servings

In small bowl, with fork, mix *2 tablespoons wine vinegar, 2 tablespoons olive oil, $^1/_4$ teaspoon salt, $^1/_4$ teaspoon sugar, $^1/_4$ teaspoon dry mustard,* and *$^1/_8$ teaspoon pepper.*

EACH TABLESPOON: About 32 calories, 0 g protein, 0 g carbohydrate, 3 g total fat (0 g saturated), 0 g fiber, 0 mg cholesterol, 145 mg sodium.

Garlicky Spinach ⓥ

PREP 5 minutes   **COOK** 5 minutes   **MAKES** 4 servings

- **1 tablespoon olive oil**
- **1 large garlic clove, minced**
- **2 bags (10 ounces each) fresh spinach, rinsed and drained but not spun dry, tough stems trimmed**
- **¹⁄₄ teaspoon salt**

In 12-inch skillet, heat oil over medium-high heat until hot. Add garlic and cook, stirring, until fragrant, 30 seconds. Stir in half the spinach with water clinging to leaves; cover and cook just until wilted, 2 minutes. Add remaining spinach and cook, uncovered, until tender, 2 minutes longer. Stir in salt.

EACH SERVING: About 64 calories, 4 g protein, 5 g carbohydrate, 4 g total fat (1 g saturated), 3 g fiber, 0 mg cholesterol, 258 mg sodium.

Eye-Opening Spinach

A number of research studies have found that people who eat a lot of spinach have a lower risk of developing two eye problems—cataracts and macular degeneration. Credit goes to lutein, an antioxidant found both in spinach and in the eyes. Sautéing spinach in oil helps the body absorb even more lutein than eating spinach raw.

Bulgur and Corn Salad Ⓥ

PREP 10 minutes   **COOK** 10 minutes   **MAKES** about 2$^1/_4$ cups or 3 servings

1 cup water

$^1/_2$ cup bulgur (cracked wheat)

1 medium ear corn, husk and silk removed

1 tablespoon rice vinegar

1 tablespoon olive oil

pinch salt

pinch ground black pepper

2 medium plum tomatoes (6 ounces), cut into $^1/_2$-inch chunks

$^1/_4$ cup fresh basil, chopped

1. In 1-quart saucepan, heat water to boiling over high heat. Stir in bulgur; heat to boiling. Reduce heat to low; cover and simmer until liquid is absorbed, 10 minutes.

2. Meanwhile, place corn on plate in microwave oven. Cook on High, turning and rearranging corn halfway through cooking, 2 to 3 minutes. Cool slightly until easy to handle. With sharp knife, cut corn kernels from cob.

3. In large bowl, with fork, mix vinegar, oil, salt, and pepper; stir in warm bulgur, corn, tomatoes, and basil until combined. If not serving right away, cover and refrigerate up to 4 hours.

EACH SERVING: About 160 calories, 4 g protein, 27 g carbohydrate, 5 g total fat (1 g saturated), 6 g fiber, 0 mg cholesterol, 191 mg sodium.

Wheat-Berry Salad
with Spinach Ⓥ

PREP 15 minutes plus soaking   **COOK** 1 hour 15 minutes   **MAKES** 6 servings

> **1¹/₂ cups wheat berries (whole-grain wheat)**
>
> **10 dried tomato halves (1 ounce)**
>
> **3 tablespoons olive oil**
>
> **2 tablespoons red wine vinegar**
>
> **¹/₂ teaspoon Dijon mustard**
>
> **1 teaspoon salt**
>
> **¹/₂ teaspoon sugar**
>
> **¹/₄ teaspoon coarsely ground black pepper**
>
> **1 cup golden raisins**
>
> **1 medium tomato, diced**
>
> **1 bunch (10 to 12 ounces) spinach, tough stems trimmed and coarsely chopped**

1. In large bowl, soak wheat berries overnight in enough *water to cover by 2 inches.*

2. Drain wheat berries. In 4-quart saucepan, heat *7 cups water* to boiling over high heat. Add soaked wheat berries; heat to boiling. Reduce heat to low; cover and simmer until wheat berries are tender, about 1 hour. Drain.

3. Place dried tomato halves in small bowl; add *1 cup boiling water.* Let stand 5 minutes. Drain well and coarsely chop.

4. In medium bowl, with wire whisk or fork, mix oil, vinegar, mustard, salt, sugar, and pepper until blended. Add wheat berries, chopped dried tomatoes, raisins, diced tomato, and spinach; toss well.

EACH SERVING: About 328 calories, 9 g protein, 61 g carbohydrate, 8 g total fat (1 g saturated), 9 g fiber, 0 mg cholesterol, 546 mg sodium.

Fattoush ⓥ

PREP 25 minutes plus standing   **MAKES** about 16 cups or 4 servings

3 tablespoons fresh lemon juice

3 tablespoons olive oil

³/₄ teaspoon salt

¹/₂ teaspoon coarsely ground black pepper

4 medium tomatoes (1¹/₄ pounds), cut into ¹/₂-inch pieces

3 green onions, chopped

1 medium cucumber (8 ounces), peeled, seeded, and cut into ¹/₂-inch pieces

1 cup loosely packed fresh parsley leaves, chopped

¹/₂ cup loosely packed fresh mint leaves, chopped

4 (4-inch) whole-wheat pitas (about 75 calories each), each split horizontally in half

1 small head romaine lettuce (1 pound), coarsely chopped

1. In large salad bowl, with wire whisk or fork, mix lemon juice, oil, salt, and pepper. Add tomatoes, green onions, cucumber, parsley, and mint; toss to coat. Let tomato mixture stand 15 minutes to allow flavors to blend.

2. Meanwhile, toast pitas; cool. Break pitas into 1-inch pieces.

3. Just before serving, toss lettuce and pitas with tomato mixture.

EACH SERVING: About 230 calories, 7 g protein, 29 g carbohydrate, 12 g total fat (2 g saturated), 0 mg cholesterol, 615 mg sodium.

Green Cabbage Salad Ⓥ

PREP 10 minutes   **MAKES** about 14 cups or 7 servings

$1/4$ **cup light mayonnaise (such as from Kraft or Hellman's)**

2 tablespoons reduced-fat sour cream

2 tablespoons cider vinegar

3 tablespoons chopped fresh dill

1 teaspoon sugar

$1/4$ **teaspoon salt**

$1/8$ **teaspoon ground black pepper**

$1/2$ **large head green cabbage ($2\,1/4$ pounds), tough ribs discarded, thinly sliced**

1.   In large bowl, whisk mayonnaise, sour cream, vinegar, dill, sugar, salt, and pepper until blended. Add green cabbage and toss until evenly coated.

2.   If not serving right away, cover and refrigerate salad. To serve, arrange on large platter.

EACH SERVING: About 58 calories, 2 g protein, 7 g carbohydrate, 3 g total fat (1 g saturated), 2 g fiber, 4 mg cholesterol, 154 mg sodium.

Soybean Salad ⓥ

PREP 20 minutes   **COOK** 5 minutes   **MAKES** about 4 cups or 6 servings

1 bag (16 ounces) frozen shelled edamame or frozen baby lima beans

¼ cup seasoned rice vinegar

1 tablespoon olive oil

1 teaspoon sugar

½ teaspoon salt

⅛ teaspoon ground black pepper

1 bunch radishes (8 ounces), each cut in half and thinly sliced

1 cup loosely packed fresh cilantro leaves, chopped

1. Cook edamame as label directs; drain. Rinse with cold water to stop cooking; drain again.

2. In medium bowl, whisk vinegar, oil, sugar, salt, and pepper until blended. Add edamame, radishes, and cilantro; toss until evenly coated. Cover and refrigerate salad up to 1 day if not serving right away.

EACH SERVING: About 164 calories, 14 g protein, 17 g carbohydrate, 6 g total fat (1 g saturated), 5 g fiber, 0 mg cholesterol, 377 mg sodium.

Green Pea and Lettuce Soup Ⓥ

PREP 5 minutes   **COOK** 15 minutes   **MAKES** about 6 cups or 4 servings

2 teaspoons butter or zero grams trans fat margarine

1 medium onion, finely chopped

1 can (14 ounces) reduced-sodium vegetable broth (preferably fewer than 350 mg sodium per cup, such as Health Valley Fat Free)

1 package (10 ounces) frozen peas

1 head Boston lettuce (10 ounces), coarsely chopped

³/₄ teaspoon salt

¹/₈ teaspoon ground black pepper

¹/₈ teaspoon dried thyme

1 cup water

¹/₂ cup fat-free (skim) milk

1 tablespoon fresh lemon juice

1. In 4-quart saucepan, melt butter over medium heat. Add onion and cook, stirring occasionally, until tender, about 5 minutes. Stir in broth, frozen peas, lettuce, salt, pepper, thyme, and water; heat to boiling over high heat. Reduce heat to low; simmer 5 minutes. Stir in milk.

2. Spoon half of pea mixture into blender; cover, with center part of cover removed to let steam escape, and puree until smooth. Pour soup into large bowl. Repeat with remaining mixture.

3. Return soup to same saucepan; heat through. Stir in lemon juice and remove from heat. Transfer soup to serving bowl.

EACH SERVING: About 107 calories, 6 g protein, 18 g carbohydrate, 2 g total fat (0 g saturated), 4 g fiber, 1 mg cholesterol, 677 mg sodium.

Antipasto Salad Ⓥ

PREP 25 minutes   **MAKES** 4 servings

1 bag (5 ounces) baby arugula

6 marinated artichokes hearts ($\frac{1}{2}$ of a 12-ounce jar; preferably fewer than 320 mg sodium per $\frac{1}{2}$ cup), drained and coarsely chopped

4 ounces fresh mozzarella cheese, cut into $\frac{1}{2}$-inch cubes

$\frac{1}{2}$ cup jarred roasted red bell pepper, cut into thin strips

2 ounces thinly sliced prosciutto, cut into strips

1 celery stalk, thinly sliced

2 teaspoons extravirgin olive oil

$1\frac{1}{2}$ teaspoons balsamic vinegar

pinch hot pepper flakes

In a large bowl, combine arugula, artichokes, mozzarella, bell pepper, prosciutto, and celery. Drizzle with oil and vinegar. Sprinkle with hot pepper flakes and toss to combine.

EACH SERVING: About 101 calories, 7 g protein, 4 g carbohydrate, 6 g total fat (2 g saturated), 2 g fiber 15 mg cholesterol, 590 mg sodium.

Artichoke and Pasta Salad ⓥ

PREP 15 minutes   **COOK** 10 minutes   **MAKES** 4 servings

4 ounces whole-wheat pasta (such as penne or fusilli)

$^1\!/_2$ cup frozen peas

1 jar (12 ounces) marinated artichokes hearts (preferably fewer than 320 mg sodium per $^1\!/_2$ cup), drained and coarsely chopped

$^1\!/_2$ cup grape tomatoes, each halved

2 green onions, finely chopped

2 tablespoons refrigerated pesto sauce

1 tablespoon red wine vinegar

1. In a large saucepot, cook pasta according to package directions without salt; stir in peas and drain. Rinse with cold water and drain well.

2. In a large bowl, combine pasta and peas, artichokes, tomatoes, green onions, pesto, and vinegar. Toss to combine.

EACH SERVING: 188 calories, 7 g protein, 27 g carbohydrate, 7 g total fat (0 g saturated), 5 g fiber, 0 mg cholesterol, 263 mg sodium.

Grilled Garlic and Herb Bread ⓥ

PREP 10 minutes   **GRILL** 10 minutes   **MAKES** 6 servings

> **6 tablespoons reduced-fat soft, spreadable cheese with garlic and herbs, such as Rondele Cheese Spread Garlic Herbs Light**
>
> **¹/₂ long (16-ounce) whole-grain loaf French or Italian bread, split horizontally in half**
>
> **1 plum tomato, seeded and chopped**

1. Prepare charcoal fire or gas grill for covered direct grilling over medium heat.

2. Evenly spread cheese on cut sides of bread. Sprinkle bottom half of bread with tomato. Replace top half of bread. Wrap bread tightly in heavy-duty foil.

3. Place foil-wrapped bread on hot grill rack. Cover and cook 10 minutes, turning over once halfway through grilling.

4. Transfer bread to cutting board. To serve, carefully remove foil. With serrated knife, cut bread crosswise into slices.

EACH SERVING: About 129 calories, 5 g protein, 21 g carbohydrate, 3 g total fat (1 g saturated), 2 g fiber, 8 mg cholesterol, 266 mg sodium.

Grilled Basil-Romano Bread ⓥ

Prepare grill as in step 1 of Grilled Garlic and Herb Bread. In step 2, brush cut sides of bread with *2 tablespoons bottled Italian salad dressing* (preferably less than 400 mg sodium per 2 tablespoons, such as Newman's Own Family Recipe Italian). Sprinkle bottom half of bread with *¹/₃ cup torn fresh basil leaves* and *¹/₄ cup freshly grated Pecorino Romano cheese*. Replace top half of bread; wrap in heavy-duty foil. Complete recipe as in steps 3 and 4.

EACH SERVING About 140 calories, 5 g protein, 20 g carbohydrate, 4 g total fat (1 g saturated), 2 g fiber, 3 mg cholesterol, 319 mg sodium.

Toasted Barley Pilaf ⓥ

PREP 20 minutes   **COOK** 30 minutes   **MAKES** about 8 cups or 12 servings

> 1 bag (1 pound) pearl barley
>
> 4 cups water
>
> 1 teaspoon salt
>
> 1 cup pecans, toasted and chopped
>
> 1 cup dried tart cherries
>
> 1 bunch fresh parsley leaves, chopped (1 cup)
>
> $^1/_2$ cup seasoned rice vinegar
>
> 2 tablespoons olive oil
>
> $^1/_4$ teaspoon ground black pepper

1. Preheat oven to 400°F.

2. In 15$^1/_2$" by 10$^1/_2$" jelly-roll pan, toast barley, shaking pan occasionally, until fragrant and lightly browned, 20 minutes.

3. In 5-quart Dutch oven, heat barley, water, and salt to boiling over high heat. Reduce heat to low; cover and simmer until barley is tender and all liquid is absorbed, 30 minutes.

4. Spoon barley into large serving bowl; stir in pecans, cherries, parsley, vinegar, oil, and pepper. Serve warm or at room temperature.

EACH SERVING: About 271 calories, 5 g protein, 46 g carbohydrate, 9 g total fat (1 g saturated), 8 g fiber, 0 mg cholesterol, 365 mg sodium.

Strawberries with Amaretto

PREP 10 minutes plus standing   **MAKES** about 5 cups or 4 servings

2 pints strawberries, hulled and each cut into quarters, or halves if small

2 tablespoons amaretto (almond-flavored liqueur)

2 tablespoons sugar

1/2 teaspoon grated fresh orange peel

In large bowl, toss strawberries with amaretto, sugar, and peel. Let stand 10 minutes, stirring occasionally. Spoon strawberries with their juice into 4 dessert bowls.

EACH SERVING: About 97 calories, 1 g protein, 21 g carbohydrate, 1 g total fat (0 g saturated), 3 g fiber, 0 mg cholesterol, 2 mg sodium.

Strawberries in White Wine

PREP 10 minutes   **MAKES** 4 servings

1/3 cup dry white wine (such as Riesling or Sauvignon Blanc)

2 tablespoons sugar

1 pint strawberries, hulled and each cut in half

fresh mint leaves, for garnish

In small bowl, stir together wine and sugar. Divide strawberries among 4 chilled dishes; pour wine mixture over berries and garnish with fresh mint.

EACH SERVING: About 99 calories, 1 g protein, 25 g carbohydrate, 0 g total fat, 2 g fiber, 0 mg cholesterol, 12 mg sodium.

Strawberry Granita

PREP 10 minutes plus cooling and freezing   **COOK** 10 minutes   **MAKES** about 4 cups or 8 servings

1 cup water

¹/₂ cup sugar

1 container (1 pound) strawberries, hulled

1 tablespoon fresh lemon juice

1. In 2-quart saucepan, heat water and sugar to boiling over high heat, stirring until sugar dissolves. Reduce heat to low and simmer 5 minutes. Set saucepan in bowl of ice water. Stir occasionally until syrup is cool, about 15 minutes.

2. Meanwhile, in food processor with knife blade attached, pulse strawberries until pureed.

3. Using whisk, stir strawberry puree and lemon juice into syrup until completely blended; pour into 9" by 9" metal baking pan. Cover and freeze until frozen around the edges, about 2 hours. Stir mixture from edges into center, breaking up chunks with side of fork. Cover and freeze until completely frozen, 3 hours longer.

4. To serve, with fork, scrape across the surface of granita to make ice crystals. Serve immediately in chilled dessert dishes.

EACH SERVING: About 40 calories, 0 g protein, 11 g carbohydrate, 0 g total fat, 1 g fiber, 0 mg cholesterol, 0 mg sodium.

Raspberry-Tea Mold

PREP 20 minutes plus chilling   **MAKES** 6 servings

> **2 envelopes unflavored gelatin**
>
> **$^1/_3$ cup sugar**
>
> **2 cups cranberry-raspberry juice**
>
> **2 Earl Grey tea bags**
>
> **1 cup boiling water**
>
> **$^1/_2$ pint raspberries**
>
> **1 cup diced ($^1/_4$-inch) cantaloupe**
>
> **mint leaves, raspberries, and diced cantaloupe, for garnish**

1. In 1-quart saucepan, mix gelatin and sugar. Stir in $^1/_2$ cup cranberry juice; let stand 3 minutes to soften gelatin. Stir over low heat until gelatin completely dissolves, about 3 minutes. Remove from heat.

2. Meanwhile, in 2-cup glass measuring cup, combine tea bags with boiling water; let steep 5 minutes. Remove tea bags and discard.

3. In medium bowl, stir together dissolved gelatin, tea, and remaining $1^1/_2$ cups juice. Refrigerate juice mixture, stirring occasionally, until it has the consistency of unbeaten egg whites, about 1 hour 45 minutes. (To quick-chill gelatin, set bowl in larger bowl of ice water and stir frequently with rubber spatula just until mixture begins to thicken.)

4. Stir raspberries and cantaloupe into thickened gelatin; pour into 5-cup mold. Cover and refrigerate until firm, 4 hours.

5. To unmold gelatin, place mold up to rim in bowl of warm, not hot, water for a few seconds. Be careful not to melt gelatin. Remove mold from water. Insert small metal spatula around edge of mold to release gelatin. Dry outside of mold. Invert platter on top of mold, then quickly invert mold and platter together. Lift off mold. Garnish with mint, raspberries, and cantaloupe.

EACH SERVING: About 118 calories, 3 g protein, 28 g carbohydrate, 0 g total fat, 1 g fiber, 0 mg cholesterol, 11 mg sodium.

Berry Sorbet

PREP 5 minutes   **MAKES** about 4 cups or 6 servings

> **1 package (20 ounces) frozen strawberries or raspberries**
>
> **1 container (8 ounces) plain low-fat yogurt**
>
> **³/₄ cup confectioners' sugar**
>
> **1 tablespoon fresh lemon juice**
>
> **fresh berries (optional)**

1. In food processor with knife blade attached, blend frozen berries until fruit resembles finely shaved ice, stopping processor occasionally to scrape down side with rubber spatula. If fruit is not finely pureed, dessert will not be smooth.

2. With processor running, add yogurt, sugar, and lemon juice and blend until mixture is smooth and creamy. Stop processor and scrape down side occasionally. Serve immediately for creamy texture or freeze and serve later for a firmer sorbet. Top each serving with some berries if you like.

EACH SERVING: About 134 calories, 3 g protein, 31 g carbohydrate, 1 g total fat (0 g saturated), 3 g fiber, 2 mg cholesterol, 28 mg sodium.

Berry Sorbet

Cool Berry Syrups

Cool Berry Syrup

Two tablespoons of this syrup over a scant $^1/_2$ cup of light vanilla ice cream or frozen yogurt is a great 125-calorie treat.

PREP 15 minutes plus standing and chilling   **COOK** 5 minutes   **MAKES** about $^3/_4$ cup or 6 servings

- **1 lemon**
- **1 orange**
- **$^1/_4$ cup sugar**
- **$^1/_4$ cup water**
- **1 cup raspberries, blackberries, blueberries, or sliced strawberries**

1. With vegetable peeler, remove a 3" by 1" strip peel from lemon and orange. Squeeze 1 tablespoon juice from each.

2. In 1-quart saucepan, combine lemon peel, orange peel, sugar, and water; heat to boiling over high heat. Reduce heat to low; add berries and simmer, uncovered, 5 minutes. Remove saucepan from heat. Let stand until cool, about 30 minutes. Remove and discard lemon and orange peels.

3. In blender, pulse berry mixture until pureed. Pour puree into medium-mesh sieve set over bowl. Press with back of spoon to remove seeds; discard seeds. Stir in lemon and orange juices. Cover and refrigerate syrup until cold, about 1 hour (or up to 1 week). Serve syrup over ice cream, yogurt, or fresh fruit, or mix with seltzer for a refreshing cooler.

EACH 2 TABLESPOONS: About 45 calories, 0 g protein, 11 g carbohydrate, 0 g total fat, 1 g fiber, 0 mg cholesterol, 0 mg sodium.

Lime Rickey

PREP 5 minutes   **MAKES** 1 serving

> **3 tablespoons Cool Berry Syrup (page 299)**
>
> **2 tablespoons fresh lime juice**
>
> **1 tablespoon sugar**
>
> **ice cubes**
>
> **club soda**
>
> **lime slice and berries, for garnish**

1. In 14-ounce tall drinking glass, combine berry syrup, lime juice, and sugar. Stir to dissolve sugar.

2. Fill glass with ice cubes and add enough soda to come to top of glass. Stir gently with long-handled spoon. Garnish with lime slice and berries.

EACH SERVING: About 125 calories, 0 g protein, 32 g carbohydrate, 0 g total fat, 1 g fiber, 0 mg cholesterol, 1 mg sodium.

Warm Berry Compote

PREP 5 minutes plus standing   **COOK** 3 minutes   **MAKES** about 5 cups or 8 servings

> **1 container (1 pound) strawberries, hulled, each cut in half, or into quarters if large**
>
> **1 cup raspberries**
>
> **1 cup blueberries**
>
> **¼ cup sugar**

1. In 12-inch skillet, place strawberries, raspberries, blueberries, and sugar; stir gently to combine. Let stand 15 minutes.

2. Cook berry mixture over medium heat, gently stirring occasionally, until sugar dissolves and berries soften slightly, 3 to 4 minutes. Serve warm over ice cream or toasted pound cake, or topped with whipped cream.

EACH SERVING: About 60 calories, 1 g protein, 14 g carbohydrate, 0 g total fat, 3 g fiber, 0 mg cholesterol, 2 mg sodium.

Lemonade Pops

PREP 10 minutes plus freezing **COOK** 5 minutes **MAKES** 10 pops

1 cup sugar

1 cup tap water

1¹⁄₂ cups fresh lemon juice (from 6 to 8 lemons)

2 cups ice water

1. In 2-quart saucepan, heat sugar and tap water to boiling over medium-high heat. Reduce heat to low; simmer, stirring, until sugar dissolves. Remove from heat. Stir lemon juice and ice water into sugar syrup.

2. Pour lemonade into ten 5-ounce paper drinking cups. Place cups in shallow pan for easier handling; freeze pops until partially frozen, about 3 hours.

3. Insert wooden ice cream bar stick into center of each cup. Freeze until frozen solid, about 4 hours longer. To serve, peel off paper cups.

EACH POP: About 85 calories, 0 g protein, 22 g carbohydrate, 0 g total fat, 0 g fiber, 0 mg cholesterol, 0 mg sodium.

Plum Yogurt Pops

PREP 15 minutes plus freezing **MAKES** 16 pops

1 pound ripe red or purple plums (4 medium), coarsely chopped

¹⁄₂ cup sugar

1 tablespoon fresh lemon juice

2 cups low-fat vanilla yogurt

1. In blender, at medium speed, puree plums, sugar, and lemon juice. Pour plum puree into medium-mesh sieve set over medium bowl. With spoon, press against sieve to push through pulp and juice. Discard solids in sieve.

2. With wire whisk, mix yogurt and plum puree until well combined.

3. Spoon yogurt mixture into sixteen 3-ounce paper cups; freeze until partially frozen, 3 hours. Insert wooden ice cream bar stick into center of each cup. Freeze until completely frozen, about 2 hours longer. (Or, spoon yogurt mixture into sixteen 2-ounce frozen-pop molds; seal and insert wooden sticks as manufacturer directs. Freeze overnight.)

EACH POP: About 60 calories, 1 g protein, 13 g carbohydrate, 1 g total fat (0 g saturated), 0 g fiber, 2 mg cholesterol, 20 mg sodium.

Nectarine-Lime Sorbet

PREP 10 minutes plus chilling and freezing   **COOK** 6 minutes   **MAKES** about 4½ cups or 8 servings

- ¾ **cup water**
- ¾ **cup sugar**
- **pinch salt**
- **4 ripe large nectarines (2¼ pounds), pitted and cut into chunks**
- **3 tablespoons fresh lime juice**

1. In 2-quart saucepan, heat water, sugar, and salt to boiling over high heat, stirring until sugar dissolves. Reduce heat to medium and cook 3 minutes. Remove saucepan from heat; cool sugar syrup to room temperature.

2. In blender or food processor with knife blade attached, in batches, puree unpeeled nectarines with sugar syrup until smooth. Pour into large bowl; stir in lime juice. Cover and refrigerate until well chilled, about 2 hours.

3. Pour nectarine mixture into ice cream maker and freeze as manufacturer directs. Serve sorbet immediately or store in freezer for up to 2 weeks.

EACH SERVING: About 120 calories, 1 g protein, 30 g carbohydrate, 0 g total fat, 2 g fiber, 0 mg cholesterol, 20 mg sodium.

Apricot Soufflés

PREP 15 minutes   **BAKE** 15 minutes   **MAKES** 4 servings

2 tablespoons sugar

$1/4$ cup plus 3 tablespoons apricot jam or preserves

$1/2$ teaspoon vanilla extract

4 large egg whites

$1/4$ teaspoon cream of tartar

1. Preheat oven to 375°F. Grease four 6-ounce custard cups or soufflé dishes; sprinkle with 1 tablespoon sugar.

2. In large bowl, with wire whisk, mix apricot jam with vanilla.

3. In another large bowl, with mixer at high speed, beat egg whites and cream of tartar until soft peaks form. Beating at high speed, gradually sprinkle in remaining 1 tablespoon sugar until mixture holds stiff peaks when beaters are lifted.

4. With rubber spatula, gently fold one-third of beaten whites into apricot mixture. Fold in remaining whites, half at a time. Spoon mixture into custard cups. (Mixture will fill cups completely.)

5. With metal spatula held at a 45-degree angle to soufflé, make a domed peak on each soufflé. Place cups on jelly-roll pan for easier handling. Bake soufflés until puffed and golden, 12 to 15 minutes. Serve immediately.

EACH SERVING: About 128 calories, 3 g protein, 29 g carbohydrate, 0 g total fat, 0 g fiber, 0 mg cholesterol, 68 mg sodium.

Orange Liqueur Soufflés

PREP 25 minutes   **BAKE** 30 minutes   **MAKES** 10 servings

3 tablespoons butter or margarine

$1/4$ cup all-purpose flour

$1/8$ teaspoon salt

$1\,1/4$ cups whole milk

$1/4$ cup plus 5 tablespoons granulated sugar

4 large eggs, separated, plus 1 large egg white

$1/4$ cup orange-flavor liqueur

1 tablespoon grated fresh orange peel

confectioners' sugar (optional)

1. In 2-quart saucepan, melt butter over medium heat. Whisk in flour and salt until blended; gradually stir in milk. Cook, stirring frequently, until mixture boils and thickens; boil 1 minute. Remove from heat.

2. Stir $1/4$ cup granulated sugar into milk mixture. Whisk in egg yolks until well blended. Transfer to medium bowl; cool slightly, about 30 minutes. Stir in liqueur and peel.

3. Preheat oven to 375°F. Grease ten 6-ounce ramekins; sprinkle with 3 tablespoons granulated sugar.

4. In large bowl, with mixer at high speed, beat egg whites and remaining 2 tablespoons sugar until stiff peaks form when beaters are lifted. With rubber spatula, gently fold one-third of whites into milk mixture; fold milk mixture gently back into remaining whites.

5. Spoon mixture into prepared ramekins. Bake just until set, 30 minutes. When soufflés are done, sprinkle with confectioners' sugar if you like. Serve immediately.

EACH SERVING: About 150 calories, 4 g protein, 17 g carbohydrate, 7 g total fat (4 g saturated), 0 g fiber, 99 mg cholesterol, 110 mg sodium.

Orange Liqueur Soufflés

Summer Fruit in Spiced Syrup

Summer Fruit in Spiced Syrup

PREP 15 minutes plus cooling and chilling   **COOK** 7 minutes   **MAKES** about 5 cups or 6 servings

- ³/₄ **cup water**
- ¹/₂ **cup sugar**
- 3 **whole cloves**
- 1 **cinnamon stick (3 inches)**
- 1 **star anise**
- 1 **strip (3" by ³/₄") fresh lemon peel**
- 2 **tablespoons fresh lemon juice**
- 6 **cups fresh fruit, such as sliced nectarines, plums, strawberries, blueberries, and/or raspberries**

1. In 1-quart saucepan, combine water, sugar, cloves, cinnamon stick, star anise, and lemon peel; heat to boiling over medium-high heat, stirring frequently. Reduce heat to medium-low; simmer 5 minutes. Remove saucepan from heat; stir in lemon juice. Cool syrup to room temperature.

2. In large bowl, combine fruits and syrup. Cover and refrigerate 2 hours, stirring occasionally.

EACH SERVING: About 125 calories, 1 g protein, 32 g carbohydrate, 1 g total fat (0 g saturated), 4 g fiber, 0 mg cholesterol, 2 mg sodium.

Fruit Compote in Spiced Wine

PREP 20 minutes plus chilling   **COOK** 25 minutes   **MAKES** 12 cups of 16 servings

- **1 lemon**
- **2 cups dry red wine**
- **2 cups water**
- **1¼ cups sugar**
- **1 tablespoon whole black peppercorns**
- **6 whole cloves**
- **1 cinnamon stick (3 inches)**
- **4 large Anjou or Bosc pears (2 pounds), peeled, cored, and each cut into 12 wedges**
- **4 large Granny Smith apples (2 pounds), peeled, cored, and each cut into 16 wedges**
- **2 cups cranberries**

1. From lemon, with vegetable peeler, remove 1-inch-wide continuous strip of peel.

2. In 4-quart saucepan, combine lemon peel, wine, water, sugar, peppercorns, cloves, and cinnamon stick; heat to boiling over high heat, stirring frequently, until sugar dissolves. Reduce heat to medium-low; cover and simmer, stirring occasionally, 10 minutes. Pour syrup through sieve set over bowl; discard peppercorns and cloves. Return syrup, lemon peel, and cinnamon stick to saucepan.

3. Add pears and apples to syrup, gently stirring to combine; heat to boiling over medium-high heat. Reduce heat to medium-low; cover and simmer until apples and pears are tender, 5 minutes. Stir in cranberries and cook, covered, 5 minutes longer.

4. Pour fruit mixture into heat-safe bowl and refrigerate at least 4 hours to blend flavors. Remove lemon peel and cinnamon stick before serving.

EACH SERVING: About 125 calories, 0 g protein, 30 g carbohydrate, 0 g total fat, 2 g fiber, 0 mg cholesterol, 5 mg sodium.

NOTE: If stored in the refrigerator, this dessert can be made up to 4 days in advance.

Marinated Orange Slices

PREP 10 minutes plus chilling   **MAKES** 8 servings

> **1/2 cup sweet orange marmalade**
>
> **1 tablespoon orange-flavor liqueur**
>
> **5 medium navel oranges, peeled and sliced crosswise**

In large bowl, combine marmalade and liqueur. Add orange slices; stir gently to coat. Cover and refrigerate at least 30 minutes or up to several hours.

EACH SERVING: About 99 calories, 1 g protein, 25 g carbohydrate, 0 g total fat, 2 g fiber, 0 mg cholesterol, 12 mg sodium.

No-Bake Chocolate Crackles

Have one of these with 1/2 cup skim milk for a 125-calorie treat.

PREP 10 minutes plus chilling   **MAKES** 9 cookies

> **3 ounces semisweet chocolate**
>
> **2 cups crispy rice cereal**
>
> **2 graham crackers (5" by 2 1/2" each), broken into small pieces**

1. Line cookie sheet with waxed paper. In 2-quart microwave-safe bowl, heat chocolate in microwave oven on High, stirring once, until melted, 1 to 1 1/2 minutes. Add cereal and crackers; stir until coated.

2. Drop mixture by 1/4 cups onto lined cookie sheet. With fingertips, shape mixture to form rounded mound if necessary. Refrigerate cookies 30 minutes to set. Store cookies in tightly covered container at room temperature.

EACH COOKIE: About 83 calories, 1 g protein, 13 g carbohydrate, 3 g total fat (2 g saturated), 1 g fiber, 0 mg cholesterol, 65 mg sodium.

Seattle Cappuccino Angel Food Cake

PREP 30 minutes plus cooling   **BAKE** 35 minutes   **MAKES** 16 servings

> **1 cup cake flour (not self-rising)**
>
> **$1/2$ cup plus 1 tablespoon confectioners' sugar**
>
> **$1^2/_3$ cups egg whites (12 large)**
>
> **4 teaspoons instant espresso-coffee powder**
>
> **$1^1/_2$ teaspoons cream of tartar**
>
> **$1/2$ teaspoon salt**
>
> **$1/2$ teaspoon plus $1/8$ teaspoon ground cinnamon**
>
> **$1^1/_2$ teaspoons vanilla extract**
>
> **$1^1/_4$ cups granulated sugar**

1.   Preheat oven to 375°F. On waxed paper, mix flour and $1/2$ cup confectioners' sugar; set aside.

2.   In large bowl, with mixer at high speed, beat egg whites, espresso, cream of tartar, salt, and $1/2$ teaspoon cinnamon until soft peaks form; beat in vanilla. Beating at high speed, sprinkle in granulated sugar, 2 tablespoons at a time, until sugar completely dissolves and whites stand in stiff, glossy peaks.

3.   Sift flour mixture over egg whites, one-third at a time, folding in with rubber spatula after each addition.

4.   Spoon batter into ungreased 10-inch tube pan. Bake cake until top springs back when lightly touched with finger, 35 to 40 minutes. Invert cake in pan on funnel or bottle; cool completely in pan.

5.   With metal spatula, carefully loosen cake from pan; place on cake plate. In cup, mix remaining 1 tablespoon confectioners' sugar with remaining $1/8$ teaspoon cinnamon; sprinkle over top of cake.

EACH SERVING: About 120 calories, 3 g protein, 26 g carbohydrate, 0 g total fat, 0 g fiber, 0 mg cholesterol, 110 mg sodium.

Soft Applesauce-Raisin Cookies

PREP 35 minutes plus cooling   **BAKE** 20 minutes   **MAKES** 45 cookies

2 cups all-purpose flour

$^1/_2$ teaspoon baking powder

$^1/_2$ teaspoon baking soda

$^1/_2$ teaspoon ground cinnamon

$^1/_4$ ground allspice

$^1/_4$ teaspoon salt

$^1/_2$ cup plus 2 tablespoons zero-grams trans fat margarine softened (or $^1/_2$ cup margarine or butter)

$^1/_2$ cup granulated sugar

$^1/_4$ cup packed brown sugar

1 large egg

1 cup unsweetened applesauce

1 teaspoon vanilla extract

1 medium Granny Smith apple, cored and finely chopped

1 cup dark raisins

1 cup walnuts, coarsely chopped

1 cup confectioners' sugar

2 tablespoons fresh lemon juice

1. Preheat oven to 375°F. Grease 2 cookie sheets. On waxed paper, combine flour, baking powder, baking soda, cinnamon, allspice, and salt.

2. In large bowl, with mixer at medium speed, beat butter, granulated sugar, and brown sugar until light and fluffy. Reduce speed to low; beat in egg, applesauce, and vanilla. Beat in flour mixture just until blended. Stir in apple, raisins, and walnuts.

3. Drop dough by rounded measuring tablespoons, 1 inch apart, on prepared cookie sheets. Bake cookies on 2 oven racks, until lightly browned around edges and set, 20 to 22 minutes, rotating cookie sheets between upper and lower racks halfway through baking.

4. While cookies bake, in small bowl, stir confectioners' sugar and lemon juice until smooth.

5. Transfer cookies to wire racks. With pastry brush, brush lemon glaze over warm cookies; cool.

EACH COOKIE: About 92 calories, 1 g protein, 14 g carbohydrate, 4 g total fat (1 g saturated), 1 g fiber, 5 mg cholesterol, 35 mg sodium.

Index

Metric Conversion Charts

The recipes that appear in this cookbook use the standard United States method for measuring liquid and dry or solid ingredients (teaspoons, tablespoons, and cups). The information on this chart is provided to help cooks outside the U.S. successfully use these recipes. All equivalents are approximate.

METRIC EQUIVALENTS FOR DIFFERENT TYPES OF INGREDIENTS

A standard cup measure of a dry or solid ingredient will vary in weight depending on the type of ingredient. A standard cup of liquid is the same volume for any type of liquid. Use the following chart when converting standard cup measures to grams (weight) or milliliters (volume).

Standard Cup	Fine Powder (ex flour)	Grain (ex.rice)	Granular (ex. sugar)	Liquid Solids (ex. butter)	Liquid (ex. milk)
1	140 g	150 g	190 g	200 g	240 ml
$3/4$	105 g	113 g	143 g	150 g	180 ml
$2/3$	93 g	100 g	125 g	133 g	160 ml
$1/2$	70 g	75 g	95 g	100 g	120 ml
$1/3$	47 g	50 g	63 g	67 g	80 ml
$1/4$	35 g	38 g	48 g	50 g	60 ml
$1/8$	18 g	19 g	24 g	25 g	30 ml

USEFUL EQUIVALENTS FOR LIQUID INGREDIENTS BY VOLUME

$1/4$ tsp	=					1 ml
$1/2$ tsp	=					2 ml
1 tsp	=					5 ml
3 tsp	=	1 tbls	=	$1/2$ fl oz	=	15 ml
		2 tbls	= $1/8$ cup =	1 fl oz	=	30 ml
		4 tbls	= $1/4$ cup =	2 fl oz	=	60 ml
		$5^1/3$ tbls	= $1/3$ cup =	3 fl oz	=	80 ml
		8 tbls	= $1/2$ cup =	4 fl oz	=	120 ml
		$10^2/3$ tbls	= $2/3$ cup =	5 fl oz	=	160 ml
		12 tbls	= $3/4$ cup =	6 fl oz	=	180 ml
		16 tbls	= 1 cup =	8 fl oz	=	240 ml
		1 pt	= 2 cups =	16 fl oz	=	480 ml
		1 qt	= 4 cups =	32 fl oz	=	960 ml
				33 fl oz	=	1000 ml = 1 l

USEFUL EQUIVALENTS FOR DRY INGREDIENTS BY WEIGHT

(To convert ounces to grams, multiply the number of ounces by 30.)

1 oz	=	$1/16$ lb	=	30 g
4 oz	=	$1/4$ lb	=	120 g
8 oz	=	$1/2$ lb	=	240 g
12 oz	=	$3/4$ lb	=	360 g
16 oz	=	1 lb	=	480 g

USEFUL EQUIVALENTS FOR LENGTH

(To convert inches to centimeters, multiply the number of inches by 2.5.)

1 in	=					2.5 cm
6 in	=	$1/2$ ft	=			15 cm
12 in	=	1 ft	=			30 cm
36 in	=	3 ft	=	1 yd	=	90 cm
40 in	=					100 cm = 1 m

USEFUL EQUIVALENTS FOR COOKING/OVEN TEMPERATURES

	Fahrenheit	Celsius	Gas Mark
Freeze Water	32° F	0° C	
Room Temperature	68° F	20° C	
Boil Water	212° F	100° C	
Bake	325° F	160° C	3
	350° F	180° C	4
	375° F	190° C	5
	400° F	200° C	6
	425° F	220° C	7
	450° F	230° C	8
Broil			Grill